PATTERNS OF DEMOCRACY

PATTERNS OF DEMOCRACY

Government Forms and Performance in
Thirty-Six Countries

SECOND EDITION

Arend Lijphart

Yale UNIVERSITY PRESS/NEW HAVEN & LONDON

First edition 1999. Second edition 2012.

Yale University Press books may be purchased in quantity for educational, business, or promotional use. For information, please e-mail sales.press@yale.edu (US office) or sales@yaleup.co.uk (UK office).

Set in Melior type by Integrated Publishing Solutions, Grand Rapids, Michigan.
Printed in the United States of America.

Library of Congress Cataloging-in-Publication Data

Lijphart, Arend.
    Patterns of democracy : government forms and performance in thirty-six countries / Arend Lijphart. — 2nd ed.
        p.   cm.
    Includes bibliographical references and index.
    ISBN 978-0-300-17202-7 (paperbound : alk. paper)   1. Democracy.
2. Comparative government.   I. Title.
    JC421.L542 2012
    320.3—dc23   2012000704

A catalogue record for this book is available from the British Library.

This paper meets the requirements of ANSI/NISO Z39.48–1992 (Permanence of Paper).
10 9 8 7 6 5 4 3 2

for
    Gisela
and for our grandchildren,
    Connor,
    Aidan,
    Arel,
    Caio,
    Senta, and
    Dorian,

in the hope that the twenty-first century—their century—will yet become more democratic, more peaceful, kinder, and gentler than the one our generation has bequeathed to them

Contents

PREFACE TO THE SECOND EDITION

I welcome the opportunity to publish an updated edition of *Patterns of Democracy*, originally published in 1999, because it gives me an opportunity to test whether my main findings and conclusions continue to be valid—especially my finding that the great variety of formal and informal rules and institutions that we find in democracies can be reduced to a clear two-dimensional pattern on the basis of the contrast between majoritarian and consensus forms of government, and my conclusion that consensus democracies (measured on the first of these dimensions) have a superior record with regard to effective policy-making and the quality of democracy compared with majoritarian democracies. The basic organization of the book has not changed, but the data on which its empirical analysis is based has changed in important ways.

First, my analysis continues to compare the same number of democracies—thirty-six—but three of the countries had to be removed because they are no longer free and democratic according to the criteria of Freedom House: Colombia, Venezuela, and Papua New Guinea. I replaced them with Argentina, Uruguay, and Korea, which returned to democracy in the 1980s.

Second, I extended the analysis from 1996 to 2010, which entails a considerable increase in the time span during which the other thirty-three democracies are analyzed: a 74 percent increase for the newest democracies included in the first edition—India and Spain—smaller but still substantial increases for the countries that became democratic between the 1950s and the early 1970s, and even a significant 28 percent increase for the older democracies analyzed from the late 1940s on.

Third, I made no major changes in the definition and measurement of the ten basic variables that make up the majoritarian-consensus contrast, with two important exceptions. In hindsight, I concluded that the way I operationalized executive dominance in Chapter 7 of the original edition was too complicated and cumbersome; I therefore use a much simpler and more straightforward operationalization in the updated edition. In Chapter 13, I was forced to change the treatment of central bank independence because from the mid-1990s on the internationalization of central banking—in particular, the creation of the European Central Bank and changes in several national central bank charters demanded by the International Monetary Fund—changed the status of central banks from domestic institutions to organizations in the international system. A less important change is that I reduced my discussion of the issue dimensions of partisan conflict—which is not an institutional variable and is not one of the basic ten variables distinguishing majoritarian from consensus democracy—from about a third of Chapter 5 to a more appropriately short addendum to that chapter.

Fourth, the biggest changes are in Chapters 15 and 16 with regard to the variables by which I measure the performance of consensus versus majoritarian democracies. Some of these variables—like economic growth, the control of inflation and unemployment, women's representation, and political equality—are the same as in the original edition, but the data on them are for later periods and therefore almost completely new. A few others, like social expenditure and environmental performance, are also the same but measured by new and different indexes. And then there are entirely new variables not used in the original edition at all. I also streamlined the presentation of the results of the regression analyses. Instead of showing the bivariate relationships between consensus democracy and the performance variables in the tables and discussing the influence of control variables, especially the impact of the level of economic development and population size, in the accompanying text, I now have tables showing multivariate regression analyses of the effects of consensus democracy with these two standard controls in place in all instances.

Generally the quality of all the new data is a great deal better than the quality of the data that I had at my disposal in the mid-1990s, and they are available for many more countries. In particular, I made grateful use of two entirely new and highly relevant datasets for the measurement of the quality of government and the quality of democracy, respectively: the Worldwide Governance Indicators and the data of the Democracy Index project of the Economist Intelligence Unit. Not only have excellent data become much more available in the past decade, but they have also become more easily accessible. In the preface to the first edition, I wrote that I might not have been able to write it without the invention of email. I can now add that this new edition might not have been possible, or would have been much more difficult to write, without all of the information that is available on the internet.

To briefly preview my conclusions in the updated edition, I find that my original conclusions are amply confirmed. In fact, the evidence with regard to the interrelationships of my ten majoritarian versus consensus characteristics and with regard to the superior performance of consensus democracy has become even clearer and stronger.

The preparation of a study of as many as thirty-six countries is impossible without the input of many comparative and country experts. I am deeply grateful to my friends and colleagues for the valuable advice and assistance I received from them. First of all,

I want to express my thanks again to everyone who helped me with the first edition of this book. Their input is still reflected in the contents of this second edition, too.

I was especially in need of assistance with regard to the three new countries in the updated edition, and I am grateful for the excellent advice on Korean politics from Taekyoon Kim, Kyoung-Ryung Seong, Jong-Sung You, and my Korean research assistant, Don S. Lee. For Argentina and Uruguay I had a huge team of aides and advisers, and I am deeply indebted to them all: David Altman, Octavio Amorim Neto, Marcelo Camerlo, Rossana Castiglioni, Sebastián Etchemendy, Mark P. Jones, Jorge Lanzaro, Andrés Malamud, M. Victoria Murillo, Sebastián M. Saiegh, and Andrew Schrank. For recent developments in several other countries I relied on the advice of Edward M. Dew, Fragano S. J. Ledgister, Ralph R. Premdas, and Rajendra Ramlogan (Barbados and the other Caribbean countries); Carl Devos and Luc Huyse (Belgium); Pradeep K. Chhibber and Ashutosh Varshney (India); Yuko Kasuya and Mikitaka Masuyama (Japan); Deborah Bräutigam, Jørgen Elklit, Shaheen Mozaffar, Linganaden Murday, and Nadarajen Sivaramen (Mauritius); Peter Aimer and Jack Vowles (New Zealand); Richard Gunther and Óscar Martínez-Tapia (Spain); Matthew Flinders, Michael Gallagher, and Thomas C. Lundberg (United Kingdom); and Gary C. Jacobson (United States).

I am equally grateful to all of the scholars who helped me in important subject areas: Krista Hoekstra, Hans Keman, Jelle Koedam, and Jaap Woldendorp (cabinet coalitions); Daniel M. Brinks, Isaac Herzog, Donald W. Jackson, and Mary L. Volcansek (judicial review); Christopher Crowe and Mauro F. Guillén (central banks); and Scott Desposato, Stephen J. K. Lee, Philip G. Roeder, and Sebastián M. Saiegh (statistical and computer issues). Other scholars whom I would like to thank without placing them in country or subject categories are Ernesto Alvarez, Jr., Julian Bernauer, Joseph H. Brooks, Royce Carroll, Josep M. Colomer, Zachary Elkins, John Gerring, Ronald F. Inglehart, Mona Lena Krook, Sanford A. Lakoff, Dieter Nohlen, Matt H. Qvortrup, Manfred G. Schmidt, Alan

Siaroff, Fabia Soehngen, Rein Taagepera, Steven L. Taylor, and Adrian Vatter.

In April 2011, I gave seminars on the findings of this updated edition at the Juan March Institute in Madrid and at the Madrid campus of Suffolk University, and in November 2011 a similar seminar in the Department of Politics of the University of Antwerp. The comments and questions I received from the participants in these seminars were very helpful. I would also like to thank William Frucht, executive editor at Yale University Press, for the strong encouragement he gave me to write an updated edition, and Laura Jones Dooley, who expertly copyedited both the first and second editions. Above all, I owe special thanks to my two research assistants, Christopher J. Fariss and Don S. Lee. Chris was my main statistical adviser, and he prepared almost all of the figures in Chapters 6 to 14 as well as the factor analysis reported in Chapter 14. Don collected and organized most of the macroeconomic and violence data for Chapter 15. I am deeply grateful for their help, hard work, and friendship.

Preface to the First Edition

My book *Democracies,* published in 1984, was a comparative study of twenty-one democracies in the period 1945–80. Its most important findings were (1) that the main institutional rules and practices of modern democracies—such as the organization and operation of executives, legislatures, party systems, electoral systems, and the relationships between central and lower-level governments—can all be measured on scales from majoritarianism at one end to consensus on the other, (2) that these institutional characteristics form two distinct clusters, and (3) that, based on this dichotomous clustering, a two-dimensional "conceptual map" of democracy can be drawn on which each of the democracies can be located. My original plan for a second edition was to reinforce this theoretical framework and the empirical findings mainly by means of an update to the mid-1990s—an almost 50 percent increase in the total time span—with only a few additional corrections and adjustments.

When I began work on the revision, however, I realized that it offered me a great opportunity for much more drastic improvements. I decided to add not just the updated materials but also fifteen new countries, new operationalizations of the institutional

variables, two completely new institutional variables, an attempt
to gauge the stability of the countries' positions on the conceptual
map, and an analysis of the performance of the different types of
democracy with regard to a large number of public policies. As a
result, while *Patterns of Democracy* grew out of *Democracies,* it
has become an entirely new book rather than a second edition.

For those readers who are familiar with *Democracies,* let me
describe the principal changes in *Patterns of Democracy* in somewhat greater detail:

1. *Patterns of Democracy* covers thirty-six countries—fifteen more
   than the twenty-one countries of *Democracies.* This new set of
   thirty-six countries is not just numerically larger but considerably more diverse. The original twenty-one democracies were all
   industrialized nations and, with one exception (Japan), Western
   countries. The fifteen new countries include four European nations (Spain, Portugal, Greece, and Malta), but the other eleven—
   almost one-third of the total of thirty-six—are developing countries in Latin America, the Caribbean, Africa, Asia, and the
   Pacific. This greater diversity provides a critical test of the two-
   dimensional pattern found in *Democracies.* A minor change
   from *Democracies* is that I dropped the French Fourth Republic (1946–58) because it lasted only twelve years—in contrast
   with the minimum of almost twenty years of democracy for all
   other cases; in this book, "France" means the Fifth Republic
   from 1958 on.
2. In *Democracies,* I analyzed the twenty-one countries from their
   first national elections in or soon after 1945 until the end of
   1980. *Patterns of Democracy* extends this period until the middle of 1996. For the original countries (except France), the
   starting-point is still the second half of the 1940s; for the others,
   the analysis begins with their first elections upon the achievement of independence or the resumption of democracy—ranging
   from 1953 (Costa Rica) to 1977 (India, Papua New Guinea, and
   Spain.)

3. The two new institutions analyzed in *Patterns of Democracy* are interest groups and central banks (Chapters 9 and 13). Two other variables that were discussed prominently in *Democracies* and given chapters of their own—the issue dimensions of partisan conflict and referendums—are "demoted" in *Patterns of Democracy.* I now discuss them more briefly in Chapters 5 and 12, and I have dropped the issue dimensions as one of the five elements of the first cluster of characteristics because, unlike all the other variables, it is not an institutional characteristic. The first cluster still consists of five variables, however, because the interest group system is now added to it. The second cluster is expanded from three to five elements: I split the variable of constitutional rigidity versus flexibility into two separate variables—the difficulty of constitutional amendment and the strength of judicial review—and I added the variable of central bank independence.

4. I critically reviewed the operationalization of all of the institutional characteristics, and I found that almost all could be, and should be, improved. My overriding objective was to maximize the validity of my quantitative indicators—that is, to capture the "reality" of the political phenomena, which are often difficult to quantify, as closely as possible. One frequent problem was that I was faced with two alternative operationalizations that appeared to be equally justified. In such cases, I consistently chose to "split the difference" by combining or averaging the alternatives instead of more or less arbitrarily picking one instead of the other. In the end, only the operationalization of the party system variables—in terms of the effective number of parliamentary parties—survived almost (but not completely) intact from *Democracies.* All of the others were modified to a significant extent.

5. In *Democracies,* I placed my democracies on the conceptual map of democracy on the basis of their average institutional practices in the thirty to thirty-five years under consideration; I did not raise the question of how much change may have oc-

curred over time. Chapter 14 of *Patterns of Democracy* does
look into this matter by dividing the approximately fifty years
from 1945 to 1996 into separate periods of 1945–70 and 1971–
96 and by showing how much—or how little—twenty-six of
the democracies (those with a sufficient number of years in the
first period) shifted their positions on the conceptual map
from the first to the second period.

6. Perhaps the most important new subject covered in *Patterns of
Democracy* is the "so what?" question: does the type of democracy make a difference for public policy and for the effectiveness of government? Chapter 15 investigates the relationship
between the degree of consensus democracy and how successful governments are in their macroeconomic management (such
as economic growth and the control of inflation and unemployment) and the control of violence. Chapter 16 looks at several indicators of the quality of democracy (such as women's
representation, equality, and voter participation) and the records
of the governments with regard to welfare policies, environmental protection, criminal justice, and economic aid to developing countries.

7. I began *Democracies* with sketches of British and New Zealand
politics as illustrative examples of the Westminster model of democracy and similar brief accounts of Swiss and Belgian democracy as examples of the consensus model. *Patterns of Democracy*
updates these four sketches and adds Barbados and the European Union as two further examples of the respective models.

8. *Democracies* presented the relationships between the different
variables by means of tables with cross-tabulations. In *Patterns
of Democracy,* I generally use scattergrams that show these relationships and the positions of each of the thirty-six democracies in a much clearer, more accurate, and visually more attractive fashion.

9. *Patterns of Democracy* adds an appendix with the values on
all ten institutional variables and the two overall majoritarian-
consensus dimensions for the entire period 1945–96 and for

the shorter period 1971–96. The ready availability of these basic data as part of the book should facilitate replications that other scholars may want to perform as well as the use of these data for further research.

It would have been impossible for me to analyze the thirty-six countries covered in *Patterns of Democracy* without the help of a host of scholarly advisers—and almost impossible without the invention of email! I am extremely grateful for all of the facts and interpretations contributed by my advisers and for their unfailingly prompt responses to my numerous queries.

On the Latin American democracies, I received invaluable assistance from Octavio Amorim Neto, John M. Carey, Brian F. Crisp, Michael J. Coppedge, Jonathan Hartlyn, Gary Hoskin, Mark P. Jones, J. Ray Kennedy, Scott Mainwaring, and Matthew S. Shugart. Thomas C. Bruneau, P. Nikiforos Diamandouros, and Richard Gunther helped me understand the Mediterranean democracies better. Ralph R. Premdas was a key consultant on the Caribbean democracies, together with Edward M. Dew, Neville R. Francis, Percy C. Hintzen, and Fragano S. J. Ledgister. Pradeep K. Chhibber and Ashutosh Varshney helped me solve a number of puzzles in the politics of India. With regard to some of the small and underanalyzed countries, I was particularly dependent on the willingness of area and country experts to provide facts and explanations: John D. Holm, Bryce Kunimoto, Shaheen Mozaffar, and Andrew S. Reynolds on Botswana; John C. Lane on Malta; Hansraj Mathur and Larry W. Bowman on Mauritius; and Ralph Premdas (again) as well as Ben Reilly and Ron May on Papua New Guinea.

Nathaniel L. Beck, Susanne Lohmann, Sylvia Maxfield, Pierre L. Siklos, and Steven B. Webb advised me on central banks; Miriam A. Golden, Stephan Haggard, Neil J. Mitchell, Daniel L. Nielson, Adam Przeworski, and Alan Siaroff on interest groups; and Martin Shapiro and Alec Stone on judicial review. On other countries and subjects I benefited from the help and suggestions of

John S. Ambler, Matthew A. Baum, Peter J. Bowman, Thomas C. Bruneau, Gary W. Cox, Markus M. L. Crepaz, Robert G. Cushing, Robert A. Dahl, Larry Diamond, Panayote E. Dimitras, Giuseppe Di Palma, James N. Druckman, Svante O. Ersson, Bernard Grofman, Arnold J. Heidenheimer, Charles O. Jones, Samuel H. Kernell, Ellis S. Krauss, Michael Laver, Thomas C. Lundberg, Malcolm Mackerras, Peter Mair, Jane Mansbridge, Marc F. Plattner, G. Bingham Powell, Jr., Steven R. Reed, Manfred G. Schmidt, Kaare Strøm, Wilfried Swenden, Rein Taagepera, Paul V. Warwick, and Demet Yalcin.

In October 1997, I gave an intensive two-week seminar, largely based on draft materials for *Patterns of Democracy,* at the Institute for Advance Studies in Vienna; I am grateful for the many helpful comments I received from Josef Melchior, Bernhard Kittel, and the graduate students who participated in the seminar sessions. In April and May 1998, I gave similar lectures and seminars at several universities in New Zealand: the University of Canterbury in Christchurch, the University of Auckland, Victoria University of Wellington, and the University of Waikato in Hamilton. Here, too, I benefited from many useful reactions, and I want to thank Peter Aimer, Jonathan Boston, John Henderson, Martin Holland, Keith Jackson, Raymond Miller, Nigel S. Roberts, and Jack Vowles in particular.

James N. Druckman expertly executed the factor analysis reported in Chapter 14. Ian Budge, Hans Keman, and Jaap Woldendorp provided me with their new data on cabinet formation before these were published. Several other scholars also generously shared their not yet published or only partly published data with me: data on the composition of federal chambers from Alfred Stepan and Wilfried Swenden's Federal Databank; data on the distance between governments and voters collected by John D. Huber and G. Bingham Powell, Jr.; and Christopher J. Anderson and Christine A. Guillory's data on satisfaction with democracy. Last, but certainly not least, I am very grateful for the work of my research assistants Nastaran Afari, Risa A. Brooks, Linda L. Christian, and Stephen M. Swindle.

Chapter 1

Introduction

There are many ways in which, in principle, a democracy can be organized and run; in practice, too, modern democracies exhibit a variety of formal governmental institutions, like legislatures and courts, as well as political party and interest group systems. However, clear patterns and regularities appear when these institutions are examined from the perspective of how majoritarian or how consensual their rules and practices are. The majoritarianism-consensus contrast arises from the most basic and literal definition of democracy—government by the people or, in representative democracy, government by the representatives of the people—and from President Abraham Lincoln's famous further stipulation that democracy means government not only *by* but also *for* the people—that is, government in accordance with the people's prefererences.[1]

Defining democracy as "government by and for the people"

1. As Clifford D. May (1987) points out, credit for this definition should probably go to Daniel Webster instead of Lincoln. Webster gave an address in 1830—thirty-three years before Lincoln's Gettysburg address—in which he spoke of a "people's government, made for the people, made by the people, and answerable to the people."

raises a fundamental question: Who will do the governing and to whose interests should the government be responsive when the people are in disagreement and have divergent preferences? One answer to this dilemma is: the majority of the people. This is the essence of the majoritarian model of democracy. The majoritarian answer is simple and straightforward and has great appeal because government by the majority and in accordance with the majority's wishes obviously comes closer to the democratic ideal of "government by and for the people" than government by and responsive to a minority.

The alternative answer to the dilemma is: as many people as possible. This is the crux of the consensus model. It does not differ from the majoritarian model in accepting that majority rule is better than minority rule, but it accepts majority rule only as a *minimum* requirement: instead of being satisfied with narrow decision-making majorities, it seeks to maximize the size of these majorities. Its rules and institutions aim at broad participation in government and broad agreement on the policies that the government should pursue. The majoritarian model concentrates political power in the hands of a bare majority—and often even merely a plurality instead of a majority, as Chapter 2 will show—whereas the consensus model tries to share, disperse, and limit power in a variety of ways. A closely related difference is that the majoritarian model of democracy is exclusive, competitive, and adversarial, whereas the consensus model is characterized by inclusiveness, bargaining, and compromise; for this reason, consensus democracy could also be termed "negotiation democracy" (Kaiser 1997, 434).

Ten differences with regard to the most important democratic institutions and rules can be deduced from the majoritarian and consensus principles. Because the majoritarian characteristics are derived from the same principle and hence are logically connected, one could also expect them to occur together in the real world; the same applies to the consensus characteristics. All ten variables could therefore be expected to be closely related. Previous research has largely confirmed these expectations—with one major exception: the variables cluster in two clearly separate dimensions (Lijphart 1984, 211–22). The first dimension groups five characteristics of the arrangement of executive power, the party and electoral systems, and interest groups. For brevity's sake, I shall refer to this first dimension as the *executives-parties dimension*. Since most of the five differences on the second dimension are commonly associated with the contrast between federalism and unitary government—a matter to which I shall return shortly—I shall call this second dimension the *federal-unitary dimension*.

The ten differences are formulated below in terms of dichotomous contrasts between the majoritarian and consensus models, but they are all variables on which particular countries may be at either end of the continuum or anywhere in between. The majoritarian characteristic is listed first in each case. The five differences on the executives-parties dimension are as follows:

1. Concentration of executive power in single-party majority cabinets versus executive power-sharing in broad multiparty coalitions.
2. Executive-legislative relationships in which the executive is dominant versus executive-legislative balance of power.
3. Two-party versus multiparty systems.
4. Majoritarian and disproportional electoral systems versus proportional representation.
5. Pluralist interest group systems with free-for-all competition among groups versus coordinated and "corporatist" interest group systems aimed at compromise and concertation.

The five differences on the federal-unitary dimension are the following:

1. Unitary and centralized government versus federal and decentralized government.
2. Concentration of legislative power in a unicameral legislature versus division of legislative power between two equally strong but differently constituted houses.

3. Flexible constitutions that can be amended by simple majorities versus rigid constitutions that can be changed only by extraordinary majorities.
4. Systems in which legislatures have the final word on the constitutionality of their own legislation versus systems in which laws are subject to a judicial review of their constitutionality by supreme or constitutional courts.
5. Central banks that are dependent on the executive versus independent central banks.

One plausible explanation of this two-dimensional pattern is suggested by the classical theorists of federalism—Ivo D. Duchacek (1970), Daniel J. Elazar (1968), Carl J. Friedrich (1950, 189–221), and K. C. Wheare (1946)—as well as by many contemporary theorists (Colomer 2011, 85–100; Hueglin and Fenna 2006; Stepan 2001, 315–61; Watts 2008). These scholars maintain that federalism has primary and secondary meanings. Its primary definition is: a guaranteed division of power between the central government and regional governments. The secondary characteristics are strong bicameralism, a rigid constitution, and strong judicial review. Their argument is that the guarantee of a federal division of power can work well only if (1) both the guarantee and the exact lines of the division of power are clearly stated in the constitution and this guarantee cannot be changed unilaterally at either the central or regional level—hence the need for a rigid constitution, (2) there is a neutral arbiter who can resolve conflicts concerning the division of power between the two levels of government—hence the need for judicial review, and (3) there is a federal chamber in the national legislature in which the regions have strong representation—hence the need for strong bicameralism; moreover, (4) the main purpose of federalism is to promote and protect a decentralized system of government. These federalist characteristics can be found in the first four variables of the second dimension. As stated earlier, this dimension is therefore called the federal-unitary dimension.

The federalist explanation is not entirely satisfactory, however, for two reasons. One problem is that, although it can explain the clustering of the four variables in one dimension, it does not explain why this dimension should be so clearly distinct from the other dimension. Second, it cannot explain why the variable of central bank independence is part of the federal-unitary dimension. A more persuasive explanation of the two-dimensional pattern is the distinction between "collective agency" and "shared responsibility" on one hand and divided agencies and responsibilities on the other suggested by Robert E. Goodin (1996, 331).[2] These are both forms of diffusion of power, but the first dimension of consensus democracy with its multiparty face-to-face interactions *within* cabinets, legislatures, legislative committees, and concertation meetings between governments and interest groups has a close fit with the collective-responsibility form. In contrast, both the four federalist characteristics and the role of central banks fit the format of diffusion by means of institutional separation: division of power between separate federal and state institutions, two separate chambers in the legislature, and separate and independent high courts and central banks. Viewed from this perspective, the first dimension could also be labeled the joint-responsibility or joint-power dimension and the second the divided-responsibility or divided-power dimension. However, although these labels would be more accurate and theoretically more meaningful, my original labels—"executives-parties" and "federal-unitary"—have the great advantage that they are easier to remember, and I shall therefore keep using them throughout this book.

The distinction between two basic types of democracy, majoritarian and consensus, is by no means a novel invention in political science. In fact, I borrowed these two terms from Robert G. Dixon, Jr. (1968, 10). Hans Hattenhauer and Werner Kaltefleiter

2. A similar distinction, made by George Tsebelis (2002), is that between "institutional veto players," located in different institutions, and "partisan veto players" such as the parties within a government coalition.

(1986) also contrast the "majority principle" with consensus, and Jürg Steiner (1971) juxtaposes "the principles of majority and proportionality." G. Bingham Powell, Jr. (1982), distinguishes between majoritarian and broadly "representational" forms of democracy and, in later work, between two "democratic visions": majoritarian and proportional (Powell 2000). Similar contrasts have been drawn by Robert A. Dahl (1956)—"populistic" versus "Madisonian" democracy; William H. Riker (1982)—"populism" versus "liberalism"; Jane Mansbridge (1980)—"adversary" versus "unitary" democracy; and S. E. Finer (1975)—"adversary politics" versus centrist and coalitional politics.

Nevertheless, there is a surprisingly strong and persistent tendency in political science to equate democracy solely with majoritarian democracy and to fail to recognize consensus democracy as an alternative and equally legitimate type. A particularly clear example can be found in Stephanie Lawson's (1993, 192–93) argument that a strong political opposition is "the *sine qua non* of contemporary democracy" and that its prime purpose is "to become the government." This view is based on the majoritarian assumption that democracy entails a two-party system (or possibly two opposing blocs of parties) that alternate in government; it fails to take into account that governments in more consensual multiparty systems tend to be coalitions and that a change in government in these systems usually means only a partial change in the party composition of the government—instead of the opposition "becoming" the government (Lundell 2011).

The frequent use of the "turnover" test in order to determine whether a democracy has become stable and consolidated betrays the same majoritarian assumption. Samuel P. Huntington (1991, 266–67) even proposes a "two-turnover test," according to which "a democracy may be viewed as consolidated if the party or group that takes power in the initial election at the time of transition [to democracy] loses a subsequent election and turns over power to those election winners, and if those election winners then peacefully turn over power to the winners of a later election." Of the twenty countries with the longest democratic history analyzed in this book, all of which are undoubtedly stable and consolidated democratic systems, no fewer than three—Luxembourg, the Netherlands, and Switzerland—fail even the one-turnover test during the more than sixty years from the late 1940s to 2010, that is, they experienced many cabinet changes but never a complete turnover, and six—the same three countries plus Belgium, Finland, and Germany—fail the two-turnover test.

This book will show that pure or almost pure majoritarian democracies are actually quite rare—limited to the United Kingdom, New Zealand (until 1996), and the former British colonies in the Caribbean (but only with regard to the executives-parties dimension). Most democracies have significant or even predominantly consensual traits. Moreover, as this book shows, consensus democracy may be considered more democratic than majoritarian democracy in most respects.

The ten contrasting characteristics of the two models of democracy, briefly listed above, are described in a preliminary fashion and exemplified by means of sketches of relatively pure cases of majoritarian democracy—the United Kingdom, New Zealand, and Barbados—and of relatively pure cases of consensus democracy—Switzerland, Belgium, and the European Union—in Chapters 2 and 3. The thirty-six empirical cases of democracy, including the five just mentioned (but not the European Union), that were selected for the comparative analysis are systematically introduced in Chapter 4. The ten institutional variables are then analyzed in greater depth in the nine chapters that comprise the bulk of this book (Chapters 5 to 13). Chapter 14 summarizes the results and places the thirty-six democracies on a two-dimensional "conceptual map" of democracy; it also analyzes shifts on the map over time and shows that most countries occupy stable positions on the map. Chapters 15 and 16 ask the "so what?" question: Does the type of democracy make a difference, especially with regard to effective policy-making and the quality of democracy? These chapters show that consensus democracies score significantly higher on a wide array of indicators of democratic quality and that they also have better records with regard to governing effectiveness, although the differences in this respect are not as large. Chapter 17 concludes with a look at the policy implications of the book's findings for democratizing and newly democratic countries.

CHAPTER 2

THE WESTMINSTER MODEL
OF DEMOCRACY

In this book I use the term *Westminster model* interchangeably with *majoritarian model* to refer to a general model of democracy. It may also be used more narrowly to denote the main characteristics of *British* parliamentary and governmental institutions (G. Wilson 1994; Mahler 1997)—the Parliament of the United Kingdom meets in the Palace of Westminster in London. The British version of the Westminster model is both the original and the best-known example of this model. It is also widely admired. Richard Rose (1974, 131) points out that, "with confidence born of continental isolation, Americans have come to assume that their institutions—the Presidency, Congress and the Supreme Court—are the prototype of what should be adopted elsewhere." But American political scientists, especially those in the field of comparative politics, have tended to hold the British system of government in at least equally high esteem (Kavanagh 1974).

One famous political scientist who fervently admired the Westminster model was President Woodrow Wilson. In his early writings he went so far as to urge the abolition of presidential government and the adoption of British-style parliamentary government in the United States. Such views have also been held by many other non-British observers of British politics, and many features of the Westminster model have been exported to other countries: Canada, Australia, New Zealand, and most of Britain's former colonies in Asia, Africa, and the Caribbean when they became independent. Wilson (1884, 33) referred to parliamentary government in accordance with the Westminster model as "the world's fashion."

The ten interrelated elements of the Westminster or majoritarian model are illustrated by features of three democracies that closely approximate this model and can be regarded as the majoritarian prototypes: the United Kingdom, New Zealand, and Barbados. Britain, where the Westminster model originated, is clearly the first and most obvious example to use. In many respects, however, New Zealand is an even better example—at least until its sharp turn away from majoritarianism in October 1996. The third example—Barbados—is also an almost perfect prototype of the Westminster model, although only as far as the first (executives-parties) dimension of the majoritarian-consensus contrast is concerned. In the following discussion of the ten majoritarian characteristics in the three countries, I emphasize not only their conformity with the general model but also occasional deviations from the model, as well as various other qualifications that need to be made.

THE WESTMINSTER MODEL IN THE UNITED KINGDOM

1. *Concentration of executive power in one-party and bare-majority cabinets.* The most powerful organ of British government is the cabinet. It is normally composed of members of the party that has the majority of seats in the House of Commons, and the minority is not included. Coalition cabinets are rare. Because in the British two-party system the two principal parties are of approximately equal strength, the party that wins the elections usually represents no more than a narrow majority, and the minority is relatively large. Hence the British one-party and bare-majority cabinet is the perfect embodiment of the principle of

majority rule: it wields vast amounts of political power to rule as the representative of and in the interest of a majority that is not of overwhelming proportions. A large minority is excluded from power and condemned to the role of opposition.

Especially since 1945, there have been few exceptions to the British norm of one-party majority cabinets. David Butler (1978, 112) writes that "clear-cut single-party government has been much less prevalent than many would suppose," but most of the deviations from the norm—coalitions of two or more parties or minority cabinets—occurred from 1918 to 1945. The only instances of minority cabinets in the postwar period were two minority Labour cabinets in the 1970s. In the parliamentary election of February 1974, the Labour party won a plurality but not a majority of the seats and formed a minority government dependent on all other parties not uniting to defeat it. New elections were held that October and Labour won an outright, albeit narrow, majority of the seats; but this majority was eroded by defections and by-election defeats, and the Labour cabinet again became a minority cabinet in 1976. It regained a temporary legislative majority in 1977 as a result of the pact it negotiated with the thirteen Liberals in the House of Commons: the Liberals agreed to support the cabinet in exchange for consultation on legislative proposals before their submission to Parliament. No Liberals entered the cabinet, however, and the cabinet therefore continued as a minority instead of a true coalition cabinet. The so-called Lab-Lib pact lasted until 1978, and in 1979 Labour Prime Minister James Callaghan's minority cabinet was brought down by a vote of no confidence in the House of Commons.

The only instance of a coalition cabinet in the postwar period is the government formed after the May 2010 election, which, as in February 1974, did not produce a clear winner. The incumbent Labour government was defeated, but the Conservatives won only a plurality instead of a majority of the seats. In order to have majority support in the House of Commons, they formed a coalition cabinet with the small Liberal Democratic party. Conservative leader David Cameron became prime minister and Liberal Democratic leader Nick Clegg deputy prime minister. However, coalition and minority cabinets are likely to remain the exception. They tend to be formed only when an election produces what in Britain is called a "hung parliament" without a majority winner—a very unusual election outcome.

2. *Cabinet dominance.* The United Kingdom has a parliamentary system of government, which means that the cabinet is dependent on the confidence of Parliament. In theory, because the House of Commons can vote a cabinet out of office, it "controls" the cabinet. In reality, the relationship is reversed. Because the cabinet is composed of the leaders of a cohesive majority party in the House of Commons, it is normally backed by the majority in the House of Commons, and it can confidently count on staying in office and getting its legislative proposals approved. The cabinet is clearly dominant vis-à-vis Parliament.

Because strong cabinet leadership depends on majority support in the House of Commons and on the cohesiveness of the majority party, cabinets lose some of their predominant position when either or both of these conditions are absent. Especially during the periods of minority government in the 1970s, there was a significant increase in the frequency of parliamentary defeats of important cabinet proposals. This even caused a change in the traditional view that cabinets must resign or dissolve the House of Commons and call for new elections if they suffer a defeat on either a parliamentary vote of no confidence or a major bill of central importance to the cabinet. The new unwritten rule is that only an explicit vote of no confidence necessitates resignation or new elections. The normalcy of cabinet dominance was largely restored in the 1980s under the strong leadership of Conservative Prime Minister Margaret Thatcher.

Both the normal and the deviant situations show that it is the disciplined two-party system rather than the parliamentary system that gives rise to executive dominance. In multiparty parliamentary systems, cabinets—which are often coalition cabinets—

tend to be much less dominant (Peters 1997). Because of the concentration of power in a dominant cabinet, former cabinet minister Lord Hailsham (1978, 127) has called the British system of government an "elective dictatorship."[1]

3. *Two-party system.* British politics is dominated by two large parties: the Conservative party and the Labour party. Other parties also contest elections and win seats in the House of Commons—in particular the Liberals and, after their merger with the Social Democratic party in the late 1980s, the Liberal Democrats (situated in the political center, between Labour on the left and the Conservatives on the right)—but they are not large enough to be overall victors. Minor parties, like the Scottish National party, the Welsh nationalists, and several Northern Ireland parties, never manage to win more than a handful of votes and seats. The bulk of the seats are captured by the two major parties, and they form the cabinets: the Labour party from 1945 to 1951, 1964 to 1970, 1974 to 1979, and 1997 to 2010, and the Conservatives from 1951 to 1964, 1970 to 1974, and in the long stretch from 1979 to 1997. The hegemony of these two parties was especially pronounced between 1950 and 1970: jointly they never won less than 87.5 percent of the votes and 98 percent of the seats in the House of Commons in the seven elections held in this period.

The interwar years were a transitional period during which

1. In presidential systems of government, in which the presidential executive cannot normally be removed by the legislature (except by impeachment), the same variation in the degree of executive dominance can occur, depending on exactly how governmental powers are separated. In the United States, president and Congress can be said to be in a rough balance of power, but presidents in France and in some of the Latin American countries are considerably more powerful. Guillermo O'Donnell (1994, 59–60) has proposed the term "delegative democracy"—akin to Hailsham's "elective dictatorship"—for systems with directly elected and dominant presidents; in such "strongly majoritarian" systems, "whoever wins election to the presidency is thereby entitled to govern as he or she sees fit, constrained only by the hard facts of existing power relations and by a constitutionally limited term of office."

the Labour party replaced the Liberals as one of the two big parties, and in the 1945 election, the Labour and Conservative parties together won about 85 percent of the votes and 92.5 percent of the seats. Their support declined considerably after 1970: their joint share of the popular vote ranged from only about 65 percent (in 2010) to less than 81 percent (in 1979), but they continued to win a minimum of 93 percent of the seats in the elections from 1974 to 1992 and about 86 percent of the seats from 1997 on. The Liberal Democrats were the main beneficiaries, but mainly in terms of votes instead of seats. In the four elections from 1997 to 2010, they won an average of 20 percent of the popular vote—but never more than 10 percent of the seats in the House of Commons.

4. *Majoritarian and disproportional system of elections.* The House of Commons is a large legislative body with a membership that has varied between 625 and 659 since 1945. The members are elected in single-member districts according to the plurality method, which in Britain is usually referred to as the "first past the post" system: the candidate with majority vote or, if there is no majority, with the largest minority vote wins. This system tends to produce highly disproportional results. The 2005 election provides the most glaring example: the Labour party won an absolute parliamentary majority of 355 out of 646 seats with only 35.2 percent of the popular vote. In all of the elections between October 1974 and 2005, the winning party won clear majorities of seats with never more than 44 percent of the vote. All of these majorities have been what Douglas W. Rae (1967, 74) aptly calls "manufactured majorities"—majorities that are artificially created by the electoral system out of mere pluralities of the vote. In fact, all the winning parties since 1945 have won with the benefit of such manufactured majorities. It may therefore be more accurate to call the United Kingdom a *pluralitarian* democracy instead of a majoritarian democracy. The disproportionality of the plurality method can even produce an overall winner who has failed to win a plurality of the votes: the Conservatives won a clear seat majority in 1951 not just with less than a majority of the votes but also with fewer votes than the Labour party had received.

The disproportional electoral system has been particularly disadvantageous to the Liberals and Liberal Democrats, who have therefore long been in favor of introducing some form of proportional representation (PR). But because plurality has greatly benefited the Conservatives and Labour, these two major parties have remained committed to the old disproportional method. Nevertheless, there are some signs of movement in the direction of PR. For one thing, PR was adopted for all elections in Northern Ireland (with the exception of elections to the House of Commons) after the outbreak of Protestant-Catholic strife in the early 1970s. For another, soon after Labour's election victory in 1997, Prime Minister Tony Blair's new cabinet decided that the 1999 election of British representatives to the European Parliament would be by PR—bringing the United Kingdom in line with all of the other members of the European Union. Proportional representation is also used for the election of the new regional assemblies for Scotland and Wales. Clearly, the principle of proportionality is no longer anathema. Still, it is wise to heed the cautionary words of Graham Wilson (1997, 72), who points out that the two major parties have a long history of favoring basic reforms, but only until they gain power; then "they back away from changes such as electoral reform which would work to their disadvantage." As part of their price for joining the Cameron cabinet in 2010, the Liberal Democrats were promised a referendum on electoral reform. Significantly, however, the option to be submitted to the voters would be not PR but the so-called alternative vote, which, like plurality, is a majoritarian electoral method (see Chapter 8). Moreover, the Conservatives' concession did not include a promise to support even this relatively small reform in the referendum campaign, and in the end they actively campaigned against it: it lost by a more than two to one margin in May 2011 (Qvortrup 2012).

5. *Interest group pluralism.* By concentrating power in the hands of the majority, the Westminster model of democracy sets up a government-versus-opposition pattern that is competitive and adversarial. Competition and conflict also characterize the ma-

joritarian model's typical interest group system: a system of free-for-all pluralism. It contrasts with interest group corporatism in which regular meetings take place between the representatives of the government, labor unions, and employers' organizations to seek agreement on socioeconomic policies; this process of coordination is often referred to as *concertation,* and the agreements reached are often called *tripartite* pacts. Concertation is facilitated if there are relatively few, large, and strong interest groups in each of the main functional sectors—labor, employers, farmers—and/or if there is a strong peak organization in each of the sectors that coordinates the preferences and desired strategies for each sector. Pluralism, in contrast, means a multiplicity of interest groups that exert pressure on the government in an uncoordinated and competitive manner.

Britain's interest group system is clearly pluralist. The one exception is the 1975 Social Contract on wages and prices concluded between the Labour government, the main labor union federation (the Trades Union Congress), and the main employers' federation (the Confederation of British Industry). This contract fell apart two years later when the government failed to get union agreement to accept further wage restraints and imposed wage ceilings unilaterally. The 1980s were characterized even more by grim confrontations between Margaret Thatcher's Conservative government and the labor unions—the very opposite of concertation and corporatism. Not much changed under the Labour government that was in power from 1997 to 2010. Michael Gallagher, Michael Laver, and Peter Mair (2011, 467, 471) write that Britain is "often cited as one of the classic examples of a pluralist rather than a corporatist system," and they predict that the country is highly unlikely "to move away from an essentially pluralist form of interest group representation."

6. *Unitary and centralized government.* The United Kingdom is a unitary and centralized state. Local governments perform a series of important functions, but they are the creatures of the central government and their powers are not constitutionally guar-

anteed (as in a federal system). Moreover, they are financially dependent on the central government. There are no clearly designated geographical and functional areas from which the parliamentary majority and the cabinet are barred. The Royal Commission on the Constitution under Lord Kilbrandon concluded in 1973: "The United Kingdom is the largest unitary state in Europe and among the most centralised of the major industrial countries in the world" (cited in Busch 1994, 60).

Two exceptions should be noted. One is that Northern Ireland was ruled by its own parliament and cabinet with a high degree of autonomy—more than what most states in federal systems have—from 1921, when the Republic of Ireland became independent, until the imposition of direct rule from London in 1972. It is also significant, however, that Northern Ireland's autonomy could be, and was, eliminated in 1972 by Parliament by means of a simple majoritarian decision. The second exception is the gradual movement toward greater autonomy for Scotland and Wales—"devolution," in British parlance. But it was not until September 1997 that referendums in Scotland and Wales finally approved the creation of autonomous and directly elected Scottish and Welsh assemblies (Trench 2007). Devolution, however, has not gone hand in hand with decentralization within England, by far the largest and most important of the United Kingdom's four component parts. The London *Economist* argues that it is still "the West's most centralised" system (Ganesh 2010).

7. *Concentration of legislative power in a unicameral legislature.* For the organization of the legislature, the majoritarian principle of concentrating power means that legislative power should be concentrated in a single house or chamber. In this respect, the United Kingdom deviates from the pure majoritarian model. Parliament consists of two chambers: the House of Commons, which is popularly elected, and the House of Lords, which used to consist mainly of members of the hereditary nobility but also contained a large number of so-called life peers, appointed by the government. The 1999 House of Lords Act removed all but

ninety-two hereditary peers, and the appointed members now form the overwhelming majority in the House of Lords. The relationship between the two houses is asymmetrical: almost all legislative power belongs to the House of Commons. The only power that the House of Lords retains is the power to delay legislation: money bills can be delayed for one month and all other bills for one year. The one-year limit was established in 1949; between the first major reform of 1911 and 1949, the Lords' delaying power was about two years, but in the entire period since 1911 they have usually refrained from imposing long delays.

Therefore, although the British bicameral legislature deviates from the majoritarian model, it does not deviate much: in everyday discussion in Britain, "Parliament" refers almost exclusively to the House of Commons, and the highly asymmetric bicameral system may also be called near-unicameralism. The change from near-unicameralism to pure unicameralism would not be a difficult step: it could be decided by a simple majority in the House of Commons and, if the Lords objected, merely a one-year delay.

8. *Constitutional flexibility.* Britain has a constitution that is "unwritten" in the sense that there is not one written document that specifies the composition and powers of the governmental institutions and the rights of citizens. These are defined instead in a number of basic laws—like the Magna Carta of 1215, the Bill of Rights of 1689, and the Parliament Acts of 1911 and 1949—common law principles, customs, and conventions. The fact that the constitution is unwritten has two important implications. One is that it makes the constitution completely flexible because it can be changed by Parliament in the same way as any other laws—by regular majorities instead of the supermajorities, like two-thirds majorities, required in many other democracies for amending their written constitutions. One slight exception to this flexibility is that opposition by the House of Lords may force a one-year delay in constitutional changes.

9. *Absence of judicial review.* The other important implication of an unwritten constitution is the absence of judicial review:

there is no written constitutional document with the status of "higher law" against which the courts can test the constitutionality of regular legislation. Although Parliament normally accepts and feels bound by the rules of the unwritten constitution, it is not formally bound by them. With regard to both changing and interpreting the constitution, therefore, Parliament—that is, the parliamentary majority—can be said to be the ultimate or sovereign authority. In A. V. Dicey's (1915, 37–38) famous formulation, parliamentary sovereignty "means neither more nor less than this, namely, that Parliament . . . has, under the English constitution, the right to make or unmake any law whatever; and, further, that no person or body is recognised by the law of England as having the right to override or set aside the legislation of Parliament."

One exception to parliamentary sovereignty is that when Britain entered the European Community—a supranational instead of merely an international organization—in 1973, it accepted the Community's laws and institutions as higher authorities than Parliament with regard to several areas of policy. Because sovereignty means supreme and ultimate authority, Parliament can therefore no longer be regarded as fully sovereign. Britain's membership in the European Community—now called the European Union—has also introduced a measure of judicial review both for the European Court of Justice and for British courts: "Parliament's supremacy is challenged by the right of the Community institutions to legislate for the United Kingdom (without the prior consent of Parliament) and by the right of the courts to rule on the admissibility (in terms of Community law) of future acts of Parliament" (Coombs 1977, 88). Similarly, Britain has been a member of the European Convention on Human rights since 1951, and its acceptance of an optional clause of this convention in 1966 has given the European Court of Human Rights in Strasbourg the right to review and invalidate any state action, including legislation, that it judges to violate the human rights entrenched in the convention (Cappelletti 1989, 202; Johnson 1998, 155–58).

10. *A central bank controlled by the executive.* Central banks are responsible for monetary policy, and independent banks are widely considered to be better at controlling inflation and maintaining price stability than banks that are dependent on the executive. However, central bank independence is clearly in conflict with the Westminster model's principle of concentrating power in the hands of the one-party majority cabinet. As expected, the Bank of England has indeed not been able to act independently and has instead been under the control of the cabinet. During the 1980s, pressure to make the Bank of England more autonomous increased. Two Conservative chancellors of the exchequer tried to convince their colleagues to take this big step away from the Westminster model, but their advice was rejected (Busch 1994, 59). It was not until 1997—one of the first decisions of the newly elected Labour government—that the Bank of England was given the independent power to set interest rates. The degree of central bank independence is commonly measured on a scale developed by Alex Cukierman, ranging from a low of 0 to a high of 1 (see Chapter 13). From 1997 to 1998, the score for the British central bank rose from 0.27 to 0.47—indicating a significant increase in its independence but still well below, for instance, the Swiss and German scores of 0.64 and 0.69 during most of the 1990s (Polillo and Guillén 2005).

The recent changes in British politics do not change the overall character of Britain as a prime example of majoritarian democracy. As Matthew Flinders (2010, emphasis added) puts it—to cite the title and subtitle of his book—the first decade of the twenty-first century was a period of "democratic drift" and "majoritarian *modification*" rather than any basic shift away from the Westminster model.

THE WESTMINSTER MODEL IN NEW ZEALAND

Many of the Westminster model's features have been exported to other members of the British Commonwealth, but only one country adopted virtually the entire model: New Zealand. A major change away from majoritarianism took place in 1996 when New Zealand held its first election by PR, but the New Zealand political system before 1996 can serve as a second instructive example of how the Westminster model works.

1. *Concentration of executive power in one-party and bare-majority cabinets.* For six decades, from 1935 to the mid-1990s, New Zealand had single-party majority cabinets without exceptions or interruptions. Two large parties—the Labour party and the National party—dominated New Zealand politics, and they alternated in office. The one-party majority cabinet formed after the last plurality election in 1993 suffered a series of defections and briefly became a quasi-coalition cabinet (a coalition with the recent defectors), then a one-party minority cabinet, and finally a minority coalition—but all of these unusual cabinets occurred in the final phase of the transition to the new non-Westminster system (Boston, Levine, McLeay, and Roberts 1996, 93–96). The only other deviations from single-party majority government happened much earlier: New Zealand had a wartime coalition cabinet from 1915 to 1919, and another coalition was in power from 1931 to 1935.

2. *Cabinet dominance.* In this respect too, New Zealand was a perfect example of the Westminster model. Just as during most of the postwar period in the United Kingdom, the combination of the parliamentary system of government and a two-party system with cohesive parties made the cabinet predominate over the legislature. In the words of New Zealand political scientist Stephen Levine (1979, 25–26), the "rigidly disciplined two-party system has contributed to the concentration of power within the Cabinet, formed from among the Members of Parliament . . . belonging to the majority party."

3. *Two-party system.* Two large parties were in virtually complete control of the party system, and only these two formed cabinets during the six decades from 1935 to the mid-1990s: the Labour party (1935–49, 1957–60, 1972–75, and 1984–90) and the right-of-center National party (1949–57, 1960–72, 1975–84, and

after 1990). Moreover, unlike in Britain, third parties were almost absent from the New Zealand House of Representatives. In eleven of the seventeen elections from 1946 to 1993, the two large parties divided all of the seats; in five elections, only one other party gained one or two seats; and, in 1993, two small parties gained two seats each (out of ninety-nine). New Zealand's two-party system was therefore an almost pure two-party system.

4. *Majoritarian and disproportional system of elections.* The House of Representatives was elected according to the plurality method in single-member districts. The only unusual feature was that there were four special large districts, geographically overlapping the regular smaller districts, reserved for the Maori minority (representing about 12 percent of the population). These four districts entailed a deviation from the majoritarianism of the Westminster model because their aim was to guarantee minority representation. From 1975 on, all Maori voters have had the right to register and vote either in the regular district or in the special Maori district in which they reside.

As in the United Kingdom, the plurality system produced severely disproportional results, especially in 1978 and 1981. In the 1978 election, the National party won a clear majority of fifty-one out of ninety-two seats even though it won neither a majority of the popular votes—its support was only 39.8 percent—nor a plurality, because Labour's popular vote was 40.4 percent; the Social Credit party's 17.1 percent of the vote yielded only one seat. In 1981, the National party won another parliamentary majority of forty-seven out of ninety-two seats and again with fewer votes than Labour, although the respective percentages were closer: 38.8 and 39.0 percent; Social Credit now won 20.7 percent of the popular vote—more than half of the votes gained by either of the two big parties—but merely two seats. Moreover, all of the parliamentary majorities from 1954 on were manufactured majorities, won with less than majorities of the popular vote. In this respect, New Zealand was, like the United Kingdom, more a pluralitarian than a majoritarian democracy.

5. *Interest group pluralism.* New Zealand's interest group sys-

tem, like Britain's, is clearly pluralist. Also, again like Britain, New Zealand has had high strike levels—indicative of confrontation instead of concertation between labor and management. In comparative studies of corporatism and pluralism, many scholars have tried to gauge the precise degree to which the interest group systems of the industrialized democracies are corporatist or pluralist. Their judgments differ considerably with regard to a few of these countries, but on Great Britain and New Zealand there is little disagreement: both belong on the extreme pluralist end of the pluralist-corporatist spectrum (Lijphart and Crepaz 1991; Siaroff 1999).

6. *Unitary and centralized government.* The "Act to Grant a Representative Constitution to the Colony of New Zealand," passed by the British parliament in 1852, created six provinces with considerable autonomous powers and functions vis-à-vis the central government, but these provinces were abolished in 1875. Today's governmental system is unitary and centralized—not as surprising, of course, for a country with a population of about four million than for the United Kingdom with its much larger population of about sixty million people.

7. *Concentration of legislative power in a unicameral legislature.* For about a century, New Zealand had a bicameral legislature, consisting of an elected lower house and an appointed upper house, but the upper house gradually lost power. Its abolition in 1950 changed the asymmetrical bicameral system into pure unicameralism.

8. *Constitutional flexibility.* Like the United Kingdom, New Zealand lacks a single written constitutional document. Its "unwritten" constitution has consisted of a number of basic laws— like the Constitution Acts of 1852 and 1986, the Electoral Acts of 1956 and 1993, and the Bill of Rights Act of 1990—conventions, and customs.[2] Some key provisions in the basic laws are "entrenched" and can be changed only by three-fourths majorities of

2. The Constitution Act of 1852 and Electoral Act of 1956 were superseded by the two later acts.

the membership of the House of Representatives or by a majority vote in a referendum; however, this entrenchment can always be removed by regular majorities, so that, in the end, majority rule prevails. Hence, like the British parliament, the parliament of New Zealand is sovereign. Any law, including laws that "amend" the unwritten constitution, can be adopted by regular majority rule. As one of New Zealand's constitutional law experts puts it, "The central principle of the Constitution is that there are no effective legal limitations on what Parliament may enact by the ordinary legislative process" (Scott 1962, 39).

9. *Absence of judicial review.* Parliamentary sovereignty also means, as in Britain, that the courts do not have the right of judicial review. The House of Representatives is the sole judge of the constitutionality of its own legislation.

10. *A central bank controlled by the executive.* Andreas Busch (1994, 65) writes that historically New Zealand "has been a country with . . . a very low degree of central bank independence," and for the period until 1989, he gives the Reserve Bank of New Zealand his lowest rating—indicating even less autonomy than that of its British counterpart. The Reserve Bank Act of 1989 increased the bank's independence, but only slightly: the Cukierman index of central bank independence rose from 0.24 to 0.31—well below the level of the Bank of England after 1997 (Cukierman, Webb, and Neyapti 1994; Polillo and Guillén 2005).

With only one exception—the parliamentary seats reserved for the Maori minority—democracy in New Zealand was, until 1996, more clearly majoritarian and hence a better example of the Westminster model than British democracy. In fact, especially in view of the minority cabinets and frequent defeats of cabinet proposals in Britain in the 1970s, Richard Rose could legitimately claim that New Zealand was "the only example of the true British system left" (personal communication, April 8, 1982). However, the adoption of PR and the first PR election of parliament in October 1996 entailed a radical shift away from the Westminster model.

The two major parties were opposed to PR, but they both unintentionally contributed to its adoption. The first impetus was the Labour party's unhappiness with the results of the 1978 and 1981 elections, mentioned above, in which the National party won parliamentary majorities not only with less than 40 percent of the popular vote but with fewer votes than the Labour party had received. When Labour was returned to power in 1984, it appointed a Royal Commission on the Electoral System to recommend improvements. The commission's terms of reference were very broad, however, and it recommended not just small adjustments but a radical change to PR as well as a referendum on whether to adopt it. The government tried to deflect the proposal by turning it over to a parliamentary committee, which, as expected, rejected PR and instead merely recommended minor changes. The election campaign of 1987 put PR back on the political agenda: the Labour prime minister promised to let the voters decide the issue by referendum, but his party retreated from this pledge after being reelected. Seeking to embarrass Labour, the National party opportunistically made the same promise in the 1990 campaign, and when they won the election, they could not avoid honoring it. The voters then twice endorsed PR in referendums held in 1992 and 1993 (Jackson and McRobie 1998).

The form of PR that was adopted was modeled after the German system. In the first PR election, held in 1996, sixty-five members were elected by plurality in single-member districts—including five special Maori districts—and fifty-five members by PR from party lists. The second set of fifty-five seats had to be allocated to the parties in a way that made the overall result as proportional as possible.[3] This crucial provision made the new system clearly and fully a PR system, although the New Zealand term of "mixed member proportional" (MMP) system seems to imply that it is a mixture of PR and something else. The same rules have governed subsequent elections, although the numbers

---

3. Each voter has two votes, one for a district candidate and one for a party list. To avoid excessive fragmentation, parties must win either a minimum of 5 percent of the list votes or at least one district seat to qualify for list seats.

of single-member and Maori districts as well as the number of party list seats have undergone slight adjustments.

The first PR election instantly transformed New Zealand politics in several respects (Vowles, Aimer, Banducci, and Karp 1998). First, the election result was much more proportional than those of the previous plurality elections. The largest party, the National party, was still overrepresented, but by less than three percentage points; it won 33.8 percent of the vote and 36.7 percent of the seats. Second, the election produced a multiparty system with an unprecedented six parties gaining representation in parliament. Third, unlike in any other postwar election, no party won a majority of the seats. Fourth, in contrast with the long line of previous single-party majority cabinets, the National party entered into a two-party coalition cabinet with the New Zealand First party, the main representative of the Maori minority, which had won seventeen seats including all five of the special Maori seats. This cabinet still enjoyed majority support in the legislature, but all of the subsequent cabinets have been minority coalition or minority single-party cabinets.

Because of these significant deviations from the majoritarian model, post-1996 New Zealand is no longer a good, let alone the best, example of the "true British system." Hence, in Kurt von Mettenheim's (1997, 11) words, "The United Kingdom [now] appears to be the only country to have retained the central features of the Westminster model." It should be noted, however, that all of the post-1996 changes in New Zealand have to do with the executives-parties dimension of the majoritarian model, comprising the first five of the ten characteristics of the model, and that, especially with regard to this first dimension, several other former British colonies continue to have predominantly Westminster-style institutions. A particularly clear and instructive example is Barbados.

THE WESTMINSTER MODEL IN BARBADOS

Barbados is a small island state in the Caribbean with a population of about a quarter of a million. It has a "strongly homogeneous society" that is mainly of African descent (Duncan 1994, 77). It gained its independence from Britain in 1966, but there continues to be "a strong and pervasive sense of British tradition and culture" (Muller, Overstreet, Isacoff, and Lansford 2011, 116)— including British *political* traditions. Barbados is often called the "Little England" of the Caribbean.

1. *Concentration of executive power in one-party and bare-majority cabinets.* Since independence in 1966, Barbados has had single-party majority cabinets. Its two large parties—the Barbados Labour party (BLP) and the Democratic Labour party (DLP)—have been the overwhelmingly dominant forces in Barbados politics, and they have alternated in office. Unlike in the British and New Zealand cases, there are no exceptions or qualifications to this pattern that need to be noted. In fact, the pattern extends back to colonial times. Ever since the establishment of universal suffrage and cabinet government in the early 1950s, the sequence of single-party majority cabinets has been unbroken.

2. *Cabinet dominance.* Barbadian cabinets have been at least as dominant as those of the two earlier examples of the Westminster model. The term *elective dictatorship,* coined by Lord Hailsham for Britain, also fits the Barbados system well (Payne 1993, 69). One special reason for the predominance of the cabinet in Barbados is the small size of the legislature. The Barbadian House of Assembly had only twenty-four members from 1966 to 1981; this number was increased slightly to twenty-seven in 1981, twenty-eight in 1991, and thirty in 2003. Many of the legislators are therefore also cabinet ministers, which in turn means that, as Trevor Munroe (1996, 108) points out, almost one-third of the members of the legislature "are in effect constitutionally debarred from an independent and critical stance in relation to the executive."

3. *Two-party system.* The same two large parties have controlled the party politics of Barbados since independence, and they have formed all of the cabinets: the left-of-center DLP from 1966 to 1976, from 1986 to 1994, and from 2008 on, and the more conservative BLP between 1976 and 1986 and between 1994 and 2008. In

eight of the ten elections since 1966, no third parties won any seats, only one small party won two seats in 1966, and another small party won one seat in 1994. The strength of the two-party system is also illustrated by the fate of the four members of parliament who defected from the ruling DLP in 1989 and formed a separate party. As Tony Thorndike (1993, 158) writes, the new party "did not long survive the logic of the 'first past the post' Westminster system and the two-party culture of Barbados. In elections in January 1991 it lost all its four seats."

4. *Majoritarian and disproportional system of elections.* In the elections before independence, including the 1966 elections, which was held several months before formal independence took place, Barbados used the plurality method but not in the usual single-member districts. Instead, two-member districts were used (Emmanuel 1992, 3; Duncan 1994, 78); these tend to increase the disproportionality of the election results because, in plurality systems, disproportionality increases as the number of representatives elected per district increases. Since 1971, all elections have been by plurality in single-member districts, but electoral disproportionality has remained high. For instance, in 1986 the DLP won twenty-four of the twenty-seven seats (88.9 percent) with 59.4 percent of the votes, and in 1999 the BLP won twenty-six of the twenty-eight seats (92.9 percent) with 64.9 percent of the votes. In three of the elections since 1966, the parliamentary majorities were "manufactured" from pluralities of the vote, but in the other seven elections the seat majorities were genuinely "earned" with popular vote majorities. On balance, therefore, Barbados has been less of a pluralitarian democracy than Britain and New Zealand. Moreover, unlike the other two countries, Barbados has not experienced any instances of a parliamentary majority won on the basis of a second-place finish in the popular vote.

5. *Interest group pluralism.* Again like the United Kingdom and New Zealand, Barbados had an interest group system that was pluralist rather than corporatist in the first decades after independence. In 1993, however, the government, business leaders,

and labor unions negotiated an agreement on wages and prices, which included a wage freeze. This tripartite pact was renewed several times and lasted about fifteen years.

6–10. *The characteristics of the second (federal-unitary) dimension of the majoritarian model.* Barbados has a unitary and centralized form of government—not surprising for a small country with only a quarter of a million people—but as far as the other four characteristics of the federal-unitary dimension are concerned, it does not fit the pure majoritarian model. It has a bicameral legislature consisting of a popularly elected House of Assembly and an appointed Senate that can delay but not veto—a case of asymmetrical bicameralism. It has a written constitution that can be amended only by two-thirds majorities in both houses of the legislature. The constitution explicitly gives the courts the right of judicial review. Finally, the central bank of Barbados has a charter that gives it a medium degree of autonomy in monetary policy; its Cukierman score has been a steady 0.38—higher than those of the New Zealand and pre-1997 British central banks (Cukierman, Webb, and Neyapti 1994; Polillo and Guillén 2005).

Anthony Payne (1993) argues that the former British colonies in the Caribbean are characterized not by Westminster systems but by "Westminster adapted." As illustrated by Barbados—but by and large also true for the other Commonwealth democracies in the region—this adaptation has affected mainly the second dimension of the Westminster model. On the first (executives-parties) dimension, the Westminster model has remained almost completely intact. The fact that Barbados deviates from majoritarianism with regard to most of the characteristics of the federal-unitary dimension does not mean, of course, that it deviates to such an extent that it is a good example of the contrasting model of consensus democracy. In order to illustrate the consensus model, I turn in the next chapter to the examples of Switzerland, Belgium, and the European Union.

CHAPTER 3

THE CONSENSUS MODEL OF DEMOCRACY

The majoritarian interpretation of the basic definition of democracy is that it means "government by the *majority* of the people." It argues that majorities should govern and that minorities should oppose. This view is challenged by the consensus model of democracy. As the Nobel Prize–winning economist Sir Arthur Lewis (1965, 64–65) has forcefully pointed out, majority rule and the government-versus-opposition pattern of politics that it implies may be interpreted as undemocratic because they are principles of exclusion. Lewis states that the primary meaning of democracy is that "all who are affected by a decision should have the chance to participate in making that decision either directly or through chosen representatives." Its secondary meaning is that "the will of the majority shall prevail." If this means that winning parties may make all the governmental decisions and that the losers may criticize but not govern, Lewis argues, the two meanings are incompatible: "to exclude the losing groups from participation in decision-making clearly violates the primary meaning of democracy."

Majoritarians can legitimately respond that, under two conditions, the incompatibility noted by Lewis can be resolved. First, the exclusion of the minority is mitigated if majorities and minorities alternate in government—that is, if today's minority can become the majority in the next election instead of being condemned to permanent opposition. This is how the British, New Zealand, and Barbadian two-party systems have usually worked, but there have also been long periods in which one of the major parties was kept out of power: the British Labour party during the thirteen years from 1951 to 1964 and the eighteen years from 1979 to 1997, the British Conservatives for thirteen years from 1997 to 2010, the New Zealand National party for fourteen years from 1935 to 1949, New Zealand Labour for twelve years from 1960 to 1972, and the Democratic Labour party in Barbados for fourteen years from 1994 to 2008.

Even during these extended periods of exclusion from power, one can plausibly argue that democracy and majority rule were not in conflict because of the presence of a second condition: the fact that all three countries are relatively homogeneous societies and that their major parties have usually not been very far apart in their policy outlooks because they have tended to stay close to the political center. A party's exclusion from power may be undemocratic in terms of the "government *by* the people" criterion, but if its voters' interests and preferences are reasonably well served by the other party's policies in government, the system approximates the "government *for* the people" definition of democracy.

In less homogeneous societies neither condition applies. The policies advocated by the principal parties tend to diverge to a greater extent, and the voters' loyalties are frequently more rigid, reducing the chances that the main parties will alternate in exercising government power. Especially in *plural societies*—societies that are sharply divided along religious, ideological, linguistic, cultural, ethnic, or racial lines into virtually separate subsocieties with their own political parties, interest groups, and media of communication—the flexibility necessary for majoritarian democracy is likely to be absent. Under these conditions, majority rule is not only undemocratic but also dangerous, because minorities that are continually denied access to power will feel excluded and discriminated against and may lose their allegiance to the regime. For instance, in the plural society of Northern Ireland, divided into a Protestant majority and a Catholic minority, majority rule meant that the Unionist party representing the Protestant majority won all the elections and formed all of the governments between 1921 and 1972. Massive Catholic protests in the late 1960s developed into a Protestant-Catholic civil war that could be kept under control only by British military intervention and the imposition of direct rule from London.

In the most deeply divided societies, like Northern Ireland, majority rule spells majority dictatorship and civil strife rather than democracy. What such societies need is a democratic regime that emphasizes consensus instead of opposition, that includes rather than excludes, and that tries to maximize the size of the ruling majority instead of being satisfied with a bare majority: consensus democracy. Despite their own majoritarian inclinations, successive British cabinets have recognized this need: they have insisted on PR in all elections in Northern Ireland (except those to the House of Commons) and, as a precondition for returning political autonomy to Northern Ireland, on broad Protestant-Catholic power-sharing coalitions. PR and power-sharing were also the key elements in the Good Friday Agreement on the political future of Northern Ireland that was finally reached in 1998. Similarly, Lewis (1965, 51–55, 65–84) strongly recommends PR, inclusive coalitions, and federalism for the plural societies of West Africa. The consensus model is obviously also appropriate for less divided but still heterogeneous countries, and it is a reasonable and workable alternative to the Westminster model even in fairly homogeneous countries.

The examples I use to illustrate the consensus model are Switzerland, Belgium, and the European Union—all multiethnic entities. Switzerland is the best example: with one exception it approximates the pure model perfectly. Belgium also provides a good example, especially after it formally became a federal state in 1993; I therefore pay particular attention to the pattern of Belgian politics in the most recent period. The European Union (EU) is a supranational organization—more than just an international organization—but it is not, or not yet, a sovereign state. Because of the EU's intermediate status, analysts of the European Union disagree on whether to study it as an international organization or an incipient federal state, but the latter approach is increasingly common (Hix 1994, 2005). This is also my approach: if the EU is regarded as a federal state, its institutions are remarkably close to the consensus model of democracy. I discuss the Swiss and Belgian prototypes first and in tandem with each other and then turn to the EU example.

THE CONSENSUS MODEL IN SWITZERLAND AND BELGIUM

The consensus model of democracy may be described in terms of ten elements that stand in sharp contrast to each of the ten majoritarian characteristics of the Westminster model. Instead of concentrating power in the hands of the majority, the consensus model tries to share, disperse, and restrain power in a variety of ways.

1. *Executive power-sharing in broad coalition cabinets.* In contrast to the Westminster model's tendency to concentrate executive power in one-party and bare-majority cabinets, the consensus principle is to let all or most of the important parties share executive power in a broad coalition. The Swiss seven-member national executive, the Federal Council, offers an excellent example of such a broad coalition: until 2003, the three large parties— Social Democrats, Radical Democrats, and Christian Democrats— each of which held about one-fourth of the seats in the lower house of the legislature during the post–World War II era, and the Swiss People's party (SPP), with about one-eighth of the seats, shared the seven executive positions proportionally according to the so-called magic formula of 2:2:2:1, established in 1959. After the 2003 election, in which the SPP became the largest party, it

was given an additional seat at the expense of the Christian Democrats. The broad coalition was interrupted in 2007 when SPP leader Christoph Blocher, who had been a member of the Federal Council since 2003, was not reelected by parliament, and a different SPP member, who was not the party's nominee, was elected in his place. The SPP declared that it was no longer represented by its two council members and that it would become an opposition party. However, the broad coalition and the magic formula were restored in January 2009 (Church and Vatter 2009). An additional informal power-sharing rule is that the linguistic groups be represented in rough proportion to their sizes: four or five German-speakers, one or two French-speakers, and frequently an Italian-speaker.

The Belgian constitution offers an example of a formal requirement that the executive include representatives of the large linguistic groups. For many years, it had already been the custom to form cabinets with approximately equal numbers of ministers representing the Dutch-speaking majority and the French-speaking minority. This became a formal rule in 1970, and the new federal constitution again stipulates that "with the possible exception of the Prime Minister, the Council of Ministers [cabinet] includes as many French-speaking members as Dutch-speaking members" (Alen and Ergec 1994). Such a rule does not apply to the partisan composition of the cabinet, but there have been only about four years of one-party rule in the postwar era, and since 1980 all cabinets have been coalitions of between four and six parties.

2. *Executive-legislative balance of power.* The Swiss political system is neither parliamentary nor presidential. The relationship between the executive Federal Council and the legislatures is explained by Swiss political scientist Jürg Steiner (1974, 43) as follows: "The members of the council are elected individually for a fixed term of four years, and, according to the Constitution, the legislature cannot stage a vote of no confidence during that period. If a government proposal is defeated by Parliament, it is not necessary for either the member sponsoring this proposal or

the Federal Council as a body to resign." This formal separation of powers has made both the executive and the legislature more independent, and their relationship is much more balanced than cabinet-parliament relationships in the British, New Zealand, and Barbadian cases in which the cabinet is clearly dominant. The Swiss Federal Council is powerful but not supreme.

Belgium has a parliamentary form of government with a cabinet dependent on the confidence of the legislature, as in the three prototypes of the Westminster model. However, Belgian cabinets, largely because they are often broad and uncohesive coalitions, are not at all as dominant as their Westminster counterparts, and they tend to have a genuine give-and-take relationship with parliament. The fact that Belgian cabinets are often short-lived attests to their relatively weak position: from 1980 to 2010, for instance, there were nine cabinets consisting of different multiparty coalitions—with an average cabinet life of only about three years.

3. *Multiparty system.* Both Switzerland and Belgium have multiparty systems without any party that comes close to majority status. In the 2007 elections to the Swiss National Council, twelve parties won seats, but the bulk of these seats—167 out of 200— were captured by the four major parties on the Federal Council. Switzerland may therefore be said to have a four-party system.

Until the late 1960s, Belgium was characterized by a three-party system consisting of two large parties—Christian Democrats and Socialists—and the medium-sized Liberals. Since then, however, these major parties have split along linguistic lines, and several new linguistic parties have attained prominence. In addition, two Green parties, Dutch-speaking and French-speaking, have emerged in recent years. About a dozen parties have usually been able to win seats in the Chamber of Representatives, and eleven of these have been important enough to be included in one or more cabinets. Belgium clearly has "one of the most fragmented party systems of any modern democracy" (Swenden, Brans, and De Winter 2009, 8).

The emergence of multiparty systems in Switzerland and Belgium can be explained in terms of two factors. The first is that the two countries are plural societies, divided along several lines of cleavage: religion, class, and language. A contrast between Switzerland and Belgium is that linguistic differences have had only a minor impact on the Swiss party system, while they have become the major differentiator for the Belgian parties. The Swiss People's party used to be mainly strong among Protestant farmers, but it has extended its appeal, and gained a great deal of electoral support, as a right-wing populist and anti-immigrant party. This description fits one of the small Flemish-nationalist parties in Belgium, too (Pauwels 2011). Both countries also have small but significant Green parties.

4. *Proportional representation.* The second explanation for the emergence of multiparty systems in Switzerland and Belgium is that their proportional electoral systems have not inhibited the translation of societal cleavages into party-system cleavages. In contrast with the plurality method, which tends to overrepresent large parties and to underrepresent small parties, the basic aim of proportional representation is to divide the parliamentary seats among the parties in proportion to the votes they receive. The lower houses of both legislatures are elected by PR.

5. *Interest group corporatism.* There is some disagreement among experts on corporatism about the degree of corporatism in Switzerland and Belgium, mainly because the labor unions in these two countries tend to be less well organized and less influential than business. The disagreement can be resolved, however, by distinguishing between two variants of corporatism: social corporatism in which the labor unions predominate and liberal corporatism in which business association are the stronger force. Peter J. Katzenstein (1985, 105, 130) uses Switzerland and Belgium as two examplars of the latter, and he concludes that Switzerland "most clearly typifies the traits characteristic of liberal corporatism." Both countries clearly show the three general elements of corporatism: tripartite concertation, relatively few and

relatively large interest groups, and the prominence of peak associations. Gerhard Lehmbruch (1993, 52) writes that "the strength of Swiss peak associations is remarkable, and it is generally acknowledged that the cohesion of Swiss interest associations is superior to that of Swiss political parties." Moreover, Klaus Armingeon (1997) argues that, although the extent and effectiveness of corporatism in many European countries has been declining in the 1990s, it continues to be strong in Switzerland. Belgian tripartite cooperation began with the Social Pact concluded in 1944, and its corporatist system "has not fundamentally changed" since then (Deschouwer 2009, 193).

6. *Federal and decentralized government.* Switzerland is a federal state in which power is divided between the central government and the government of twenty cantons and six so-called half-cantons, produced by splits in three formerly united cantons. The half-cantons have only one instead of two representatives in the Swiss federal chamber, the Council of States, and they carry only half the weight of the regular cantons in the voting on constitutional amendments; in most other respects, however, their status is equal to that of the full cantons. Switzerland is also one of the world's most decentralized states.

Belgium was a unitary and centralized state for a long time, but from 1970 on it gradually moved in the direction of both decentralization and federalism; in 1993, it formally became a federal state. The form of federalism adopted by Belgium is a "unique federalism" (Fitzmaurice 1996) and one of "Byzantine complexity" (McRae 1997, 289), because it consists of three geographically defined regions—Flanders, Wallonia, and the bilingual capital of Brussels—and three nongeographically defined cultural communities—the large Flemish and French communities and the much smaller German-speaking community. The main reason for the construction of this two-layer system was that the bilingual area of Brussels has a large majority of French-speakers but is surrounded by Dutch-speaking Flanders. There is a considerable overlap between regions and communities, but they do not match exactly. Each has its own legislature and executive, except that in Flanders the government of the Flemish community also serves as the government of the Flemish region.

7. *Strong bicameralism.* The principal justification for instituting a bicameral instead of a unicameral legislature is to give special representation to minorities, including the smaller states in federal systems, in a second chamber or upper house. Two conditions have to be fulfilled if this minority representation is to be meaningful: the upper house has to be elected on a different basis than the lower house, and it must have real power—ideally as much power as the lower house. Both of these conditions are met in the Swiss system: the National Council is the lower house and represents the Swiss people, and the Council of States is the upper or federal chamber representing the cantons, with each canton having two representatives and each half-canton one representative. Hence the small cantons are much more strongly represented in the Council of States than in the National Council. Swiss bicameralism is also symmetrical: the "absolute equality of the two chambers in all matters of legislation" is a sacrosanct rule (Linder 2010, 51).

The two Belgian chambers of parliament—the Chamber of Representatives and the Senate—had virtually equal powers in prefederal Belgium, but they were both proportionally constituted and hence very similar in composition. The new Senate, elected for the first time in 1995, especially represents the two cultural-linguistic groups, but it is still largely proportionally constituted and not designed to provide overrepresentation for the French-speaking and German-speaking minorities. Moreover, only forty of its seventy-one members are popularly elected, and its powers were reduced in comparison with the old Senate; for instance, it no longer has budgetary authority (De Winter and Dumont 2009, 102; Deschouwer 2009, 171–72). Hence the new federal legislature of Belgium exemplifies a relatively weak rather than strong bicameralism.

8. *Constitutional rigidity.* Both Belgium and Switzerland have

a written constitution—a single document containing the basic rules of governance—that can be changed only by special majorities. Amendments to the Swiss constitution require the approval in a referendum of not only a nationwide majority of the voters but also majorities in a majority of the cantons. The half-cantons are given half weight in the canton-by-canton calculation; this means that, for instance, a constitutional amendment can be adopted by 13.5 cantons in favor and 12.5 against. The requirement of majority cantonal approval means that the populations of the smaller cantons and half-cantons, with less than 20 percent of the total Swiss population, can veto constitutional changes.

In Belgium, there are two types of supermajorities. All constitutional amendments require the approval of two-thirds majorities in both houses of the legislature. Moreover, laws pertaining to the organization and powers of the communities and regions have a semiconstitutional status and are even harder to adopt and to amend: in addition to the two-thirds majorities in both houses, they require the approval of majorities within the Dutch-speaking group as well as within the French-speaking group in each of the houses. This rule gives the French-speakers an effective minority veto.

9. *Judicial review.* Switzerland deviates in one respect from the pure consensus model: its supreme court, the Federal Tribunal, does not have the right of judicial review. A popular initiative that tried to introduce it was decisively rejected in a 1939 referendum (Codding 1961, 112). Parliament seriously considered the creation of a constitutional court as part of the comprehensive judicial reform adopted in 2000 but ultimately decided not to incorporate this proposal in the reform package (Vatter 2008, 22–23).

There was no judicial review in Belgium either until 1984, when the new Court of Arbitration was inaugurated. The court's original main responsibility was the interpretation of the constitutional provisions concerning the separation of powers among the central, community, and regional governments. Its authority was greatly expanded by the constitutional revision of 1988, and the Court of Arbitration can now be regarded as a "genuine constitutional court" (De Winter and Dumont 2009, 109).

10. *Central bank independence.* Switzerland's central bank has long been regarded as one of the strongest and most independent central banks, together with the German Bundesbank and the Federal Reserve System in the United States. Its independence, as measured by the Cukierman index, has been a high 0.63 since 1980 (Vatter 2008, 26). In contrast, the National Bank of Belgium was long one of the weakest central banks. However, its autonomy was substantially reinforced in the early 1990s, roughly at the same time as the transition to a federal system, but mainly as a result of the 1992 Maastricht Treaty, which obligated the EU member states to enhance the independence of their central banks. In 1993, its Cukierman score rose from a very low 0.17 to a more respectable 0.41 (Polillo and Guillén 2005).

THE CONSENSUS MODEL IN THE EUROPEAN UNION

The principal institutions of the European Union do not fit the classification into executive, legislative, judicial, and monetary organs as easily as those of the five sovereign states discussed so far. This is especially true for the European Council (not to be confused with the Council of the European Union, described below), which consists of the heads of government of the twenty-seven member states—"the most prominent political leaders in Europe" (Crepaz and Steiner 2011, 287)—meeting at least twice a year. It is the most powerful EU institution, and most of the major steps in the development of the European Community and, since 1993, the EU have been initiated by the Council. Its presidency used to rotate every six months among its members, but the 2007 Lisbon Treaty created a permanent president of the European Council—also called president of the European Union—elected for two and a half years. The first president, elected in 2009, was former Belgian prime minister Herman Van Rompuy. Of the other institutions, the European Commission serves as the executive of the EU and can be compared to a cabinet; the European Parliament is the lower house of the legislature; and the Council of the European Union can be regarded as the upper house. The responsibilities of the European Court of Justice and the European Central Bank are clear from their names.

1. *Executive power-sharing in broad coalition cabinets.* The European Commission consists of twenty-seven members, each with a specific ministerial responsibility, appointed by the governments of the member states. Because all twenty-seven nations that belong to the EU are represented on it, the Commission is a broad and permanent international coalition. In practice, the Commission is also a coalition that unites the left, center, and right of the political spectrum in Europe.

2. *Executive-legislative balance of power.* After each five-yearly parliamentary election, the new European Commission must be approved by a vote in the European Parliament. Parliament also has the power to dismiss the Commission, but only by a two-thirds majority. Parliament has strong budgetary powers, and its other legislative powers were enhanced by the 2007 Lisbon Treaty; for 95 percent of European legislation, the Parliament has become an equal colegislator with the more powerful Council of the European Union—composed of ministers from the governments of the twenty-seven member states. George Tsebelis and Jeannette Money (1997, 180) call the Council "the European equivalent of [an] upper house." The Council is also clearly the strongest of the three institutions. Overall, therefore, the Commission is much more like the equal partner in the consensus model than the dominant cabinet in the Westminster model.

3. *Multiparty system.* The 736-member European Parliament had seven officially recognized parties (comprising the minimum of 25 members from seven countries required for recognition) after the 2009 elections. The largest of these was the European People's party (mainly Christian Democrats), with 36 percent of the seats in Parliament—far short of a parliamentary majority. The next largest was the Socialist party with 25 percent, followed

by the Liberals with almost 12 percent of the seats. None of the other parties held more than 10 percent of the seats. The political fragmentation is even greater than appears from the multiparty pattern because the parties in the European Parliament are considerably less cohesive and disciplined than the parties in the national parliaments. The partisan composition of the "upper house," the Council of the European Union, changes as the cabinets of the member countries change, and it also depends on the subject matter being discussed, which determines which particular minister will attend a particular session. For instance, if farm policies are on the Council's agenda, the national ministers of agriculture are likely to attend. In practice, however, the Council is also a multiparty body.

4. *Proportional representation.* The European Parliament has been directly elected since 1979. It is supposed to be elected in each country according to a uniform electoral system, but the member countries have not been able to agree on such a system. Nevertheless, the prevalent method is some variant of PR, and PR is used in all of the member countries, including, since 1999, Great Britain. Nevertheless, the overrepresentation of the small states and underrepresentation of the large states in the European Parliament result in a significant degree of disproportionality. At the extremes, Germany has ninety-six and Malta six representatives, even though Germany's population is about two hundred times larger than Malta's. In this respect, the European Parliament combines in one legislative chamber the principles of proportional representation and of equal national representation that, for instance, in Switzerland are embodied in two separate houses of the legislature.

5. *Interest group corporatism.* The EU has not yet developed a full-fledged corporatism, largely because the most important socioeconomic decisions are still made at the national level or subject to national vetoes. As the EU becomes more integrated, the degree of corporatism is bound to increase. In the title of Michael J. Gorges's book *Euro-Corporatism?* the question mark is deliber-

ate, and Gorges answers the question mainly in the negative for the present situation, but he also sees significant corporatist elements in certain sectors as well as a clear trend toward greater corporatism. One important factor is that the European Commission has long favored a corporatist mode of negotiating with interest groups. For instance, it sponsored a series of tripartite conferences during the 1970s, and although these did not lead to the institutionalization of tripartite bargaining, "the Commission never abandoned its goal of promoting a dialogue between the social partners and of improving their participation in the Community's decision-making process" (Gorges 1996, 139). Vivien A. Schmidt (2006, 104) describes the current European interest group system as more pluralist than corporatist but also states that "the EU's societal actors enjoy a pluralism that is more close and cooperative than that of the [highly pluralist] United States." Similarly, but stated in more positive terms, Gerda Falkner (2006, 223) finds evidence that "corporatist variants of policy networks are not alien to the EU."

6. *Federal and decentralized government.* Compared with other international organizations, the supranational EU is highly unified and centralized, but compared with national states—even as decentralized a state as Switzerland—the EU is obviously still more "confederal" than federal as well as extremely decentralized.

7. *Strong bicameralism.* The two criteria of strong bicameralism are that the two houses of a legislature be equal in strength and different in composition. The EU's legislature fits the second criterion without difficulty: the Council has equal representation of the member countries and consists of representatives of the national governments, whereas the Parliament is directly elected by the voters and the national delegations are weighted by population size. In national legislatures, deviations from equal power tend to be to the advantage of the lower house. In the EU it is the other way around: the upper house (Council) used to be considerably more powerful than the lower house (Parliament) and still has somewhat greater legislative power, even after the adoption

of the Lisbon Treaty, noted earlier—not fully in accordance with the consensus model but even less with the majoritarian model.

8. *Constitutional rigidity.* The EU's "constitution" consists of the founding Treaty of the European Economic Community, signed in Rome in 1957, and a series of both earlier and subsequent treaties. Because these are international treaties, they can be changed only with the consent of all of the signatories. Hence they are extremely rigid. In addition, most important decisions in the Council require unanimity; on less important matters, it has become more common since the 1980s to make decision by "qualified majority voting," that is, by roughly two-thirds majorities and by means of a weighted voting system (similar to the weighted allocation of seats in the European Parliament).

9. *Judicial review.* A key EU institution is the European Court of Justice. The Court has the right of judicial review and can declare both EU laws and national laws unconstitutional if they violate the various EU treaties. Moreover, the Court's approach to its judicial tasks has been creative and activist. Alec Stone Sweet (2004, 1) writes that the Court "has no rival as the most effective supranational body in the history of the world, comparing favorably with the most powerful constitutional courts anywhere."

10. *Central bank independence.* The European Central Bank, which started operating in 1998, was designed to be a highly independent central bank; indeed the *Economist* (November 8, 1997) wrote that "its constitution makes it the most independent central bank in the world." It is the guardian of the European common currency, the Euro, used by seventeen EU members. Christopher Crowe and Ellen E. Meade (2007) give the bank an independence score of 0.83 on the Cukierman scale—considerably higher than that of any of the national central banks mentioned earlier in this chapter and in Chapter 2.

In the beginning of this chapter, I emphasized that the majoritarian model was incompatible with the needs of deeply divided, plural societies. The EU is clearly such a plural society: "Deep-seated and long-standing national differences, of which language is only one, have not and will not disappear in Europe" (Kirchner 1994, 263). Hence it is not surprising that the EU's institutions conform largely to the consensus instead of the majoritarian model (Colomer 2010, 67–72; Hendriks 2010, 76–77). Many observers predict that the EU will eventually become a federal state, especially as a result of the adoption of the Euro. For instance, Martin Feldstein (1997, 60) asserts that the "fundamental long-term effect of adopting a single currency [will] be the creation of a political union, a European federal state with responsibility for a Europe-wide foreign and security policy as well as for what are now domestic economic and social policies." If and when the EU develops into a sovereign European state, its institutions are likely to change, but it is not likely to stray far from the consensus model, and it is almost certain to take the form of a *federal* United States of Europe.

CHAPTER 4

THIRTY-SIX DEMOCRACIES

The remainder of this book is a systematic comparison of the thirty-six countries (with populations of at least a quarter of a million) that were democratic in the middle of 2010 and that had been continuously democratic since 1989 or earlier. Each democracy is analyzed from its first democratic election in or after 1945 until June 30, 2010; the time span for the thirty-six democracies varies from sixty-five years (1945–2010) for several European countries to twenty-two years (1988–2010) for Korea. In this chapter, I explain the criteria for selecting the thirty-six democracies and for choosing the minimum number of years of democratic experience. I also discuss the principal social and economic characteristics that can be expected to influence the types of democracy and democratic performance of the thirty-six countries.

DEFINITIONS OF DEMOCRACY

Although political scientists have disagreed on some of the details of defining and measuring democracy (Coppedge and Gerring 2011), the eight criteria proposed by Robert A. Dahl (1971, 3) in his seminal book *Polyarchy* still command widespread support: (1) the right to vote, (2) the right to be elected, (3) the right of political leaders to compete for support and votes, (4) elections that are free and fair, (5) freedom of association, (6) freedom of expression, (7) alternative sources of information, and (8) institutions for making public policies depend on votes and other expressions of preference. These requirements are already implied by Lincoln's simple definition of democracy as government by the people (or by representatives of the people) and for the people. For instance, "by the people" implies universal suffrage, eligibility for public office, and free and fair elections; and elections cannot be free and fair unless there is freedom of expression and association both before and between elections. Similarly, "for the people" implies Dahl's eighth criterion of responsiveness by the government to the voters' preferences. Nevertheless, it is instructive to spell out the specific criteria especially for the purpose of deciding which countries qualify as democracies and which countries do not.

Democracy, as defined by Dahl, is a twentieth-century phenomenon, and Göran Therborn (1977, 11–17) credits Australia and New Zealand with having established the first genuinely democratic systems of government in the first decade of the twentieth century. New Zealand has the strongest claim because, as early as 1893, it was the first country to institute truly universal suffrage, that is, the right to vote for both men and women *and* for the Maori minority; women, however, did not have the right to be candidates for public office until 1919. Australia adopted suffrage for both men and women in 1902, but Aboriginal Australians—admittedly a small minority comprising about 2 percent of the population—could not vote in federal elections until 1962.

Table 4.1 lists the countries that can be regarded as democratic in 2010 and as having been democratic for more than twenty years: these are the thirty-six countries analyzed in this book, classified by the decade and first year from which the analysis of each country starts. In order to decide which countries qualify as democracies, I relied to a large extent—following the example of many other researchers—on the ratings for all countries in the world that Freedom House has produced since 1972 (Gastil 1989, 50–61). In the Freedom House surveys, countries are rated as free, partly free, or not free, and these ratings are based on two sets of criteria similar to those suggested by Dahl: political rights, such as the right to participate in free and competitive elections, and civil liberties, such as freedom of speech and association. Hence the "free" countries can also be regarded as democratic countries.

I have included three borderline cases: India, Argentina, and Trinidad and Tobago. In Freedom House's judgment, India slipped from "free" to only "partly free" during seven years in the 1990s mainly because of high levels of political violence. This judgment is too severe, given India's huge size and the fact that most violence was confined to the country's periphery. Larry Diamond's (1989, 1) description of India as "the most surprising and important case of democratic endurance in the developing world" continues to be valid. Argentina and Trinidad fell just below the "freedom" cutoff point for a few years—two and four years, respectively—in the early twenty-first century but quickly regained their "free" status. It is also preferable to err on the side of inclusion because India is the world's most populous democracy and because all three countries make the set of democracies analyzed in this book much more interesting and diverse: India is the least developed of the thirty-six countries, and both India and Trinidad are among the most ethnically divided societies. Argentina is one of only six presidential democracies and one of only three Latin American democracies among the thirty-six countries.[1]

1. Of the other two Latin American democracies, Uruguay, like Argentina, is included from the 1980s on. Costa Rica has a much longer democratic record and is often lauded as "the Switzerland of Central America" (Seligson and Martínez Franzoni 2010, 307). This book is not designed to contribute to the scholarly debate about the viability of parliamentary versus presidential regimes (see Linz and Valenzuela 1994), but it seems significant that there are merely six presidential systems among the thirty-six long-term democracies and that three of these—Argentina, Uruguay, and Korea—joined this select group only in the 1980s.

TABLE 4.1

The thirty-six democracies included in this study, classified by decade and first year of the period (until the middle of 2010) analyzed

Decade	First year analyzed	Democracies
1940s	1945	Austria, Canada, Denmark, Finland, Luxembourg, Norway, United Kingdom
	1946	Australia, Belgium, Iceland, Italy, Japan, Netherlands, New Zealand, United States
	1947	Switzerland
	1948	Ireland, Sweden
	1949	Germany, Israel
1950s	1953	Costa Rica
	1958	France
1960s	1961	Trinidad and Tobago
	1962	Jamaica
	1965	Botswana
	1966	Barbados, Malta
1970s	1972	Bahamas
	1974	Greece
	1976	Mauritius, Portugal
	1977	India, Spain
1980s	1984	Argentina
	1985	Uruguay
	1988	Korea

I am also somewhat lenient with regard to several other countries that are on the list of long-term democracies in Table 4.1 in spite of the absence of fully universal suffrage—the most fundamental of democratic requisites. In pre-1971 Switzerland, women did not yet have the right to vote. In Australia, as noted earlier, Aborigines could not vote until 1962. And, in spite of President Bill Clinton's claim in his 1993 inaugural address that the United

States is "the world's oldest democracy" (*New York Times,* January 21, 1993, A11), universal suffrage was not firmly established in the United States until the passage of the Voting Rights Act in 1965. The principle of universal suffrage was also violated by the United Kingdom, France, the Netherlands, and Belgium while these countries were colonial powers, by the three Allied Powers while they were occupying Germany and Japan, and by post-1967 Israel on account of its control over the occupied territories.[2] Focusing on the post-1945 period minimizes these problems because the colonial empires were rapidly dissolved and because women finally received the right to vote in Belgium, France, and Italy.

In comparative analyses of democracy, the smallest and least populous ministates are usually excluded; the cutoff point tends to vary between populations of one million and of a quarter of a million (Anckar 2008, 69–71). Here, too, I opted to be inclusive by selecting the lower cutoff point.

There are two reasons for the requirement that countries be not just democratic but democratic for an extended period. The substantive reason is that it provides assurance that the democracies studied are not ephemeral entities but reasonably stable and consolidated systems. The second reason is procedural: in order to study, for instance, the results that elections tend to have, the kinds of cabinets that tend to be formed, and the durability of these cabinets in a particular country, we need to be able to measure more than just one or a few of these elections and cabinets. Obviously somewhat arbitrarily, I selected a time span of more than twenty years as the minimum period; all thirty-six countries included in this study have been continuously democratic since the late 1980s or earlier.

Table 4.1 shows the first year of the period analyzed for each of the thirty-six democracies. Generally, this is the year of the first

---

2. Postwar control of conquered countries or areas is the least serious violation of the universal-suffrage standard because such control is meant to be temporary; the longer it lasts, however, the more it creates a dilemma for democracy.

democratic election since 1945 or since independence. In countries where democracy was interrupted in the postwar period— in France in 1958, Greece from 1967 to 1974, India from 1975 to 1977—it is the election that marks the resumption of democracy. In the countries that became independent in the 1960s and 1970s, it is the year of the election held closest to the achievement of independence—which in three cases means the election in the year before independence (the Bahamas, Botswana, and Trinidad).[3] The only exception is Mauritius, which held a democratic election in 1967, one year before formal independence in 1968, but where democracy lapsed for several years in the early 1970s: a state of emergency was in force from 1971 to 1976; opposition leaders were imprisoned; labor unions were banned; and the 1972 election was postponed to 1976 (Bowman 1991, 73–74; Bräutigam 1997, 50). The 1976 election marks the restoration of democracy, and Mauritius is therefore included in the analysis from 1976 on.

The requirement of a minimum time span of more than twenty years of democratic experience necessarily means that quite a few democracies had to be omitted from the analysis. Shortening the required time span to ten years would have resulted in the inclusion of twenty-five more countries (see Table 4.2). Among these newer democracies are several large countries—especially Mexico, South Africa, and Poland—but of the combined total population of more than two and a half billion people in the sixty-one democracies, the thirty-six older democracies contain more than 85 percent.[4]

3. Trinidad and Tobago—for brevity's sake hereinafter simply referred to as "Trinidad"—and Jamaica became independent in 1962, Malta in 1964, Barbados and Botswana in 1966, Mauritius in 1968, and the Bahamas in 1973. I also use the short name "Korea" for the country that is often informally called South Korea and is officially called the Republic of Korea.

4. Freedom House also includes Cyprus (the Greek part of the island) and Belize among the long-term democracies. Cyprus is omitted from my analysis because of the continued division of the island and its unsettled final status. Belize's population did not reach the minimum of 250,000 until early in the twenty-first century.

TABLE 4.2

The twenty-five other democracies that have been continuously democratic since 1990–2000, classified by year of (re-)democratization

Year of democratization	Democracies
1990	Chile, Hungary, Namibia, Poland
1991	Benin, Bulgaria, Cape Verde, Lithuania, Mongolia, Slovenia
1993	Czech Republic, Estonia
1994	Latvia, Panama, South Africa
1995	Mali
1996	Romania, Taiwan
1997	El Salvador
1998	Dominican Republic, Slovakia
2000	Croatia, Ghana, Mexico, Suriname

Source: Based on information in Freedom House 2011 and earlier volumes of the *Freedom in the World* annual survey

THIRTY-SIX DIVERSE DEMOCRACIES

Our set of thirty-six democracies includes representatives of each of the three waves of democratization identified by Samuel P. Huntington (1991, 13–26). Using a rather lenient definition of "universal" suffrage—the right to vote for at least 50 percent of adult males[5]—Huntington sees a long first wave starting as early as 1828 and lasting until 1926, a short second wave from 1943 to 1962, and a third wave starting in 1974; two reverse waves, in which democracy collapsed in many countries, occurred between the three waves of democratization. Several countries that experienced reverse waves participated in more than one for-

5. Huntington (1991, 14) concedes that he includes both democratic and "semidemocratic" systems.

ward wave; among our thirty-six democracies, Argentina, Greece, and Uruguay were involved in all three forward waves and in both reverse waves. All of the countries listed in Table 4.1 as having been continuously democratic since the late 1940s, except Israel, were already part of the first of Huntington's waves. About half were also in the second wave: those in which democracy failed in the first reverse wave, like Germany and Italy, and countries where democracy was interrupted by German occupation during the Second World War.

The countries listed in Table 4.1 as having been democratic since the 1950s and 1960s belong to the second wave; for the 1960s group, democratization came about as a result of decolonization. Huntington uses 1962 as the year in which the second wave ended, but Botswana, Barbados, Malta, and even the Bahamas (not independent until 1973) should be included in the second wave. The end of the Portuguese dictatorship in 1974 initiated the third wave, which also encompasses the other democracies in the 1970s and 1980s groups (except the Bahamas) and which continued in the 1990s, especially in Eastern Europe, Latin America, and Africa (Whitehead 2009).

The twenty democracies that have been continuously democratic since the 1940s (or earlier) are a rather homogeneous group in several key respects, except their degree of pluralism: they are all economically developed, industrialized, and urbanized; with the exception of Japan, they belong to the Western Judeo-Christian world; and most are geographically concentrated in the North Atlantic area. However, the addition of the second-wave and third-wave democracies adds a great deal of diversity. Three major differences are highlighted in Table 4.3: the degree to which the thirty-six democracies are plural societies, their levels of socio-economic development, and their population sizes.

The first difference is the degree of societal division. This variable is commonly operationalized as the number and relative sizes of the ethnic groups in different countries (Colomer 2011, 95). This ethnic-groups measure captures an important element of so-

TABLE 4.3

Population sizes (in thousands) and levels of development of thirty-six democracies, classified by extent of pluralism, ca. 2010

	Population (000s), 2009	Human development index, 2010
Plural societies		
India	1,155,348	0.519
Spain	45,958	0.863
Canada	33,740	0.888
Belgium	10,789	0.867
Switzerland	7,731	0.874
Israel	7,442	0.872
Trinidad	1,339	0.736
Mauritius	1,275	0.701
Semiplural societies		
United States	307,007	0.902
Germany	81,880	0.885
France	62,616	0.872
Italy	60,221	0.854
Korea	48,747	0.877
Netherlands	16,531	0.890
Austria	8,364	0.851
Finland	5,338	0.871
Luxembourg	498	0.852
Nonplural societies		
Japan	127,560	0.884
United Kingdom	61,838	0.849
Argentina	40,276	0.775

TABLE 4.3 *continued*

	Population (000s), 2009	Human development index, 2010
Australia	21,875	0.937
Greece	11,283	0.855
Portugal	10,632	0.795
Sweden	9,302	0.885
Denmark	5,529	0.866
Norway	4,827	0.938
Costa Rica	4,579	0.725
Ireland	4,450	0.895
New Zealand	4,316	0.907
Uruguay	3,345	0.765
Jamaica	2,670	0.688
Botswana	1,950	0.633
Malta	415	0.815
Bahamas	342	0.784
Iceland	319	0.869
Barbados	256	0.788

Source: Based on data in World Bank 2011 and United Nations Development Programme 2010, 142–45

cietal division; for instance, all other things being equal, a country consisting of three ethnic groups of equal size is less divided than one with four such equal groups, and a country with two ethnic groups comprising 90 and 10 percent of the population is less divided than one with two groups of 50 percent each. Another advantage is that it can be precisely quantified.[6]

6. The measure described by Colomer (2011, 95) is the "effective number of ethnic groups," which is conceptually similar to the effective number of political parties that I introduce and explain in Chapter 5.

Its disadvantage is that it leaves out a number of important aspects of division. First, ethnic divisions are not the only relevant differences; in particular, religious cleavages, such as those among Hindus, Muslims, and Sikhs in India, may be as important or even more important. Second, the measure could, in principle, be adjusted so as to include religious as well as ethnic differences, but it would then still miss important cleavages within religious groups, such as the difference between faithfully practicing Catholics on one hand and infrequently and nonpracticing Catholics on the other and the related split between prochurch and anticlerical forces that has historically shaped much of the politics of France and Italy.

Third, it fails to take the depth of division into account. It is misleading, for instance, to treat the Protestant-Catholic division in Northern Ireland on a par with that in Switzerland, Germany, and the Netherlands, or to equate ethnic divisions in which linguistic differentiation is relatively unimportant, such as between Welsh and English or Frisians and Dutch, with ethnic divisions that coincide with sharp linguistic divisions, as in Belgium, Switzerland, India, Spain, and Finland. Fourth, it fails to indicate the extent to which the ethnic, religious, and possibly other groups differentiate themselves organizationally. A high degree of this can historically be seen in Austria, Belgium, the Netherlands, and Israel, where religious and ideological groups have organized themselves into more or less separate subsocieties with their own political, socioeconomic, cultural, educational, and recreational associations.

The threefold classification into plural, semiplural, and non-plural societies in Table 4.3 takes these considerations into account. It is obviously a more subjective and much rougher measure than one based exclusively on the number and sizes of ethnic groups, but it is also a more valid and meaningful measure. Three further comments on the trichotomous classification are in order. First, all but one of the plural societies are linguistically divided countries; India, with its more than a dozen officially recognized languages, is an extreme case. The population of Mauritius is about two-thirds of Indian and one-third of African descent; the Indian community is a microcosm of the linguistic and religious divisions of India (Kasenally 2011). Israel is a plural society not just because of the division between Jewish and Arab citizens but even more as a result of the sharp split between religious and secular Jews. The only exceptional case is Trinidad, where there is a common language but where a deep cleavage separates the Afro-Creole and Indian communities (Premdas 2007, 17–44). Most of the semiplural societies have significant, but only moderately divisive, ethnic or religious differences. Korea is also in this category on account of its pronounced regional rivalries.

Second, the threefold classification reflects the situation in the early twenty-first century, but it would not have looked very different if it had been based on a much longer time span. The only exceptions would be Austria, the Netherlands, and Luxembourg, which are classified as semiplural here but which should have been rated as plural in the first two postwar decades, when their religious and ideological segments were organizationally much more distinct. Third, it is important not to equate "nonplural" with "homogeneous": most of the nonplural societies are religiously divided to at least some extent, and most contain at least one or more small minorities. Examples that have already been mentioned are the ethnic minorities in the United Kingdom, Australia, and New Zealand. Another example is Botswana, which is often regarded as the most homogeneous state in Africa but where there is a significant ethnic minority, the Kalanga, and where the dominant Tswana ethnic group is divided internally into eight tribes.

Table 4.3 also indicates the level of socioeconomic development in the thirty-six democracies. This variable has traditionally been operationalized as gross national product (GNP) per capita, although it has long been recognized that GNP per capita is a flawed measure because of its excessive sensitivity to exchange rate fluctuations and its exaggeration of the poverty of less developed nations. A considerable improvement is to adjust per capita GNP for the different price levels in different countries, yielding so-called purchasing power parities (Dogan 1994, 44–46). A further big improvement is the human development index, designed by the United Nations Development Programme in 1990. Nobel Prize–winning economist Amartya Sen (2010, vi), who participated in the development of the index, explains that it was "devised explicitly as a rival to GNP," concentrating on the three fundamental dimensions of "longevity, basic education and minimal income." It is a more accurate indicator of development because it is more broadly based than the two older measures, and it quickly found wide acceptance among social scientists (Diamond 1992, 100–102; Lane and Ersson 1994, 214–28; Vanhanen 1997, 75–79).

The human development index can, in principle, range from a high of 1 to a low of 0. As Table 4.3 shows, most of the countries that are commonly regarded as highly developed and industrialized have indices higher than 0.8. Those of most of the developing countries are between 0.7 and 0.8, but three nations have lower indices: the lowest is India (0.519), followed in ascending order by Botswana and Jamaica.

By far the greatest difference among the thirty-six countries is in their population sizes. Table 4.3 highlights these differences by listing the countries in each of the three degree-of-pluralism categories in descending order of size. India is by far the largest country, with a population exceeding one billion—larger than the combined populations of the thirty-five other countries. Another way to emphasize these enormous differences is to calculate India's weekly population growth from its annual growth of about fifteen million people; its population growth *per week* is about 290,000—more than the entire population of Barbados.

The above variables are important in this comparative analysis because they can be expected to influence the form of democracy adopted in different countries as well as their democratic performance. For instance, I have hinted in previous chapters that consensus democracy is especially appropriate for plural societies and that federalism makes more sense for large than for small countries. Moreover, the level of development is likely to have an effect on the macroeconomic performance of governments. These relationships are explored in Chapters 14 and 15.

The only significant relationship among the three variables is between population size (logged) and degree of pluralism. It is logical to expect larger countries to be more heterogeneous than smaller countries (Dahl and Tufte, 1973, 13–14); in our set of thirty-six democracies, the correlation coefficient is 0.29, not very strong but still significant at the 5 percent level. There is virtually no relationship between population size and pluralism on one hand and level of development on the other. Finally, the length of continuous democratic experience between 1945 and 2010 (measured by decade, as indicated in Table 4.1) is very strongly correlated with development—the older democracies are the wealthier countries ($r=0.58$, significant at the 1 percent level)—but there is no significant relationship with either population size or degree of pluralism.

Chapter 5

Party Systems: Two-Party and Multiparty Patterns

The first of the ten variables that characterize the majoritarian-consensus contrast, presented in Chapter 1, was the difference between single-party majority governments and broad multiparty coalitions. This first difference can also be seen as the most important and typical difference between the two models of democracy because it epitomizes the contrast between concentration of power on one hand and power-sharing on the other. Moreover, the factor analysis reported in Chapter 14 shows that it correlates more strongly with the "factor" representing the first (executives-parties) dimension than any of the other four variables that belong to this dimension. It would therefore make sense to devote this chapter—the first of nine chapters that will discuss the ten basic variables[1]—to this first and most typical variable.

For practical reasons, however, it is necessary to discuss the subject of party systems first. The classification of cabinets—single-party cabinets versus multiparty coalition cabinets, and bare-majority cabinets versus minority cabinets and cabinets that have

1. Two of the variables—constitutional rigidity and judicial review—will be discussed in one chapter (Chapter 12).

"unnecessary" parties in them—depends a great deal on how political parties and the numbers of parties in party systems are
defined. Hence these definitional problems have to be solved before the question of cabinet types can be properly addressed. It is
worth noting, however, that the type of party system is also a strong
component of the executives-parties dimension. To preview the factor analysis in Chapter 14 once more, the party-system variable
correlates with the first "factor" almost as strongly as the type of
cabinet and more strongly than the remaining three variables.

Two-party systems typify the majoritarian model of democracy and multiparty systems the consensus model. The traditional literature on party systems is staunchly majoritarian and
emphatically favors the two-party system. Two-party systems are
claimed to have both direct and indirect advantages over multiparty systems. The first direct benefit is that they offer the voters
a clear choice between two alternative sets of public policies.
Second, they have a moderating influence because the two main
parties have to compete for the swing voters in the center of the
political spectrum and hence have to advocate moderate, centrist
policies. This mechanism is especially strong when large numbers of voters are located in the political center, but its logic continues to operate even when opinions are more polarized: at the
two ends of the spectrum, the parties will lose some of their supporters, who will decide to abstain instead of voting for what is,
to them, a too moderate program, but a vote gained in the center,
taken away from the other party, is still twice as valuable as a
vote lost by abstention. Both claims are quite plausible—but also
contradictory: if the programs of the two parties are both close to
the political center, they will be very similar to each other and,
instead of offering a meaningful "choice" to the voters, are more
likely to "echo" each other.[2]

2. Most two-party theorists do not make both of the competing claims
simultaneously. The advantage of party moderation is typically asserted
by the American school of thought, whereas the claim of a clear-cut
choice reflects the British two-party school.

In addition, two-party systems are claimed to have an important indirect advantage: they are necessary for the formation of single-party cabinets that will be stable and effective policy-makers. For instance, A. Lawrence Lowell (1896, 70, 73–74), one of the first modern political scientists, wrote that the legislature must contain "two parties, and two parties only, . . . in order that the parliamentary form of government should permanently produce good results." He called it an "axiom in politics" that coalition cabinets are short-lived and weak compared with one-party cabinets: "the larger the number of discordant groups that form the majority the harder the task of pleasing them all, and the more feeble and unstable the position of the cabinet."

In the next two chapters I confirm Lowell's hypothesis linking party systems to types of cabinets and his "axiom" that single-party majority cabinets are more durable and dominant than coalition cabinets. The majoritarians' preference for two-party systems is therefore clearly and logically linked to their preference for powerful and dominant one-party cabinets. Furthermore, in Chapter 8 I show a strong connection between party systems and electoral systems, which further explains the majoritarians' strong preference for plurality, instead of proportional representation, because of its bias in favor of larger parties and its contribution to the establishment and maintenance of two-party systems. However, whether this syndrome of features actually translates into more capable and effective policy-making than its consensual counterpart is another matter entirely. Lowell simply assumes that concentrated strength means effective decision-making; in Chapter 15 I show that this assumption is largely incorrect.

In this chapter I first address the question of how the number of parties in party systems should be counted and argue that the "effective number of parliamentary parties" is the optimal measure. I also try to solve the problem of how to treat factionalized parties as well as closely allied parties: Should such parties be treated as one party or as more than one party? Next, the average effective numbers of parliamentary parties in our thirty-six democracies are presented and discussed; these numbers exhibit a wide range—from well below two to more than five parties. I close with a brief discussion of the relationship between the numbers of parties and the numbers and types of issue dimensions that divide the parties.

THE EFFECTIVE NUMBER OF PARTIES

Pure two-party systems with, in Lowell's words quoted above, "two parties, and two parties only," are extremely rare. In Chapter 2, the party systems of Britain, pre-1996 New Zealand, and Barbados were also described as two-party systems in spite of the usual presence of one or more additional small parties in the legislature. Is this a correct description, or should it be modified in some way? This question points to the most important problem in determining the number of parties in a party system: whether to count small parties and, if not, how large a party has to be in order to be included in the count.

One well-known solution was proposed by Giovanni Sartori (1976, 122–23). He suggests, first of all, that parties that fail to win seats in parliament be disregarded, that the relative strengths of the other parties be measured in terms of parliamentary seats, and that not all parties regardless of size can be counted, but that one cannot establish an arbitrary cut-off point of, say, 5 or 10 percent above which parties are counted and below which they should be ignored. These preliminary assumptions are unexceptionable. More controversial are his "rules for counting." He argues that only those parties should be counted as components of the party system that are "relevant" in terms of having either "coalition potential" or "blackmail potential." A party has coalition potential if it has participated in governing coalitions (or, of course, in one-party governments) or if the major parties regard it as a possible coalition partner. Parties that are ideologically unacceptable to all or most of the other coalition partners, and that therefore lack coalition potential, must still be counted if they are large enough. Examples are the strong French and Italian

Communist parties until the 1970s. This is Sartori's "subsidiary counting rule based on the power of intimidation, or more exactly, the *blackmail potential* of the opposition-oriented parties."[3]

Sartori's criteria are very useful for distinguishing between the parties that are significant in the political system and those that play only a minor role, but they do not work well for counting the number of parties in a party system. First, although Sartori's criteria are based on two variables, size and ideological compatibility, size is the crucial factor. Only sufficiently large parties can have blackmail potential, but sufficiently large size is also the chief determinant of coalition potential: very small parties with only a few seats in the legislature may be quite moderate and hence ideologically acceptable to most other parties, but they rarely possess coalition potential because they simply do not have sufficient "weight" to contribute to a cabinet. Hence the parties to be counted, whether or not they are ideologically compatible, are mainly the larger ones. Second, although size figures so prominently in Sartori's thinking, he does not use this factor to make further distinctions among the relevant parties: for instance, both the Christian Democratic party that dominated Italian politics until the 1990s and its frequent but very small coalition partner, the Republican party, which never won more than 5 percent of the lower house seats, are counted equally.

To remedy this defect, Jean Blondel (1968, 184–87) proposed a classification of party systems that takes into account both their number and their relative sizes. His four categories are shown in Table 5.1. Two-party systems are dominated by two large parties, although there may be some other small parties in parlia-

3. Sartori (1976, 123) is too critical of his own criterion of coalition potential when he states that it is merely "postdictive," since "the parties having a coalition potential, coincide, in practice, with the parties that have in fact entered, at some point in time, coalition governments." For instance, immediately after the first electoral success of the Dutch party Democrats '66 in 1967, it was widely regarded as an acceptable coalition partner, although it did not enter a cabinet until 1973.

TABLE 5.1

Classification of party systems based on the numbers and relative sizes of political parties

Party systems	Hypothetical examples of seat shares	Effective number of parties
Two-party system	55–45	2.0
Two-and-a-half party system	45–40–15	2.6
Multiparty system with a dominant party	45–20–15–10–10	3.5
Multiparty system without a dominant party	25–25–25–15–10	4.5

Source: Adapted from Blondel 1968, 184–87

ment. Blondel's examples include our British and New Zealand prototypes. If, in addition to the two large parties, there is a considerably smaller party but one that may have coalition potential and that plays a significant political role—such as the German and Luxembourg Liberals, the Irish Labour party, and the Canadian New Democrats—Blondel calls this a "two-and-a-half" party system. Systems with more than two-and-a-half significant parties are multiparty systems, and these can be subdivided further into multiparty systems with and without a dominant party. Examples of the former are pre-1990 Italy with its dominant Christian Democratic party and the three Scandinavian countries with their strong Socialist parties. Representative instances of party systems without a dominant party are Switzerland, the Netherlands, and Finland.

The concepts of a "dominant" party and a "half" party—still widely used by political scientists (Colomer 2011, 184; Siaroff, 2003a, 2009, 201–2)—are extremely useful in highlighting, respectively, the relatively strong and relatively weak position of one of the parties compared with the other important parties in the system, but they are obviously imprecise. What we need is an index that tells us exactly how many parties there are in a party system, taking their relative sizes into account. Such an index was developed by Markku Laakso and Rein Taagepera (1979), and it is now the index most commonly used by comparativists in political science: the effective number of parties. This number (N) is calculated as follows:

$$N = \frac{1}{\Sigma s_i^2}$$

in which s_i is the proportion of seats of the i-th party.[4]

It can easily be seen that in a two-party system with two equally strong parties, the effective number of parties is exactly 2.0. If one party is considerably stronger than the other, with, for instance, respective seat shares of 70 and 30 percent, the effective number of parties is 1.7—in accordance with our intuitive judgment that we are moving away from a pure two-party system in the direction of a one-party system. Similarly, with three exactly equal parties, the effective-number formula yields a value of 3.0. If one of these parties is weaker than the other two, the

---

4. It is also possible to calculate the effective number of parties based on their vote shares instead of their seat shares, but I consistently use seat shares because this study's focus is on the strengths and patterns of parties in parliaments and on their effects on the formation of cabinets. The effective number of parties (N) carries the same information as Douglas W. Rae and Michael Taylor's (1970, 22–44) index of fragmentation (F) and can easily be calculated from F as follows:

$$N = \frac{1}{1 - F}$$

The advantage of N is that it can be visualized more easily as the number of parties than the abstract Rae-Taylor index of fragmentation. It has not been without critics (for instance, Dunleavy and Boucek 2003), but I agree with Taagepera (2007, 47) that, although not ideal in every respect, all of the alternatives "are worse."

effective number of parties will be somewhere between 2.0 and 3.0, depending on the relative strength of the third party. In the hypothetical example of the two-and-a-half party system in Table 5.1—with three parties holding 45, 40, and 15 percent of the parliamentary seats—the effective number of parties is in fact very close to two and half, namely 2.6.

In all cases where all the parties are equal, the effective number will be the same as the raw numerical count. When the parties are not equal in strength, the effective number will be lower than the actual number. This can also be seen in Table 5.1. The two hypothetical examples of multiparty systems contain five parties each. When there is a dominant party, the effective number of parties is only 3.5. Without a dominant party, the seat shares are more equal and the effective number increases to 4.5, close to the raw number of parties in which all parties are counted regardless of size.

CLOSELY ALLIED PARTIES

The problem of how to count parties of different sizes is solved by using the effective-number measure. This measure, however, does not solve the question of what a political party is. The usual assumption in political science is that organizations that call themselves "political parties" are, in fact, political parties. This assumption works well for most parties and most countries but is problematic in two situations: parties that are so tightly twinned that they look more like one party than two and, conversely, parties that are so factionalized that they look more like two or more parties than one. The former problem is less difficult to solve than the latter. Let me turn to the relatively easier issue first.

The cases in point are the following five closely allied parties: the Christian Democratic Union (CDU) and Christian Social Union (CSU) in Germany, the Liberal and National parties in Australia, and, in Belgium, the two Christian Democratic parties that resulted from a split along linguistic lines in 1968, the two similarly divided Liberal parties since 1971, and the two Socialist

parties since 1978. In particular, the two German and two Australian parties are often treated as single parties. For instance, Blondel
(1968, 185) regards the Liberals and Nationals as one party when
he calls the Australian party system a two-party instead of a two-
and-a-half party system, and he treats the CDU and CSU as one
party when he calls the German system a two-and-a-half instead
of a two-and-two-halves party system. Another example is Manfred G. Schmidt's (1996, 95) statement that the three "major established parties" in Germany until the mid-1990s were "the CDU-
CSU, the SPD [Socialists] and the Liberals."

Four criteria can be applied to decide whether closely allied
parties—which do have different names and separate party organizations—are actually two parties or more like one party. First,
political parties normally compete for votes in elections; do the
problematic five pairs of parties do so? The CDU and CSU do not
compete for votes because they operate in different parts of the
country: the CSU in Bavaria and the CDU in the rest of Germany.
Neither do the three pairs of Belgian parties because they compete for votes in either Flanders or Wallonia and among either
French-speakers or Dutch-speakers in Brussels. In the Australian
single-member district elections, the pattern is mixed: Liberals
and Nationals usually do not challenge an incumbent representative of the other party, but they may each nominate a candidate
in Labor-held districts and in districts without an incumbent.

The second criterion revolves around the degree of cooperation between the parties in parliament and, in particular, whether
the two parties form a single parliamentary party group and also
caucus together. Only the CDU and CSU do so. Third, do the parties behave like separate parties in cabinet formations: Are they
either in the cabinet together or in opposition together, or can
one be in the cabinet and the other in the opposition? In this respect, each of the five pairs operates strictly like a single party—
with one small exception: the French-speaking Socialists entered
the Belgian cabinet without their Flemish counterparts in 2007
(De Winter, Swyngedouw, and Dumont 2009, 89–90). Australia is a

particularly striking example of the more usual pattern because, although the Liberals won clear seat majorities in the 1975, 1977, and 1996 elections, and could therefore have governed by themselves, they nevertheless included the Nationals in all three cabinets that they formed.

The fourth criterion is time: it only makes sense to consider counting tightly allied parties as one party if the close collaboration is of long standing. Both duration and degree of closeness distinguish the above five pairs of parties from other examples of electoral alliances that are mere "marriages of convenience." Plurality and other majoritarian electoral systems give small and medium-sized parties a strong incentive to form such alliances, but these alliances tend to be ad hoc, temporary, and shifting; examples are France, India, and Mauritius.[5] Electoral alliances also occur in PR systems, such as, in Portugal, the three-party Democratic Alliance that presented a single list of candidates and was highly successful in the 1979 and 1980 elections but that reverted to mutually competitive parties frc a 1983 on. In Italy, too, after the switch to a less proportional ystem in 1994, groupings like the Freedom Alliance and Olive ee Alliance have been, as their names indicate, mere party allia ces and not parties.

Unfortunately, the four criteria do not provide an unequivocal answer to the question of how the five problematic pairs of parties in Australia, Belgium, and Germany should be treated. They are all genuinely somewhere in between two parties and one party. Therefore, instead of arbitrarily opting for either the one-party or two-party solution—or by simply flipping a coin!—I propose to

5. Like the Australian alternative vote system, the French two-ballot electoral system actually encourages parties not to merge but to make electoral alliances with like-minded parties (see Chapter 8). However, unlike the Australian Liberal-National alliance, the French Socialist-Communist and Gaullist-Republican alliances fail to meet the criteria for closely allied parties, especially because Socialist cabinets have usually not included the Communists and because Gaullists and Republicans usually challenge each other in presidential elections.

split the difference: calculate two effective numbers of parties, based first on the two-party assumption and next on the one-party assumption, and average these two numbers. This means that each twinned pair of parties is counted like one-and-a-half parties. Like any compromise, it may not be the most elegant solution, but it reflects the reality of these partisan actors better than either of the more extreme options.

FACTIONALIZED PARTIES

I propose a similar solution for highly factionalized parties: the Indian Congress party, the Italian Christian Democrats, the Liberal Democratic party in Japan, the Democratic party in the United States, and the Frente Amplio (Broad Front), Colorado, and Blanco parties in Uruguay. These are not the only parties in modern democracies that lack perfect cohesion—in fact, it is generally wrong to view parties as "unitary actors" (Laver and Schofield 1990, 14–28)—but they are the most extreme cases in which analysts have tended to conclude that the party factions are very similar to separate parties. For instance, Japan experts generally view the factions of the Liberal Democratic party as "parties within the party" (Reed and Bolland 1999); Junichiro Wada (1996, 28) writes that the Liberal Democrats are "not a single party but a coalition of factions"; and Raymond D. Gastil (1991, 25) pointedly states the "the 'real' party system in Japan is the factional system within the Liberal Democratic party." In spite of the 1994 electoral reform, which reduced the incentives for factionalism, the Liberal Democrats continue to be a clearly factionalized party (Krauss and Pekkanen 2004). Until their demise in the early 1990s, the Italian Christian Democrats, too, were "more a collection of factions than a unified party" (Goodman 1991, 341).

The Congress party in India was another highly factionalized party and also a dominant party for a major part of its history. Paul R. Brass (1990, 97) argues that for this reason it was more accurate to speak of the Indian "factional system" than the Indian party system. However, the Congress party has become gradually less divided as several factions have split off, making the party smaller and more unified. The last important split occurred in 1999. The American Democrats, according to Klaus von Beyme (1985, 229), "generally act as two parties in Congress," the southern Dixiecrats and the northern liberals. This split has continued in the form of the conservative Blue Dog Democrats versus the liberal northern wing of the party. Finally, the Uruguayan parties have traditionally all been extremely faction-ridden. The listing of party factions on the ballot for the presidential race was eliminated by the 1997 constitutional reform, but it was left unchanged for legislative elections, and factions have continued to be very strong and important (Cason 2002).

These kinds of strong intraparty factions also tend to operate much like political parties during cabinet formations and in coalition cabinets. As mentioned earlier, coalition cabinets tend to be less durable than one-party cabinets. If factions behave like parties, we would also expect cabinets composed of factionalized parties to be less durable than cabinets with more cohesive parties. In an eight-nation comparative study, James N. Druckman (1996) found that this was indeed the case.

The big challenge in finding a compromise solution for counting factionalized parties is that the two numbers to be compromised are not immediately obvious: At one end, there is the one-party alternative, but what is the number of parties at the other end? In Italy and Japan, where the intraparty factions have been highly distinct and identifiable, the number of factions has been quite large: if these factions are counted as parties, measured in terms of the effective number of parties discussed earlier, both the Christian Democrats and the Liberal Democrats would have to be counted as five to six parties. This is clearly excessive, since it would make the overall party systems of these two countries the most extreme multiparty systems in the world. My proposal for the alternative at the multiparty end is much more modest: treat each factionalized party as two parties of equal size. The compromise is then to average the effective number of parties based on the one-party assumption and the effective number based on the two-equal-parties assumption.

The upshot is that factionalized parties are counted as one-and-a-half parties—exactly the same solution that I proposed for closely allied parties. Of course, my solution for factionalized parties is both a rougher approximation and more unconventional—and therefore likely to be more controversial. However, especially because this book focuses on the degree of multipartism as one of the elements of concentration versus fragmentation of power, it is absolutely necessary that severe intraparty fragmentation be taken into account. My own only doubt is not whether an adjustment is necessary and justified, but whether the proposed adjustment is substantial enough.[6]

THE PARTY SYSTEMS OF THIRTY-SIX DEMOCRACIES

Table 5.2 shows the effective numbers of parties in thirty-six democracies—based on the partisan composition of the lower, and generally most important, house of bicameral legislatures or the only chamber of unicameral legislatures[7]—averaged over all

6. Whether closely allied parties and factionalized parties are counted as one-and-a-half parties, or more conventionally as, respectively, two parties and one party also affects how cabinets are classified (one-party versus coalition cabinets and minimal winning versus other types of cabinets), and it affects the calculation of electoral disproportionality.

7. The effective number of parties is based on the parties in the legislature when it first meets after an election. In most cases, there is no difference between the seats won by parties in an election and the seats they occupy in the legislature. However, several minor changes have occurred in two countries. In Japan since the 1950s, several successful independent candidates have joined the Liberal Democrats after their election. In the Botswana lower house, four "specially" elected legislators are coopted by the popularly elected ones; this has increased the legislative majorities of the ruling Botswana Democratic party by four seats (Holm 1989, 197)—and it has necessarily also slightly decreased the effective number of parliamentary parties. Two other minor measurement questions: (1) The two instances of elections boycotted by a major party—in Trinidad in 1971 and in Jamaica in 1983—resulted in the election of one-party legislatures; I dis-

elections between 1945 and the middle of 2010. They are listed in decreasing order of effective party numbers. The range is wide: from a high of 5.20 in Switzerland to a low of 1.38 in Botswana. The mean for the thirty-six democracies is 3.19 and the median 2.99 parties.

Toward the bottom of the list, as expected, we also find our prototypical majoritarian cases of the United Kingdom, New Zealand, and Barbados. The average of 2.16 parties in the British House of Commons reflects the numerous small parties in this still basically two-party system. New Zealand's average is a relatively high 2.28 as a result of the increase in the number of parties after the introduction of proportional representation in 1996. In the five PR elections from 1996 on, the average was 3.35—much higher than the average of 1.96 in the seventeen prior elections under plurality rules when there were fewer third parties and where the winning party's seat share tended to be large. Similarly, the average effective number for Barbados is below 2.00. At the other end of the range, Switzerland is at the top, but Belgium has only the seventh highest multipartism over the entire period. However, in the ten elections since 1978, after all of the major parties had split along linguistic lines, the average effective number was 6.05, and it grew to 6.36 parties in the five elections after the adoption of federalism in 1993. Both of these numbers exceed Switzerland's average of 5.20.

Table 5.2 also indicates the range of variation within each of the thirty-six democracies by showing the lowest and the highest effective numbers of parties in all of their elections (the number of which is given in the last column). The Maltese pure two-party system with two, and only two, highly equal parliamentary par-

---

regarded these election results because they are quite atypical. (2) Any independent members of the legislatures were counted as tiny one-member parties—which means, of course, that they are virtually ignored in the calculation of the effective number of parties, which weights parties by their seat shares.

TABLE 5.2

Average, lowest, and highest effective numbers of parliamentary parties resulting from elections in thirty-six democracies and the number of elections on which these averages are based, 1945–2010

	Mean	Lowest	Highest	Number of elections
Switzerland	5.20	4.71	6.70	16
Israel	5.18	3.12	8.68	18
Finland	5.04	4.54	5.58	18
Netherlands	4.87	3.49	6.74	20
Italy	4.84	3.08	6.97	17
India	4.80	2.51	6.53	10
Belgium	4.72	2.45	7.03	21
Denmark	4.57	3.50	6.86	25
Uruguay	4.40	3.61	4.92	6
Iceland	3.72	3.20	5.34	20
Norway	3.64	2.67	5.35	17
Japan	3.62	2.17	5.76	19
Luxembourg	3.48	2.68	4.34	14
Sweden	3.47	2.87	4.29	19
France	3.26	2.15	4.52	13
Argentina	3.15	2.54	5.32	13
Portugal	3.13	2.23	4.26	12
Germany	3.09	2.48	4.40	17
Ireland	2.89	2.38	3.63	18
Korea	2.85	2.39	3.54	6
Mauritius	2.85	2.07	3.48	9
Austria	2.68	2.09	4.27	20
Costa Rica	2.67	1.96	3.90	15
Spain	2.66	2.34	3.02	10
Canada	2.52	1.54	3.22	21
United States	2.39	2.20	2.44	32
New Zealand	2.28	1.74	3.76	22

TABLE 5.2 *continued*

	Mean	Lowest	Highest	Number of elections
Greece	2.27	1.72	2.62	13
Australia	2.22	2.08	2.30	25
United Kingdom	2.16	1.99	2.57	18
Malta	1.99	1.97	2.00	10
Trinidad	1.87	1.18	2.23	12
Bahamas	1.69	1.34	1.97	8
Barbados	1.68	1.15	2.18	10
Jamaica	1.67	1.30	1.99	10
Botswana	1.38	1.17	1.71	10

Source: Based on data in Mackie and Rose 1991; Bale and Caramani 2010 and earlier volumes of the "Political Data Yearbook"; Nohlen 2005; Nohlen, Grotz, and Hartmann 2001; Nohlen, Krennerich, and Thibaut 1999; Nohlen and Stöver 2010; official election websites; and data provided by Royce Carroll, Mark P. Jones, Dieter Nohlen, Ralph Premdas, and Nadarajen Sivaramen

ties shows the least variation: between 1.97 and 2.00 in ten elections. The largest differences between the lowest and highest numbers can be seen among the countries with the greatest multipartism at the top of the table. The biggest gap is Israel's 5.56, followed in descending order by Belgium, India, Italy, Japan, and Denmark. Four countries have experienced major increases in multipartism: Belgium and New Zealand, as already noted, and also India and Israel. Portugal is the only example of a clear trend toward fewer parties. In most of the other countries, there is either little variation over time or fluctuation without any clear long-term trend. Nevertheless, the overall tendency is toward greater multipartism: in twenty-eight of the thirty-six countries, the highest numbers of parties were recorded in elections held later than those in which the lowest numbers occurred.

ADDENDUM: ISSUE DIMENSIONS OF PARTISAN CONFLICT

The descriptions of the prototypical majoritarian and consensus party systems in Chapters 2 and 3 showed that they differ not only in terms of numbers of parties but also in the numbers of programmatic differences among them. The major parties in the British, New Zealand, and Barbadian two-party systems are mainly divided by a single issue dimension—socioeconomic or left-right issues—whereas additional issues, like religious and linguistic matters, divide the Swiss and Belgian parties. These two variables mutually influence each other. On one hand, when there are several lines of political conflict in a society, one would expect that a relatively large number of parties is needed to express all of these, unless they happen to coincide. On the other hand, an established two-party system cannot easily accommodate as many issue dimensions as a multiparty system.

There are seven issue dimensions that can be observed in our thirty-six democracies between 1945 and 2010: socioeconomic, religious, cultural-ethnic, urban-rural, regime support, foreign policy, and postmaterialist issues. The socioeconomic issue dimension has been important in all thirty-six countries and is often the most salient dimension. Differences between religious and secular parties and sometimes between different religions—as in the Netherlands before 1977 between Catholics and Protestants and in India between Hindus and Muslims—constitute the second most important issue dimension. The cultural-ethnic-linguistic dimension has been especially salient in the countries described as plural societies in Chapter 4. Differences between rural and urban areas and interests occur in all democracies, but they constitute the source of partisan conflict in only a few and only with medium salience; for instance, the old agrarian parties in the Nordic countries became less exclusively rural and changed their names to "Center party" around 1960, and the Australian National party, the traditional defender of rural and farming concerns, used to be called the "Country party." The dimension of support versus opposition to the democratic regime has become rare in recent decades but used to be salient in countries with strong Communist parties in southern Europe, India, and Japan. The Flemish separatist parties are more recent examples. A great variety of foreign policy issues have divided the parties of many of our countries, such as membership in NATO (North Atlantic Treaty Organization) and the EU in several European countries and the relationship with the United States in Japan. Finally, the postmaterialist dimension is most clearly seen in the emergence of many Green parties in recent decades (Inglehart 1977; Inglehart and Welzel 2005).

Earlier research has found a strong empirical relationship between the effective number of parties and the number of issue dimensions (Lijphart 1999, 78–89), roughly in line with the equation suggested by Rein Taagepera and Bernard Grofman (1985):

$$N = I + 1$$

in which N stands for the effective number of parties and I for the number of issue dimensions. In abstract terms, the typical single-issue two-party Westminster system fits this formula perfectly. Concretely, the fit is also very close: the single-issue party systems of Britain, New Zealand (before 1996), and Barbados have 2.11, 1.96, and 1.68 effective parties, respectively—close to the predicted 2.00. At the other end of the spectrum, Switzerland with its four issue dimensions—clear left-right, religious, and environmentalist dimensions, as well as weaker urban-rural and linguistic differences that must be given only half-weight—should be expected to have about five parties; the actual number is 5.20. For the post-1977 Belgian party system with five issue dimensions (all seven potential dimensions except urban-rural and foreign policy), about six parties can be predicted; the actual number is 6.05. The empirical fit is quite close for the in-between moderately multiparty systems, too.

Unlike the effective number of parties, and unlike the four

variables discussed in the next four chapters, the number of issue dimensions is not an institutional variable and should therefore not be used as one of the components of the overall executives-parties dimension. However, because it is so closely related to the number of parties, it would fit this dimension very closely and, if it were included, would barely affect the shape of this dimension.

CHAPTER 6

CABINETS: CONCENTRATION VERSUS SHARING OF EXECUTIVE POWER

The second of the ten basic variables that characterize the difference between majoritarian and consensus forms of democracy, to be discussed in this chapter, concerns the breadth of participation by the people's representatives in the executive branch of the government. As I stated at the beginning of Chapter 5, this variable can be regarded as the most typical variable in the majoritarian-consensus contrast: the difference between one-party majority governments and broad multiparty coalitions epitomizes the contrast between the majoritarian principle of concentrating power in the hands of the majority and the consensus principle of broad power-sharing.

Single-party majority cabinets and broad multiparty coalitions differ from each other in two respects: whether the cabinet is a one-party cabinet or a coalition cabinet and the kind of parliamentary support base that the cabinet has. As far as the support base is concerned, the standard threefold classification in coalition theory distinguishes among (1) minimal winning cabinets, which are "winning" in the sense that the party or parties in the cabinet control a majority of parliamentary seats but "minimal" in the sense that the cabinet does not include any party that is not necessary to reach a majority in parliament, (2) oversized cabinets, which do contain more parties than are necessary for majority support in the legislature, and (3) minority or "undersized" cabinets, which are not supported by a parliamentary majority. The most majoritarian type of cabinet is one that is single-party and minimal winning—that is, a one-party majority cabinet. The most consensual type of cabinet is multiparty and oversized. As I argue below, minority cabinets resemble oversized cabinets, and multiparty minority cabinets therefore also belong to the consensus end of the spectrum. This leaves two kinds of cabinets in an intermediate position: multiparty minimal winning cabinets and one-party minority cabinets.

In this chapter I review the major coalition theories and explain why they are such poor predictors of the kinds of cabinets that are actually formed in democracies. One important reason is that they are based almost entirely on majoritarian assumptions; another is that they tend to ignore institutional features that encourage the formation of minority and oversized cabinets. Next, after discussing the precise criteria for assigning cabinets to the different categories, I present the empirical findings concerning the types of cabinets found in thirty-six democracies in the period 1945–2010; our democracies differ a great deal on this variable—from 100 percent cabinets that are one-party and minimal winning in five countries to 4 percent in Switzerland. Last, I analyze the relationship between types of cabinets and the effective numbers of parties in our set of thirty-six countries.

COALITION THEORIES

In parliamentary systems of government, cabinets have to be formed so that they will enjoy the confidence of—or will at least be tolerated by—a parliamentary majority. Can we predict which particular cabinet will form if we know the strengths of the different parties in parliament? If one party has a majority of the parliamentary seats, a prediction appears to be easy: the majority party is likely to form a one-party cabinet. This prediction is correct in most cases, but it is also possible that the majority will form a coalition with one or more minority parties; for instance, the British Conservatives had a clear majority in the House of Commons during the Second World War, but Winston Churchill's war cabinet was a broad coalition of the Conservative, Labour, and Liberal parties. If no party has a parliamentary majority, it is likely—barring the formation of a one-party minority cabinet—that a coalition cabinet will be formed, but which coalition is the most likely one? Several theories have been proposed to predict which coalitions will form in parliamentary systems. The six most important of these coalition theories predict the following kinds of coalitions:[1]

1. *Minimal winning coalitions.* William H. Riker's (1962, 32–46) "size principle" predicts that minimal winning coalitions will be formed: winning (majority) coalitions in which only those parties participate that are minimally necessary to give the cabinets majority status. Table 6.1 presents an example. Coalition ABC (a cabinet coalition of parties A, B, and C) is a winning coalition because A, B, and C control a majority of fifty-five out of one hundred parliamentary seats. It is minimal because all three parties are necessary to form a majority. The elimination of the smallest coalition partner, party A, would reduce the coalition's parliamentary support from a majority of the seats, fifty-five, to a minority of only forty-seven. The addition of party D to the coalition would make it larger than minimal, because in coalition ABCD either A or D could be eliminated without losing majority support.

The basic assumption of minimal winning coalition theory is both simple and quite plausible: political parties are interested in maximizing their power. In parliamentary systems, power means participation in the cabinet, and maximum power means holding as many of the cabinet positions as possible. To enter the cabinet,

1. The political science literature on the formation and durability of government coalitions is extensive. Useful summaries and critical reviews can be found in Strøm, Müller, and Bergman 2008.

TABLE 6.1

Cabinet coalitions predicted by six coalition theories for a hypothetical distribution of parliamentary seats

Parties:	A (Left)	B	C	D	E (Right)		
Seats:	8	21	26	12	33		
Theories:							
Minimal winning coalition	ABC		ADE	BCD	BE	CE	
Minimum size			ADE				
Bargaining proposition					BE	CE	
Minimal range	ABC			BCD		CE	
Minimal connected winning	ABC			BCD		CDE	
Policy-viable coalition	ABC			BCD		CE	

a minority party will have to team up with one or more other parties, but it will resist the inclusion of unnecessary parties in the coalition because this would reduce its share of ministers in the cabinet. For instance, in cabinet coalition CE in Table 6.1, party C contributes almost half of the parliamentary support, and hence it is likely to receive almost half of the ministerial appointments. If party B were added to the coalition, C's share of cabinet positions would probably be only a third.

Only when there is a majority party in parliament can minimal winning coalition theory make a single specific prediction: a one-party, noncoalition cabinet formed by the majority party. When there is no majority party, the theory always predicts more than one outcome. In the example of Table 6.1, five coalitions are predicted. The next three coalition theories to be discussed attempt to improve minimal winning coalition theory by introducing additional criteria to arrive at more specific predictions.

2. *Minimum size coalitions.* Minimum size coalition theory is based on the same assumption of power maximization as minimal winning coalition theory, but it follows this rationale to its logical conclusion. If political parties want to exclude unneces-

sary partners from a coalition cabinet to maximize their share of cabinet power, they should also be expected to prefer the cabinet to be based on the narrowest possible parliamentary majority. For instance, it is more advantageous for party E to form coalition ADE with fifty-three seats than CE with fifty-nine seats. In the former, E's thirty-three seats in parliament contribute 62 percent of the cabinet's parliamentary support, and in the latter only 56 percent. In a cabinet with twenty ministers, this difference is easily worth an additional ministerial appointment for party E. According to this reasoning, cabinets of minimum size are predicted. In the example of Table 6.1, coalition ADE with fifty-three parliamentary seats is predicted rather than the other four minimal winning coalitions whose sizes range from fifty-four to fifty-nine seats.

3. *Coalitions with the smallest number of parties.* A different criterion that may be used to choose among the many coalitions predicted by minimal winning coalition theory is Michael Leiserson's (1970, 90) "bargaining proposition." He argues that those minimal winning coalitions will tend to form that involve the smallest possible number of parties, because "negotiations and bargaining [about the formation of a coalition] are easier to complete, and a coalition is easier to hold together, other things being equal, with fewer parties." Of the five minimal winning coalitions in Table 6.1, the bargaining proposition predicts that coalitions BE or CE will form because they involve only two parties rather than one of the three-party coalitions.

4. *Minimal range coalitions.* The preceding theories base their predictions on the sizes and numbers of political parties but ignore their programs and policy preferences. Minimal range coalition theory makes the plausible assumption that it is easier to form and maintain coalitions among parties with similar policy preferences than among parties that are far apart in this respect. Of the several slightly different versions of this theory, Table 6.1 presents the most basic one: the parties are placed on a left-right scale, with party A at the extreme left and E at the extreme right, and the distance between them is measured in terms of the num-

ber of "spaces" separating them. The five minimal winning coalitions have ranges of two, three, and four "spaces." If parties seek to form a coalition with like-minded partners, coalition ABC, with a range of two "spaces," is much more likely than coalition ADE, with a range of four "spaces" covering the entire left-right spectrum. Minimal range theory also predicts coalitions BCD and CE, which have the same minimal range of two "spaces" as ABC.

5. *Minimal connected winning coalitions.* A closely related theory has been proposed by Robert Axelrod (1970, 165–87). He predicts that coalitions will form that are both "connected"—that is, composed of parties that are adjacent on the policy scale—and devoid of unnecessary partners. The underlying assumption of this theory is that parties will try to coalesce with their immediate neighbors and that other adjacent parties will be added until a majority coalition is formed. The example of Table 6.1 shows that minimal *connected* winning coalitions are not necessarily minimal winning coalitions. According to the latter theory, coalition CDE contains a superfluous partner—party D—but in Axelrod's theory, party D is necessary to make the coalition a connected one.

6. *Policy-viable coalitions.* The focus on the policy preferences of parties is taken to its ultimate conclusion by policy-viable coalition theory. If we assume that parties truly care only about policy instead of holding office, real power resides in the legislature, where major new policies have to be enacted, rather than in the cabinet. In the legislature, it is the "core" party that is of pivotal importance; the core party is the party that, on a one-dimensional policy scale like the left-right scale, contains the median member of parliament: party C in the example of Table 6.1. This pivotal party can virtually dictate policy because neither the party or parties on its left nor those on its right have the majorities necessary to enact any policy contrary to its wishes. This means that, in strict policy terms, it is completely irrelevant how many and which parties participate in the cabinet. In fact, as Michael Laver and Norman Schofield (1990, 88) state, for the formation of policy-viable cabinets "it does not [even] matter whether or not the pivotal party" participates.

And yet, Laver and Schofield (1990, 55) concede that a distinction should be made between big policy questions and more detailed matters of policy. To influence detailed matters of policy, it can be quite important after all to be in the cabinet and at the head of a ministerial department, and this consideration "may provide a strong incentive for parties concerned not at all with the intrinsic rewards of office nonetheless to slug it out for a seat at the cabinet table." The importance of which party holds which cabinet portfolio is also emphasized in the work of Michael Laver and Kenneth A. Shepsle (1996). The implication is that parties are presumably also interested in "slugging it out" for as many cabinet seats and ministerial portfolios as possible—which takes us back to the logic of minimal winning coalitions, with the provision that the pivotal party be included in such coalitions: coalitions ABC, BCD, and CE in Table 6.1. In the final analysis, policy-viable coalition theory either makes no prediction about the composition of cabinets or predicts minimal winning coalitions similar to those predicted by minimal range theory.[2]

INCENTIVES FOR THE FORMATION OF MINORITY AND OVERSIZED CABINETS

Of the above six coalition theories, the policy-based ones have been able to predict actual cabinet coalitions more successfully than the policy-blind theories (de Swaan 1973). Some of this success has to be discounted because the assignment of parties to positions on the left-right scale may involve circular reasoning.

2. Two alternative interpretations of policy-viable coalition theory are that the core party should be able to govern by itself or that the coalition should include the core party (Strøm, Budge, and Laver 1994, 328). The first interpretation yields the prediction that a one-party minority cabinet will be formed—not a prediction that is likely to be successful because fewer than 20 percent of cabinets formed in minority situations are one-party minority cabinets (see Table 6.2 below). The problem with the second interpretation is that it produces a large number of predictions: in the situation of Table 6.1, fifteen coalitions can be formed that include party C. One of these may well be the cabinet that is formed; if so, the one correct prediction is still outweighed by fourteen incorrect ones.

Where a party stands on left-right issues may be inferred from its formal program, its votes in parliament, and so on, but is also likely to be influenced by whether the party is or has been a member of the government and with which other parties it has formed a coalition. In Germany, for instance, the Free Democratic party has often been assigned a center position on the policy scale—in contrast with the right-of-center position of other European Liberal parties—because it was in several cabinet coalitions with the leftist Social Democrats from 1969 to 1982. Explaining the coalition in terms of the two parties' adjacent policy positions, which are in turn derived from their coalition behavior, obviously does not explain very much.

The basic problem of all of the theories is that they predict minimal winning coalitions of one kind or another; Axelrod's theory is only a partial exception because few of his minimal connected winning coalitions are larger than minimal winning. The minimal winning prediction is based on a majoritarian assumption, and it conflicts with the large numbers of actual minority and oversized coalitions that are formed in parliamentary democracies. Laver and Schofield (1990, 70–71) classify 196 cabinets formed in "minority situations" (that is, where there is no majority party in parliament) in twelve European democracies from 1945 to 1987. Only 77 of these—39.3 percent—were minimal winning coalitions; 46 were oversized and 73 were minority cabinets. Paul Mitchell and Benjamin Nyblade (2008, 205–8) present a similar classification of 406 cabinets in seventeen European parliamentary democracies from 1945 to 1999, but they do include "majority situations" in which one-party majority cabinets are usually formed. Only 178 of these—43.8 percent—were minimal winning cabinets. Excluding the single-party majority governments, 125 of the remaining 353 cabinets—35.4 percent—were minimal winning coalitions; 87 were oversized and 141 were minority cabinets.

Table 6.2 presents similar data on the cabinets in the thirty-one parliamentary systems investigated in this book (including

TABLE 6.2

Proportions of time during which five types of cabinets were in power
in thirty-one parliamentary democracies, 1945–2010

	All cabinets (%)	All cabinets except minimal winning, one-party cabinets (%)
Type of cabinet		
Minimal winning, one-party	36.3	—
Minimal winning coalition	24.8	38.9
Minority, one-party	10.9	17.1
Minority coalition	7.3	11.4
Oversized coalition	20.7	32.6
Total	100.0	100.0

Source: Based on data in Woldendorp, Keman, and Budge 2010; Bale and Caramani 2010
and earlier volumes of the "Political Data Yearbook"; Muller, Overstreet, Isacoff, and Lansford 2011 and earlier volumes of the *Political Handbook of the World;* and data provided
by Krista Hoekstra, Jelle Koedam, and Linganaden Murday

semiparliamentary Switzerland and the three phases of parliamentary government in the French Fifth Republic). The table
covers twelve non-European in addition to nineteen European
countries during the longer period from 1945 to 2010. Several of
these are countries that usually have majority parties in their parliament; this accounts for the large proportion of one-party majority cabinets: 36.3 percent. As indicated earlier, when one party
has a majority of the seats in parliament, it is easy, and almost
always correct, to predict the formation of a one-party cabinet.
When these cabinets are excluded, in the second column of Table
6.2, the proportion of minimal winning coalitions is 38.9 percent—which happens to be very close to the 39.3 percent found
by Laver and Schofield and the 35.4 percent found by Mitchell
and Nyblade, in spite of the different countries, time periods,

and definitions of cabinets used in their and my analyses.[3] Oversized coalitions comprise 32.6 percent of the total and minority cabinets 28.5 percent; together they outnumber minimal winning cabinets by a margin of more than three to two.[4]

How can all of these oversized and minority cabinets be explained? The kind of rational incentives on which the above coalition theories are based can also account for the formation of other than minimal winning cabinets. One important consideration is the parties' time perspective. Even if it is correct to assume that parties seek power and that power means participation in the cabinet, it is not necessarily true that parties want to enter cabinets at all times; they may well believe that not carrying government responsibility for a while may be electorally advantageous and, hence, that a period in the opposition will offer the opportunity of both electoral gains and the possibility of enhanced cabinet participation in the future (Strøm 1990, 44–47). If this consideration is important for several parties, it creates a high probability that a minority cabinet will be formed.

Riker himself explicitly acknowledges a reason for the forma-

3. Laver and Schofield (1990) and Mitchell and Nyblade (2008) count each cabinet at the time of its formation and regardless of how long it lasts, whereas I weight the cabinets by their duration.

4. The classification into minimal winning, oversized, and coalition cabinets is not exhaustive because it misses two borderline cases: so-called blocking cabinets—composed of parties with exactly 50 percent of the seats in parliament—and cabinets that become blocking if the smallest cabinet partner leaves. An example of the former is the 1989–93 Spanish cabinet under Prime Minister Felipe González, whose Socialist party controlled 175 of the 350 seats in the lower house of parliament. An example of the latter is the 1992–93 four-party coalition of Prime Minister Giuliano Amati in Italy: together the four parties controlled 331 of the 630 seats in the Chamber of Deputies, but without the smallest party only 315. For the classification of such cabinets, the best solution is to split the difference. Half of the time that blocking cabinets are in power can be credited to minimal winning and half to minority cabinets. Similarly, cabinets like the Amati cabinet can be counted half as oversized and half as minimal winning.

tion of larger than minimal winning cabinets. He calls it the "information effect": in the negotiations about the formation of a cabinet, there may be considerable uncertainty about how loyal one or more of the prospective coalition parties, or individual legislators belonging to these parties, will be to the proposed cabinet. Therefore, additional parties may be brought into the coalition as insurance against defections and as guarantee for the cabinet's winning status. In Riker's (1962, 88) words, "If coalition-makers do not know how much weight a specific uncommitted participant adds, then they may be expected to aim at more than a minimum winning coalition."

Second, the policy-based theories also take the size principle into account. They represent additions, instead of alternatives, to minimal winning theory: minimal range coalitions are also minimal winning coalitions, and minimal connected winning coalitions either equal or are only slightly larger than minimal winning size. In reality, however, the parties' policy preferences may exert strong pressures to enlarge instead of to minimize the size and range of coalitions. Each party naturally prefers to form a cabinet that will follow policies close to its own policy preferences; a cabinet in which it participates with parties of about equal weight on both its left and its right is ideal in this respect. In the example of Table 6.1 above, if B and C are inclined to participate in a coalition together, coalition ABC is more attractive to B because B occupies the center position in it, whereas for the same reason C prefers coalition BCD. In such a situation, it is not at all unlikely that the oversized coalition ABCD will be formed.

Third, policy considerations also lead to oversized coalitions if it is the overriding objective of all or most of the parties to work together to defend the country or the democratic regime against external or internal threats. Wars are the main external threats, and wartime grand coalitions, such as Churchill's war cabinet in Britain, have occurred frequently. Internal threats may be posed by antidemocratic parties and movements and by deep differences among prodemocratic parties in plural societies. Ian Budge and Valentine Herman (1978, 463) tested the following hypothesis in twenty-one countries during the period 1945–78: "Where the democratic system is immediately threatened (externally or internally), all significant pro-system parties will join the government, excluding anti-system parties." They found that of the cabinets formed under such crisis conditions, 72 percent were indeed such broad coalitions.

In addition, several institutional features may favor the formation of minority and oversized instead of minimal winning cabinets (Mitchell and Nyblade 2008). For instance, it is easier to form a minority cabinet in the absence of an investiture requirement—that is, if a new cabinet can take office without the need for a parliamentary vote formally electing or approving it; a minority cabinet is more likely to be formed when a parliamentary majority is allowed to tolerate it instead of having to give it explicit approval. There are many parliamentary democracies without investiture rules: examples are the United Kingdom and most former British colonies (but not Ireland), the Scandinavian countries, and the Netherlands.

The requirement of a "constructive" vote of no confidence— that is, the provision that a no-confidence motion must simultaneously propose an alternative cabinet—may have two different effects. A successful no-confidence vote, supported by a parliamentary majority, is akin to investiture and hence encourages the formation of majority cabinets. And yet, the constructive no-confidence requirement may also maintain a minority cabinet in power if the parliamentary majority opposing the cabinet is too divided to agree on an alternative. Germany was the first country to adopt the constructive vote of no confidence in its postwar constitution. It is now also used by Spain and, since 1993, by federal Belgium.

Minority cabinets are also encouraged by an innovative rule in the constitution of the French Fifth Republic. It gives the cabinet the right to make its legislative proposals matters of confidence and stipulates that such proposals be automatically adopted unless an absolute majority of the National Assembly votes to dismiss the cabinet: the Government bill "shall be considered as adopted, unless a motion of censure . . . is voted under the conditions laid down in the previous paragraph." This previous paragraph prescribes that "the only votes counted shall be those favorable to the motion of censure, which may be adopted only by a majority of the members comprising the Assembly" (Article 49). Aided by this rule, the minority Socialist cabinets serving under President François Mitterrand managed not only to stay in power from 1988 to 1993 but also to pass much of their legislative program.

Probably the most important institutional feature favoring minority cabinets is the strength of parliamentary committees; powerful committees with a great deal of influence on the general thrust as well as the details of proposed legislation give parties the ability to influence policy from their positions in the legislature— and decrease their incentives to try to enter the cabinet (Strøm 1990, 70–72). The strength of legislative committees is one aspect of the general question of the balance of power between executives and legislatures (the subject of the next chapter): all other factors being equal, the incentives to participate in cabinets decrease, and the probability of minority cabinets increases, when legislatures are relatively strong vis-à-vis executives.

Oversized cabinets may also be encouraged by particular institutional provisions like the prescription of linguistic balance in Belgium. It has indirectly tended to enlarge the cabinet. If, for instance, the Flemish Socialists are invited into the cabinet, the requirement of linguistic balance increases the probability that the Francophone Socialists will be included, too, even if they are not needed to give the cabinet a parliamentary majority.

Finally, special majorities necessary for the adoption of constitutional amendments or regular legislation may be strong reasons for forming oversized cabinets. If the policy agenda of a new cabinet includes one or more important amendments to the constitution, any special majorities required for this purpose are likely to broaden the composition of the cabinet. The two-thirds majority rule for constitutional amendments in Belgium was one of the reasons for its many oversized cabinets during the long process of constitutional reform that led to the establishment of a federal state in 1993. Until the early 1990s, Finland's tendency to have oversized cabinets was similarly reinforced by the requirement of two-thirds and even five-sixths majorities for certain types of economic legislation. Moreover, "even ordinary laws passed by simple majority could be deferred until after the next election by a vote of one-third of the members, a striking provision for a temporary minority veto. These procedures rewarded consensual behavior and made a minimum-majority coalition less valuable than a broader one" (McRae 1997, 290).

MINORITY CABINETS

The threefold classification into minimal winning, oversized, and minority cabinets and the twofold classification into one-party and coalition cabinets appear simple and straightforward, but they raise a number of problems that need to be resolved before they can be used to measure the degree of concentration of executive power. The most important of these problems are the treatment of minority cabinets and presidential cabinets.

It is clear that minimal winning and one-party cabinets represent majoritarian characteristics and that oversized and coalition cabinets express consensus traits. But where do minority cabinets fit? In principle, there can be two kinds of minority cabinets. One is a genuine minority cabinet that has to negotiate continually with one or more noncabinet parties both to stay in office and to solicit support for its legislative proposals; this bargaining relationship, typically with different noncabinet parties for different purposes, makes such minority cabinets resemble oversized coalitions. The other kind is described by Strøm (1997, 56) as "majority governments in disguise"—minority cabinets that are more like majority cabinets because they have received a firm commitment of support from one or more specific parties in the legislatures, although these have opted not to take portfolios in the cabinet.

In his earlier study, Strøm (1990, 95) found that only 11 percent of the many minority cabinets he analyzed could be regarded as such disguised majorities—allowing him to conclude that, by a large margin, most minority cabinets are *not* "simply majority governments in disguise. . . . Instead, the typical minority cabinet is a single-party government . . . which may have to look for legislative support from issue to issue on an *ad hoc* basis." On the basis of Strøm's findings as well as two additional considerations— that the commitment of a support party is never as solid as that of a party actually in the cabinet and that it is often difficult to determine whether a party qualifies as a support party—it makes the most sense, both theoretically and practically, to treat minority cabinets like oversized cabinets. Accordingly, the contrast will be between minimal winning cabinets on one hand and oversized and minority cabinets on the other.

PRESIDENTIAL CABINETS

The classifications into one-party versus coalition cabinets and minimal winning versus oversized versus minority cabinets have been applied mainly to cabinets in parliamentary systems of government, which has been the almost exclusive focus of coalition theorists. Can they also be applied to presidential cabinets? Two crucial adjustments are needed for this purpose. The differences between parliamentary and presidential systems are more fully and systematically discussed in the next chapter, but one major difference is that the executive (cabinet) in parliamentary systems depends on majority support in the legislature both to stay in office and to get its legislative proposals approved, whereas the executive in presidential systems needs legislative majority support only for the president's legislative proposals; presidents are elected for a fixed term of office, and neither they nor the cabinet they appoint are dependent on the confidence of the legislature for their survival in office. Therefore, in one respect—

staying in office—presidents and presidential cabinets are minimal winning by definition; in the other respect—legislative support for proposed laws—presidential cabinets may be minimal winning, oversized, or minority cabinets depending on the party affiliations of the presidents and of their cabinet members and the sizes of the respective parties in the legislature. This means that whereas cabinets in parliamentary systems can vary between 0 and 100 percent minimal winning, the variation for presidential cabinets is only between 50 and 100 percent.

The other difference between parliamentary and presidential systems that is of critical relevance here is that parliamentary executives are collegial cabinets, whereas presidential executives are one-person executives; in presidential systems, executive power is concentrated in the president, and his or her cabinet consists of advisers to the president instead of more or less coequal participants. For the distinction between one-party and coalition executives, this means that in one respect presidential cabinets are one-party cabinet by definition—the one party being the president's party because of the president's dominant status in the cabinet. On the other hand, it does make a difference whether a president appoints only members of his or her own party to the cabinet or whether members of one or more other parties are also included. On the assumption that these two aspects can be weighted equally, presidential cabinets can vary between 50 and 100 percent one-party cabinets in contrast with parliamentary cabinets, where the range of variation is the full 0 to 100 percent. As is explained more fully in the next chapter, the six presidential systems are the United States, France (except in three short parliamentary phases), Costa Rica, Argentina, Uruguay, and Korea.[5] So-called semipresidential systems other than France can be treated like parliamentary systems. Switzerland is an intermediate case, but for the purpose of classifying the composition of its executive, it can be treated as a parliamentary system.

5. In addition, Israel's brief experience under the "directly elected prime minister" should also be treated like a presidential phase (see Chapter 7).

GRAND COALITIONS, "TOKEN" MINISTERS,
AND "PARTIAL" COALITIONS

The great variety of forms that cabinets can assume can be illustrated further by five of our democracies: Austria, the United States, Argentina, Uruguay, and Japan. Even these unusual cabinets, however, can still be classified in terms of the basic criteria distinguishing one-party cabinets from coalitions and minimal winning from oversized and minority cabinets.

The so-called grand coalition cabinets in Austria from 1949 to 1966 exemplify the rather frequent occurrence of very broad coalitions, composed of a country's two largest parties—which are, however, minimal winning cabinets in purely technical terms. These Austrian coalitions were composed of the Socialists and the conservative People's party, which together controlled on average more than 92 percent of the parliamentary seats during this period. Since each of the parties had fewer than half of the seats, however, their cabinets were technically minimal winning because the defection of either would have turned the cabinet into a minority cabinet. In substantive terms, such broad coalitions should obviously be regarded as oversized. Accordingly, I classified as oversized any coalition cabinet based on a large supermajority of four-fifths—80 percent—or more of the seats in the legislature.[6]

Coalition cabinets are not formed frequently in presidential systems, but they are not completely exceptional either. One important reason for their formation is that presidents may not have

6. The other cases of substantively oversized cabinets are a later Austrian cabinet (1987–90), the 1961–65 Belgian cabinet, the well-known "grand coalition" of Christian Democrats and Social Democrats in Germany from 1966 to 1969, and the 1954–59 cabinet in Luxembourg. However, I deviate from my own 80 percent rule in the case of the French Gaullist-Republican cabinet that took office in 1993, because its huge parliamentary majority (81.8 percent) was manufactured from a mere 39.9 percent of first-ballot votes. Technically—according to the 80 percent rule—this was an oversized cabinet, but substantively it can be regarded only as minimal winning.

majority support in the legislature and that legislative majorities are needed to get laws passed (Amorim Neto 2006). Examples of such presidential coalition cabinets are the coalition of the National Congress for New Politics and the United Liberal Democrats under President Kim Dae Jung in Korea (1998–2000), the Peronist-Radical coalition under President Eduardo Duhalde in Argentina (2002–3), and the two successive Colorado-Blanco coalitions under Presidents Julio María Sanguinetti and Jorge Batlle in Uruguay (1995–2002).

More frequent, however, are partisan cabinets with one or two "token" members drawn from a different party or parties; token participation in cabinets means a share of cabinet seats that is much lower than what a party could expect on the basis of proportionality. The first Sanguinetti administration had such token Blanco and Civic Union members in its cabinet (1985–90), and President Cristina Fernández de Kirchner was elected in Argentina in 2007 on a joint Peronist-Radical ticket with a Radical vice-presidential candidate who, however, played no significant role in her administration. American cabinets also provide clear examples. Republicans C. Douglas Dillon and Robert S. McNamara served in President John F. Kennedy's cabinet, and Democrat John B. Connally served in President Richard M. Nixon's cabinet; the example of Connally is especially striking because he had been an active Democratic politician and had served as Democratic governor of Texas (Jones 1994, 107–8). More recent examples are the appointment of former Republican senator William S. Cohen as secretary of defense in the second Clinton administration and the appointment of Republican Robert M. Gates, also as secretary of defense, in the Obama administration. Richard F. Fenno's (1959, 68) conclusion is still valid: "Typically, the entire Cabinet is of the same political party as the President. . . . The few exceptions serve only to prove the rule. Many deviations from this norm are more apparent than real, involving men whose ideas and sympathies obviously do not coincide with their partisan labels." It is worth noting that Connally later switched parties and became a candidate for the Republican presidential nomination in 1980. One important general finding concerning coalition cabinets is that approximate proportionality in the division of cabinet positions tends to be closely adhered to (Verzichelli 2008). It is therefore not at all difficult to distinguish tokenism from genuine coalitions, and token ministers—just like nonpartisan ministers in otherwise partisan cabinets[7]—can be ignored in the classification of cabinets.

The Liberal Democratic (LDP) cabinets in Japan from 1976 to 1993 present the unusual case of a numerically minimal winning cabinet behaving like a minority cabinet. T. J. Pempel (1992, 11) writes that the LDP, instead of using "its parliamentary majority to ram through controversial legislation," tended to follow "the norm of cross-party consensus building. Usually the LDP [tried] to ensure support for its proposals by at least one, and often more, opposition parties." In Japan, this was called the strategy of "partial coalition" with the parliamentary opposition (Krauss 1984, 263). Especially because experts on Japanese politics link this behavior to strong consensual norms "that operate against what the Japanese usually refer to as 'tyranny of the majority'" (Pempel 1992, 11), these LDP cabinets should be counted as minority rather than minimal winning.[8]

7. Because all of the classifications of cabinets are based on their partisan composition, cabinets that are entirely "nonparty" or "business" cabinets have to be disregarded, but fortunately these do not occur frequently.

8. Two final issues of classification need to be mentioned briefly. First, the logical consequence of the treatment of factionalized and closely linked parties as one-and-a-half parties, explained in Chapter 5, is that cabinets composed of such parties have to be classified as half one-party cabinets and half two-party coalition cabinets. For instance most of the Liberal-National cabinets in Australia have to be counted as in between one-party and coalition cabinets; moreover, when the Liberals have had a majority of seats in parliament, such cabinets are halfway between minimal winning and oversized. Second, any major interelection changes in the legislative seats controlled by cabinet parties must be taken into consideration. For instance, the British Labour cabinet that began as a mini-

CABINETS IN THIRTY-SIX DEMOCRACIES

The first and second columns of Table 6.3 present the types of cabinets in thirty-six democracies in terms of the time that minimal winning and one-party cabinets were in power. The values in the third column are the averages of those in the first two; they measure the overall degree of majoritarianism in the formation of cabinets. The countries are listed in ascending order of the majoritarian nature of their cabinets.

The scores in the first two columns are strongly correlated ($r=0.58$, significant at the 1 percent level), mainly because at the top of the table both scores tend to be low and at the bottom they tend to be high. Most one-party cabinets are also minimal winning, and oversized cabinets are coalitions by definition. In the middle of the table, however, are several countries in which the two elements are unequally combined: some that have mainly minimal winning cabinets but few one-party cabinets—especially Germany, Iceland, and Luxembourg—and some with relatively few minimal winning but many one-party cabinets—especially Spain and Sweden. The range of variation on both variables is wide: from 8 percent to 100 percent on minimal winning cabinets and from 0 to 100 percent on one-party cabinets. Five countries always had minimal winning cabinets without exception, and eight countries always had one-party cabinets; by contrast, four countries never had one-party cabinets. The tendency to have minimal winning cabinets is slightly stronger than the tendency toward one-party cabinets: the mean and median of the values in the first column are 64.2 and 71.4 percent, compared with 56.4 and 67.6 percent in the second column. The third column ranges from 4 to 100 percent with a mean of 60.3 and a median of 55 percent.

---

mal winning cabinet in October 1974 became a minority cabinet in the middle of 1976 (see Chapter 2). A reverse example is the Indian Congress cabinet that started off as a minority cabinet in 1991 but became a minimal winning cabinet in December 1993 when several defectors from other parties were welcomed into the Congress party.

TABLE 6.3

Proportions of time during which minimal winning and one-party cabinets were in power in thirty-six democracies, 1945–2010

	Minimal winning cabinets (%)	One-party cabinets (%)	Mean (%)
Switzerland	8.0	0.0	4.0
Finland	11.4	8.5	10.0
Italy	15.5	8.0	11.7
Israel	22.1	6.0	14.0
Mauritius	30.6	0.0	15.3
Denmark	13.7	33.6	23.6
Netherlands	53.6	0.0	26.8
India	37.0	24.0	30.5
Belgium	68.1	6.5	37.3
Germany	74.3	1.3	37.8
Japan	42.4	37.8	40.1
Austria	60.1	26.5	43.3
Luxembourg	90.8	0.0	45.4
Iceland	90.3	2.3	46.3
Sweden	25.1	71.1	48.1
Ireland	57.2	41.8	49.5
Portugal	48.3	58.5	53.4
France	62.0	47.5	54.8
Norway	44.0	66.6	55.3
Spain	38.6	100.0	69.3
Uruguay	79.5	81.0	80.3
United States	71.5	89.2	80.4
Australia	92.7	68.7	80.7
New Zealand	80.9	82.0	81.4
Argentina	71.2	93.5	82.4
Costa Rica	71.6	100.0	85.8
Korea	83.3	88.7	86.0

continued

TABLE 6.3 *continued*

	Minimal winning cabinets (%)	One-party cabinets (%)	Mean (%)
Canada	76.8	100.0	88.4
Trinidad	99.2	89.5	94.3
United Kingdom	94.8	99.8	97.3
Greece	98.4	97.8	98.1
Bahamas	100.0	100.0	100.0
Barbados	100.0	100.0	100.0
Botswana	100.0	100.0	100.0
Jamaica	100.0	100.0	100.0
Malta	100.0	100.0	100.0

Source: Based on data in Woldendorp, Keman, and Budge 2010; Bale and Caramani 2010 and earlier volumes of the "Political Data Yearbook"; Muller, Overstreet, Isacoff, and Lansford 2011 and earlier volumes of the *Political Handbook of the World;* and data provided by Octavio Amorim Neto, Marcelo Camerlo, Krista Hoekstra, Jelle Koedam, Jorge Lanzaro, Andrés Malamud, and Linganaden Murday

As expected, Switzerland turns up at the top of the table; its only minimal winning coalitions occurred from 1955 to 1959, when there was a three-party executive without the Social Democrats instead of the usual four-party executive, and during 2008 when the Swiss People's party was in the opposition. Belgium is farther down in the table but would have had a higher position had only more recent decades been analyzed. Toward the majoritarian end at the bottom of the table, we find, as expected, the United Kingdom and Barbados, but New Zealand has a higher position in the table as a result of its political evolution since 1996. More generally, there are two groups of countries on the majoritarian side: presidential systems, which, as discussed earlier, owe much of their majoritarian character to the constitutional position and power of their presidents, and democracies with a British political heritage: all but one of the sixteen countries at the bottom of the table fit one of these categories. Ireland, India, and Mauritius, also former British colonies, are exceptions: Ireland is near the middle of the table, and India and Mauritius, both deeply plural societies, are in eighth and fifth place, respectively, near the consensual top of the table. Greece, in contrast, is a rather surprising presence among the British-heritage countries at the majoritarian end.

CABINETS AND PARTY SYSTEMS

There is an extremely strong relationship between party systems and types of cabinets, as Figure 6.1 shows.[9] As the effective number of parliamentary parties increases, the incidence of one-party minimal winning cabinets decreases. The correlation coefficient is −0.85 (significant at the 1 percent level). Most countries are located very close to the regression line, and there are no extreme outliers. The most deviant cases are Uruguay and Mauritius. Uruguay's mainly majoritarian cabinets are similar to those of the Argentine, Costa Rican, Korean, and American cabinets, but unlike the other four presidential democracies, it has a high effective number of parties due to the strong factionalism of its three main parties. In Mauritius, the plurality system of elections has reduced the effective number of parties, but not to the extent of creating a two-party system, and moderate multipartism and coalition cabinets have gone hand in hand; moreover, the usual inclusion in the cabinet of one of the parties representing the distant island of Rodrigues has tended to make the coalitions oversized.

The strong relationship between party systems and cabinet types is part of the cluster of five closely related variables that comprise the executives-parties dimension of the contrast between majoritarian and consensus democracy, described in the first three

9. In Figure 6.1 and in similar figures in later chapters, the thirty-six democracies are identified by the first three characters of their English names, except that AUL means Australia, AUT Austria, CR Costa Rica, JPN Japan, NZ New Zealand, UK United Kingdom, and US United States.

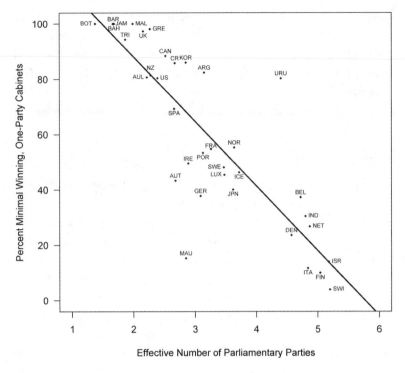

FIG. 6.1 The relationship between the effective number of parliamentary parties and type of cabinet in thirty-six democracies, 1945–2010

chapters of this book. The next three chapters will analyze the other three variables in this cluster: executive-legislative relations, electoral systems, and interest groups. This analysis will again show strong empirical relationships, although not quite as strong and significant as the strikingly close link between party systems and cabinets.

ADDENDUM: PRIME MINISTERIAL POWER

What is the strength of the head of a cabinet within his or her cabinet? In presidential systems, the cabinet is the president's cabinet and the president's constitutional position makes him or her preeminent. This position can be called, in Giovanni Sartori's (1994, 109) words, "a *primus solus,* as in the case of the American president (whose government is only his private cabinet)." In parliamentary systems, the power of the prime minister who heads the cabinet can vary greatly from—again using Sartori's terminology—a strong "first *above unequals*" to a medium "first *among unequals*" to a relatively weak "first *among equals*."

In this chapter, I have measured the concentration of power and the degree of majoritarianism in the cabinet in terms of the breadth of representation and the numbers of parties included in the cabinet. A logical corollary would be to expect the degree of prime ministerial power to be related to the concentration of power in the cabinet. The threefold classification of the within-cabinet power of prime ministers in parliamentary democracies— similar to Sartori's trichotomous scheme—presented by Jaap Woldendorp, Hans Keman, and Ian Budge (2000, 68) allows a test of this hypothesis. Among the prime ministers whom they judge to have a high degree of influence within their cabinets are the British, Australian, German, Greek, Indian, Jamaican, and New Zealand prime ministers. Those in Austria, Belgium, Denmark, Japan, and Sweden are in a medium position. And examples of prime ministers with a low degree of influence are the Dutch, Icelandic, Italian, and Norwegian. A comparison of these examples with the scores in the third column of Table 6.1 shows that prime ministers indeed appear to have greater power in countries with majoritarian than in those with consensual cabinets. The Woldendorp-Keman-Budge data are available for twenty-four of our democracies. The coefficient of the correlation between type of cabinet and prime ministerial power is 0.44 (significant at the 5 percent level).

More of our democracies can be included in the test by extending the threefold classification of prime ministers into a fivefold classification of all heads of government. At the top we can add a new category for Sartori's *primus solus* presidential chief executives. At the other end, we can give Switzerland a category of its own; its head of government, the annually rotating chair of the seven-member Federal Council, is not even a "first among equals"—merely an "equal among equals." Botswana's strong president, who is also the head of government in an essentially parliamentary system, can be placed in the same category as the British and New Zealand prime ministers. For thirty-two of our democracies—all except the Bahamas, Barbados, Mauritius, and Trinidad—the correlation coefficient is now a strong 0.60 (significant at the 1 percent level). The sharing of executive power generally also means greater equality in the executive branch of government.

CHAPTER 7

EXECUTIVE-LEGISLATIVE RELATIONS:
PATTERNS OF DOMINANCE AND BALANCE
OF POWER

The third difference between the majoritarian and consensus models of democracy concerns the relationship between the executive and legislative branches of government. The majoritarian model is one of executive dominance, whereas the consensus model is characterized by a more balanced executive-legislative relationship. In real political life, a variety of patterns between complete balance and severe imbalance can occur.

In this chapter I first contrast the two most prevalent formal arrangements of executive-legislative relations in democratic regimes: parliamentary government and presidential government. I propose a classificatory scheme based on the three major differences between these types of government and show that almost all of the thirty-six democracies included in this study fit either the pure parliamentary or the pure presidential type. The next topic is the question of how to measure degrees of executive dominance. I propose an index that is mainly, but not entirely, based on the durability of cabinets; several important adjustments are required, especially for presidential systems. After presenting the empirical findings concerning the different levels of executive dominance in thirty-six democracies between 1945 and

2010, I explore two relationships: the link between the five basic types of cabinet and the durability of these cabinets in parliamentary systems and the relationship between the incidence of one-party majority government and the degree of executive dominance in the thirty-six democracies. I close with a brief discussion of the power exercised by heads of state—monarchs and presidents—and some of the problems associated with monarchical and presidential power.

PARLIAMENTARY AND PRESIDENTIAL FORMS OF GOVERNMENT

Parliamentary and presidential systems of government have three crucial differences. First, in a parliamentary system, the head of government—who may have such different official titles as prime minister, premier, chancellor, minister-president, *taoiseach* (in Ireland), or, rather confusingly, even "president" (in Botswana) but whom I generically term the prime minister—and his or her cabinet are responsible to the legislature in the sense that they are dependent on the legislature's confidence and can be dismissed from office by a legislative vote of no confidence or censure. In a presidential system, the head of government—always called president—is elected for a constitutionally prescribed period and in normal circumstances cannot be forced to resign by a legislative vote of no confidence (although it may be possible to remove a president for criminal wrongdoing by the process of impeachment).[1]

The second difference between presidential and parliamentary governments is that presidents are popularly elected, either directly or via a popularly elected presidential electoral college, and that prime ministers are selected by legislatures. The process of selection may take a variety of forms. For instance, the German

1. In addition, as I argue below, we can still speak of presidential government if the legislature can dismiss the president, but only if two conditions apply: (1) that the president also has the right to dissolve the legislature, and (2) that in either event new elections of both the president and the legislature take place.

chancellor is formally elected by the Bundestag, the Irish taoiseach by the Dáil, the Japanese prime minister by the House of Representatives, and the Botswanan "president" by the National Assembly. In Italy and Belgium, cabinets emerge from negotiations among the parties in parliament and especially among party leaders, but they also require a formal parliamentary vote of investiture. In the United Kingdom, the king or queen normally appoints the leader of the majority party to the prime ministership, and in many multiparty systems, too, the cabinets that emerge from interparty bargaining are appointed by the heads of state without formal election or investiture; these cabinets are assumed to have the legislature's confidence unless and until it expresses its lack of confidence.

The third fundamental difference is that parliamentary systems have collective or collegial executives whereas presidential systems have one-person, noncollegial executives. As I indicated at the end of the previous chapter, the prime minister's position in the cabinet can vary from preeminence to virtual equality with the other ministers, but there is always a relatively high degree of collegiality in decision-making; in contrast, the members of presidential cabinets are mere advisers and subordinates of the president. The most important decisions in parliamentary systems have to be made by the cabinet as a whole, not just by the prime minister; the most important decisions in presidential systems can be made by the president with or without, and even against, the advice of the cabinet.

Because parliamentary and presidential governments are defined in terms of three dichotomous criteria, their joint application yields the eight possible combinations shown in the typology of Figure 7.1. In addition to the pure parliamentary and presidential types, there are six hybrid forms of government, labeled I through VI in the typology. Thirty-five of our thirty-six democracies fit the criteria of the two pure types, although France and Israel have to be classified differently in different periods. Six countries have been mainly or wholly presidential—the United

			Collegial executive		One-person executive	
			Not dependent on	Dependent on	Not dependent on	
		Dependent on	legislative	legislative	legislative	
		legislative confidence	confidence	confidence	confidence	
		Parliamentary	Hybrid I	Hybrid II	Hybrid III

Executive selected by legislature		AUL GRE MAU
		AUS* ICE* NET
		BAH IND NZ
		BAR IRE* NOR
		BEL ITA POR*
		BOT JAM SPA
		CAN JPN SWE
		DEN LUX TRI
		FIN* MAL UK
		GER
		FRA* (1986–88,
		  1993–95, 1997–
		  2002)
		ISR (1949–96, 2003–)
			SWI		

Executive selected by voters		Hybrid IV	Hybrid V	Hybrid VI	Presidential

					ARG CR
					KOR US
					URU
					FRA* (1958–86,
					  1988–93, 1995–97,
					  2002–)
					ISR (1996–2003)

*Semipresidential systems

FIG. 7.1 Parliamentary, presidential, and hybrid forms of government in thirty-six democracies, 1945–2010: a typology

States, France, Costa Rica, Argentina, Uruguay, and Korea—and twenty-nine have been mainly or wholly parliamentary. Switzerland fits hybrid form I, and it is the only example among our thirty-six democracies that can be classified in any of the hybrid categories. This hybrid is parliamentary in two respects and presidential in one: the Swiss "cabinet," the collegial Federal Council, is elected by parliament, but the seven councilors stay in office for a fixed four-year term and cannot be dismissed by a legislative vote of no confidence.

Hybrid types III and V are presidential in two respects and parliamentary in one. The United States would have provided an example of type III if the Constitutional Convention of 1787 had not changed its mind at the last moment. The Virginia plan included the election of the president by the national legislature, and the Constitutional Convention voted three times in favor of this plan before finally settling on the electoral college solution. It should also be noted that if no presidential candidate wins a majority in the electoral college, the US Constitution prescribes hybrid III as the next step: election by the House of Representatives. An interesting example of type V is the 1952–67 Uruguayan political system, which had a collegial presidency: a Swiss-inspired nine-member body, collegial and serving for a fixed term, like the Swiss Federal Council, but popularly elected.

There are no empirical examples of hybrid types II, IV, and VI—which is not surprising because the logic of legislative confidence militates against them. Type II would be a parliamentary system except that the prime minister's relationship to the cabinet would resemble that of a president to his or her cabinet. On paper, the German constitution appears to call for such a system, but because the chancellor needs the Bundestag's confidence, the negotiation of a collegial coalition cabinet takes place before the formal election of the chancellor by the Bundestag. Types IV and VI are problematic because a legislative vote of no confidence in a popularly elected executive would be seen as defiance of the popular will and of democratic legitimacy. The only democratically acceptable form of these two types would be one in which a legislative vote of no confidence in the executive would be matched by the executive's right to dissolve the legislature, and where either action would trigger new elections of both legislature and executive. Such an amended type VI system appears to be what the Committee on the Constitutional System proposed for the United States in 1987, but, as I argue below, this proposal entailed a special form of presidential government rather than a hybrid type.

The only serious problem of classifying democracies according to the eightfold typology is raised by systems that have both a popularly elected president and a parliamentary prime minister, usually referred to as "semipresidential" (Duverger 1980) or "premier-presidential" systems (Shugart and Carey 1992). Among our thirty-six democracies, there are six of these semipresidential systems: Austria, Finland, France, Iceland, Ireland, and Portugal. These cases can be resolved by asking the question: Who is the *real* head of government—the president or the prime minister? The Austrian, Icelandic, and Irish presidents are weak though popularly elected, and these three democracies operate much like ordinary parliamentary systems. In semipresidential Portugal, the president continues to exercise significant power, even after his formal prerogatives were severely reduced in the constitutional revision of 1982 (Amorim Neto and Costa Lobo 2009), but it can still be treated like a mainly parliamentary system.

The French case is more problematic. Until 1986, the French president, popularly elected for a fixed seven-year term, was clearly the head of the government and not the prime minister. Presidential power, however, was based more on the support by strong parliamentary majorities than on constitutional prerogatives, and in the early 1980s, two well-known French political scientists predicted that, if the president were to lose this majority support, the presidential system would change to a parliamentary one. Raymond Aron (1982, 8) wrote: "The President of the Republic is the supreme authority as long as he has a majority in the National Assembly; but he must abandon the reality of power to the prime minister if ever a party other than his own has a majority in the Assembly." Based on the same logic, Maurice Duverger (1980, 186) predicted that the French Fifth Republic would develop a pattern of alternation between presidential and parliamentary phases. This is exactly what happened when the Gaullists and Republicans won a legislative victory in 1986 and Jacques Chirac became prime minister: "Except for some issues concerning foreign relations and defense . . . [Socialist president] Mitterrand stood on the legislative sidelines while Chirac functioned as France's political executive" (Huber 1996, 28). The situation repeated itself from 1993 to 1995 when Gaullist premier Édouard Balladur replaced President Mitterrand as the real head of government, and Socialist premier Lionel Jospin inaugurated the third parliamentary phase under President Chirac, which lasted for five years (1997–2002).

The Finnish semipresidential system is the most difficult case. Finland has an elected president—indirectly elected via an electoral college until the early 1990s—with less power than the French president usually has but more than that of the presidents in the other semipresidential systems. Yet there is a close resemblance to the French system in its parliamentary phases during which the prime minister is head of government and the president's power is limited to a special role in foreign affairs. If these phases in the French system can be regarded as parliamentary, the similar situation in Finland should be considered parliamentary, too. The classification may be somewhat debatable for the long period from 1956 to 1981 during which the formidable Urho Kekkonen served as president, but it clearly fits the period since his departure from the political scene.[2] A constitutional amendment in 1991 reduced presidential power by removing the president's right to dissolve parliament—a right that the French president does have—but at the same time increased presidential prestige by abolishing the presidential electoral college and instituting direct popular election. On balance, Finnish democracy can be classified as a parliamentary system in the typology of Figure 7.1; it is certainly much closer to a parliamentary than a presidential system.

Finally, Israel shifted from a system that was unambiguously parliamentary in every respect to the direct popular election of the prime minster in 1996—presenting another intriguing puzzle of classification. The basic rules were that the prime minister was elected directly by the voters, that parliament was elected simultaneously, that parliament retained the right to dismiss the prime minister, that the prime minister also had the right to dissolve parliament, and that either action resulted in new elections of both prime minister and parliament (Hazan 1997). The Israelis

2. G. Bingham Powell (1982, 56) classified Finland as a parliamentary system even during the Kekkonen era.

entered uncharted territory with this innovation, but it resembles one of the solutions proposed by the Committee on the Constitutional System (1987, 16) for the problem of executive-legislative deadlock in the United States: "If it were possible for a President to call new elections, or for Congress to do so, we would have a mechanism for resolving deadlocks over fundamental policy issues." Such a mutual right to call new elections, both presidential and congressional, would be a change *in* rather than a change *of* the presidential system—that is, the United States would still be a presidential system according to all three basic criteria.

The Israeli system, which lasted until 2003, was very similar to this special form of presidentialism except that the president was called "prime minister." The prime minister was (1) popularly elected instead of being selected by parliament, (2) elected for a fixed period of four years, except if the special rule of mutual dismissal and new elections were to become operative, and (3) predominated over the cabinet by virtue of the democratic legitimacy conferred by popular elections. As far as the third point is concerned, the Israeli rule that the other members of the cabinet needed a parliamentary vote of investiture before taking office sounds like the retention of one aspect of the old parliamentarism, but remember that in the United States, too, the president can appoint the members of his or her cabinet only with the "advice and consent" of the Senate. The directly elected prime minister was therefore much more like a president in a presidential system than like a prime minister in a parliamentary system.[3]

3. According to Matthew Soberg Shugart and Scott Mainwaring (1997, 15), presidentialism can be defined in terms of two basic characteristics: "separate origin" (separate popular elections) and "separate survival" (fixed terms of office for both president and legislature). According to the second criterion, the proposal of the Committee on the Constitutional System and the 1996–2003 Israeli system would clearly not qualify as presidential, but neither would the French Fifth Republic because the National Assembly can be dissolved prematurely. Moreover, a fixed term of office for the legislature can also be a characteristic of parliamentary systems, as in the case of Norway.

Israel's experiment with the directly elected prime minister did not last long; pure parliamentarism was restored in 2003.

ADDITIONAL PARLIAMENTARY-PRESIDENTIAL CONTRASTS

A few eminent political scientists have argued that in addition to the three crucial differences between parliamentary and presidential systems discussed above, there are three other important differences (esp. Verney 1959, 17–56). On closer examination, these contrasts turn out to have serious empirical exceptions and not to be essential for the distinction between the two major forms of government.

First, separation of powers in presidential systems is usually taken to mean not only the mutual independence of the executive and legislative branches but also the rule that the same person cannot simultaneously serve in both. In contrast, the non-separation of powers in parliamentary systems means not only that the executive is dependent on the legislature's confidence but also that the same persons can be members of both parliament and the cabinet. With regard to the latter, however, there is a great deal of variation within the parliamentary type of government. On one end of the spectrum, many parliamentary systems—especially those in the United Kingdom and the former British colonies—make it an almost absolute requirement that cabinet members be members of the legislature, too. On the other end, there are three countries—the Netherlands, Norway, and Luxembourg—in which membership in the cabinet cannot be combined with membership in parliament; in all three, however, cabinet members can and do participate in parliamentary debates. Because the incompatibility rule emphasizes the separate status of the cabinet, it tends to strengthen the cabinet's authority vis-à-vis parliament, but it cannot be considered more than a minor variation within the parliamentary type. It would certainly be incorrect to argue that these three countries fit or even approximate the presidential form of government in this respect.

Second, it is often claimed that a key difference between presidential and parliamentarism is that presidents do not have the right to dissolve the legislature whereas prime ministers and their cabinets do have this right. One exception on the presidential side is that the French president does have the power to dissolve the National Assembly; another exception is the Israeli 1996–2003 example of mutual dismissal and new elections for both, discussed earlier. In parliamentary systems, there is again a wide range of variation. In the British and many British-inspired systems, the power to dissolve is virtually unlimited and it is a specifically prime ministerial prerogative. In Germany and several other countries, parliament can be dissolved only under special circumstances and not at the sole discretion of the executive. In Norway, parliament is elected for a four-year term and cannot be dissolved at all. Executive authority is obviously affected by whether the executive does or does not have such power over the legislature, but this factor cannot be considered an essential distinction between the parliamentary and presidential forms of government.

Third, parliamentary systems usually have dual executives: a symbolic and ceremonial head of state (a monarch or president) who has little power and a prime minister who is the head of the government and who, together with the cabinet, exercises most executive power. The normal rule in presidential systems is that the president is simultaneously the head of state and the head of the government. However, there are major exceptions on both sides. Botswana has a prime minister, elected by and subject to the confidence of the legislature, who is the head of the government but who also serves as head of state—and who therefore has the formal title of "president." Another example is democratic South Africa, whose first head of the government was President Nelson Mandela—not a president in a presidential system but a combined head of government and head of state in a parliamentary system.

If the directly elected Israeli prime minister in the period 1996–2003 can indeed be seen as a president in a presidential system, Israel provides an example of a presidential system with a dual instead of a single executive: in addition to the presidential prime minister, there was a president who was the head of state. Another example showing that a dual executive is, in principle, compatible with a presidential form of government is the proposal for a directly elected prime minister in the Netherlands (Andeweg 1997, 235). This plan, widely debated in the late 1960s and early 1970s, entailed the popular election of the prime minister for a fixed four-year term and not subject to parliamentary confidence—but not to change the monarchy. In effect, such a "prime minister" would be head of the government in a presidential system—but not the head of state, because the monarch would continue in that position. The prestige of being head of state obviously enhances the influence of most presidents and is an advantage that most prime ministers lack, but it is not an essential distinction between the two forms of government.

SEPARATION OF POWER AND BALANCE OF POWER

The distinction between parliamentary and presidential systems is of great importance in several respects. For instance, as discussed in the previous chapter, presidential cabinets are fundamentally different, and have to be classified differently, from cabinets in parliamentary systems; moreover, both later on in this chapter and in the next chapter, presidential systems are again treated differently from parliamentary systems in the measurement of key variables. However, the parliamentary-presidential distinction does not bear directly on the distribution of power in executive-legislative relationships. In parliamentary systems, one can find a rough balance of power between cabinet and parliament, as in Belgium, but one can also find clear executive dominance as in the United Kingdom, New Zealand, and Barbados (see Chapters 2 and 3). The same range of variation occurs in presidential systems. The United States and France are good examples at opposite ends of the scale. In the United States, separation of powers has usually also meant a rough balance of power between president and Congress. The same applies to Switzerland, the one separation-of-powers system that is not a presidential system. The French presidential system is at the opposite end; in Anthony King's (1976, 21) words, "the French legislature has . . . become even more subordinate to the executive than the British."

Presidential powers derive from three sources. One is the power of presidents defined in constitutions, consisting of "reactive powers," especially presidential veto power, and "pro-active powers," especially the ability to legislate by decree in certain areas (Shugart and Mainwaring 1997, 41). The second source of power is the strength and cohesion of presidents' parties in the legislature. Third, presidents derive considerable strength from their direct popular election and the fact that they can claim that they (and their vice presidents, if any) are the only public officials elected by the people as a whole.

The frequent dependence of presidents on their partisan powers means that the relative power of presidents and legislatures can and often does change abruptly and that it is generally less stable than in parliamentary systems. Substantial changes have occurred in the historical experience of the United States. Woodrow Wilson (1885) decried the predominance of Congress and stated that the American "presidential" system should more realistically be called, as the title of his famous book indicates, *Congressional Government.* More recent critics have charged that, especially under Presidents Lyndon B. Johnson, Richard M. Nixon, and George W. Bush, an "imperial presidency" tended to overshadow Congress. In the much shorter history of the French presidential system, John T. S. Keeler and Martin A. Schain (1997, 95–100) see four alternations between "hyperpresidential" and "tempered presidential" phases in the period from 1962 to 1993.

MEASURING DEGREES OF DOMINANCE
AND BALANCE OF POWER

How can the relative power of the executive and legislative branches of government be measured? For parliamentary systems, the best indicator is cabinet durability. A cabinet that stays in power for a long time is likely to be dominant vis-à-vis the legislature, and a short-lived cabinet is likely to be relatively weak.[4] Coalition theorists have paid great attention to the duration of cabinets, but they usually assume—either explicitly or, more often, implicitly—that cabinet durability is an indicator not just of the cabinet's strength compared with that of the legislature but also of regime stability. The argument is that short-lived cabinets do not have sufficient time to develop sound and coherent policies and that ineffective policy-making will endanger the viability of democracy: cabinet instability is assumed to lead to, and is therefore taken as an indicator of, regime instability. An explicit statement to this effect is Paul V. Warwick's (1994, 139): "A parliamentary system that does not produce durable government is unlikely to provide effective policy making, to attract widespread popular allegiance, or perhaps even to survive over the longer run."

This view is as wrong as it is prevalent. F en the proverbially short-lived cabinets of the Fourth French] ₃public were far from completely ineffective policy-makers. M   y members of each defunct cabinet served again in the new ɾ ɪe, and their average life as ministers was considerably longer than that of the cabinets as a whole. The contemporary French observer André Siegfried (1956, 399) explained this "paradox of stable policy with unstable cabinets" as follows: "Actually the disadvantages are not as serious as they appear. . . . When there is a cabinet crisis, certain ministers change or the same ministers are merely shifted around; but no civil servant is displaced, and the day-to-day administration continues without interruption. Furthermore, as the same

4. This interpretation is supported by the contrast between democracies in general and nondemocratic systems. In the latter we find the strongest executives and the most subservient legislatures or no legislatures at all—and we also find, "not surprisingly," as Henry Bienen and Nicolas van de Walle (1991, 103) state, the greatest incidence of "long-lasting leaders."

ministers hold over from one cabinet to another, they form as it were teams of government."[5] Mattei Dogan (1989) attacks the equation of cabinet stability with regime stability head-on and argues emphatically that cabinet stability is *not* a valid indicator of the health and viability of the democratic system; the major reason is that in most systems with seemingly unstable cabinets, there is a highly stable "core" of ministerial personnel—similar to the situation in the Fourth Republic described by Siegfried.

What should be added to Dogan's argument is that, in relatively short-lived cabinets, there tends to be continuity not only of personnel but also of participating parties. One-party cabinets tend to be more durable than coalition cabinets, but a change from a one-party cabinet to another is a wholesale partisan turnover, whereas a change from one coalition cabinet to another usually entails only a piecemeal change in the party composition of the cabinet. I return to the general issue of the effectiveness of policy-making in Chapter 15; there the question is whether majoritarian democracies with their typically more dominant and durable executives are better policy-makers than consensus democracies with their usually shorter-lived and less dominant executives—and the answer is that consensus democracies actually have a somewhat better record in this respect.

The next step—after having decided that cabinet duration can be used as an indicator of executive dominance—is to decide how to measure it. This question concerns the events that are con-

5. In their comparative nineteen-nation analysis of cabinet durability, Michael Taylor and Valentine M. Herman (1971, 29) state: "A considerable empirical study would be necessary before it could be said that [cabinet durability] was an indicator of *anything.*" They argue that their article does not make any assumption about the broader significance of cabinet durability, but they also state that their "results would be of greater interest if Siegfried's observation that the instability of the Fourth Republic made no difference to public policy-making were found to be untrue of instability generally." Their unspoken assumption, of course, is that the significance of studying cabinet durability has much to do with its putative link with regime viability.

sidered to end the life of one cabinet and to herald the beginning of a new one. There are two major alternatives. One is to focus exclusively on the partisan composition of cabinets and to count a cabinet as one cabinet if its party composition does not change; one pioneering study of cabinet duration took this approach (Dodd 1976). It is much more common, however, to regard two additional events as marking the end of one and the beginning of the next cabinet: a parliamentary election and a change in the prime ministership (Müller, Bergman, and Strøm 2008, 6; Damgaard 2008, 303). A big advantage of Dodd's broad definition is that it measures cabinet durations that can be interpreted very well as indicators of executive dominance. In particular, cabinets that win several successive elections—and which Dodd therefore counts as the same cabinet—are less and less likely to meet serious challenges from their parliaments.

Average cabinet life serves as the index of executive dominance for twenty-eight of the thirty-six democracies in Table 7.1, but adjustments are needed for Switzerland, Botswana, and the six presidential systems. Switzerland and Botswana present no major challenges. Botswana has had only one cabinet since independence in 1965 and hence the very long "average" cabinet life of more than forty-five years, but its executive dominance must be judged to be only slightly greater than that of other former British colonies like the Bahamas and Jamaica. The Swiss average of 12.51 years—based on only five different party compositions from 1947 to 2010—is obviously completely wrong as a measure of executive dominance because Switzerland is a prime example of executive-legislative balance. Hence we can give these two countries values at the top and bottom of Table 7.1.

Finding the proper values for the presidential democracies is considerably more difficult. For one thing, experts on presidential government tend to disagree on the relative powers of presidents in different countries. For instance, should the Argentine or Uruguayan president be regarded as the more powerful (García Montero 2009, 102–3; Shugart and Haggard 2001, 80)? And is

TABLE 7.1

Index of executive dominance and average cabinet duration (in years) in thirty-six democracies, 1945–2010

	Index of executive dominance	Average cabinet duration
Switzerland	1.00	12.51
Israel	1.46	1.46
Italy	1.49	1.49
Finland	1.55	1.55
Mauritius	2.39	2.39
Belgium	2.57	2.57
Netherlands	2.91	2.91
Costa Rica	3.00	5.15
Iceland	3.20	3.20
Denmark	3.23	3.23
Portugal	3.26	3.26
India	3.33	3.33
Japan	3.37	3.37
Germany	3.80	3.80
United States	4.00	7.05
Uruguay	4.00	4.22
Norway	4.04	4.04
Ireland	4.16	4.16
Greece	4.45	4.45
New Zealand	4.54	4.54
Sweden	5.61	5.61
Luxembourg	5.87	5.87
Trinidad	6.95	6.95
Argentina	8.00	5.30
France	8.00	3.22
Korea	8.00	2.77
Austria	8.07	8.07

TABLE 7.1 *continued*

	Index of executive dominance	Average cabinet duration
Canada	8.10	8.10
United Kingdom	8.12	8.12
Spain	8.26	8.26
Malta	8.85	8.85
Barbados	8.87	8.87
Australia	9.10	9.10
Bahamas	9.44	9.44
Jamaica	9.64	9.64
Botswana	9.90	45.33

Source: Based on data in Woldendorp, Keman, and Budge 2010; Bale and Caramani 2010 and earlier volumes of the "Political Data Yearbook"; Muller, Overstreet, Isacoff, and Lansford 2011 and earlier volumes of the *Political Handbook of the World;* and data provided by Octavio Amorim Neto, Marcelo Camerlo, Krista Hoekstra, Jelle Koedam, Jorge Lanzaro, Andrés Malamud, and Linganaden Murday

the American or the Korean president the stronger chief executive (Shugart and Haggard 2001, 80; Siaroff 2003b, 297)? For another, experts also differ profoundly on the relative powers of the chief executives in presidential and parliamentary systems. Sebastián M. Saiegh (2011, 84–89) finds prime ministers to be generally more powerful than presidents, but Torsten Persson and Guido Tabellini (2003, 275) argue that "presidential states typically have stronger executives than parliamentary states." On the first issue, I follow the lead of Matthew S. Shugart and Stephan Haggard (2001) and assign the United States, Costa Rica, and Uruguay a considerably lower position on the scale of executive dominance than the other three countries. Within the first group of three countries, the United States and Uruguay should be slightly higher than Costa Rica. An important consideration in the American case is the president's preeminent power over foreign policy and the fact that the superpower status of the United States means that many crucial decisions in this area have to be made. Korea has been called a "prime example of majoritarian presidentialism" (Croissant and Schächter 2010, 191), and this label fits Argentine and French presidentialism, too. On the second issue, I see no valid reason to regard the average president as either much more or much less powerful than the average executive in parliamentary systems. In Table 7.1, the average values for the six presidential and twenty-nine parliamentary systems are very close to each other: 5.83 and 5.40, respectively.[6]

Table 7.1 lists the thirty-six democracies in ascending order of executive dominance. The index ranges from 1.00 to 9.90, the values assigned to Switzerland and Botswana, as explained above. The mean value is 5.35, roughly in the middle of the range, and the median is a lower 4.30. The six countries at the majoritarian end include Barbados, and they are all former British colonies. The United Kingdom itself is in a slightly higher position and is preceded by Canada, another former British colony. New Zealand is near the middle of the table, partly due to its short three-

6. There are two partly comparable measures of executive-legislative relationships. The Woldendorp-Keman-Budge (2000, 56–57) index of executive-legislative balance, available for twenty-six of our democracies, measures such variables as whether a formal vote of investiture is required, whether the cabinet can ignore a vote of no confidence, and whether the cabinet or prime minister can dissolve parliament. M. Steven Fish and Matthew Kroenig (2009, 756–57) construct a "parliamentary powers index," based on thirty-two formal powers that legislatures may or may not possess, for most of the countries in the world, including thirty-one of our democracies. Because both of these indexes are based entirely on formal rules, we cannot expect them to correlate strongly with our index of executive dominance. However, confidence in our index would be increased if there were a substantial degree of correspondence with these formal indexes. The correlation coefficients show that this is indeed the case: –0.43 (statistically significant at the 5 percent level) and –0.45 (significant at the 1 percent level), respectively.

year parliamentary terms, which increase the likelihood of government turnovers, but, more important, reflecting the impact of the shift to PR elections from 1996 on: cabinets lasted an average of 6.15 years until early 1996 but only 2.39 years thereafter. Several British-heritage countries are on the left, more consensual, side of the table, especially Mauritius and, although less strikingly, India. Of the two prototypes of consensus democracy, Switzerland and Belgium, Switzerland was assigned to the top of the table. Belgium is farther down but still in sixth place, just behind Mauritius.

CABINET TYPES AND CABINET DURABILITY

How are the different cabinet types, analyzed in the previous chapter, related to the degree of executive dominance? There are three reasons to expect a positive relationship between minimal winning and one-party cabinets on one hand and executive dominance on the other. First, as discussed in Chapter 1, both variables belong to the same cluster of variables that make up the executives-parties dimension of the majoritarian-consensus contrast. Second, minority cabinets are by their nature at the mercy of the legislature in parliamentary systems and can therefore not be expected to dominate their legislatures. Third, studies of the independence shown by individual legislators in voting against their own cabinet in Britain have found that this kind of independent parliamentary behavior has tended to vary directly with the size of the cabinet's majority in the House of Commons: bare-majority cabinets have generally received solid support from their partisans in parliament, whereas cabinets with ample majorities have frequently found their parliamentary party to be more rebellious (Crowe 1980). Analogizing from this tendency in the British House of Commons to the other parliamentary systems, we can expect greater legislative independence when cabinets are oversized rather than minimal winning.

Table 7.2 and Figure 7.2 show the strength of these relationships. Table 7.2 classifies the cabinets that have been in power in thirty parliamentary systems—including the three parliamentary phases in France but excluding the other presidential democracies and Switzerland—according to the five basic types of cabinet, and it presents the average duration of these cabinets.[7] Minimal winning one-party cabinets have the longest average life span. And both types of minimal winning cabinets last longer than minority and oversized cabinets. Oversized coalitions and one-party minority cabinets—which in terms of their parliamentary support appear to be at a maximum distance from each other—actually have very similar durations; the oversized cabinets last only slightly less long. Minority coalitions have the shortest life. An important explanation is that in multiparty systems such coalitions are often temporary caretakers after a cabinet has fallen and while awaiting a new election. In countries where they are more like regular cabinets, as in the Scandinavian countries, minority coalition cabinets last longer. For instance, Denmark had nine minority coalition cabinets that lasted an average of 3.79 years.

Figure 7.2 shows the relationship between types of cabinet and executive dominance in terms of the combination of the two characteristics in each of our thirty-six democracies (based on the data in the third column of Table 6.3 and the first column of Table 7.1). The pattern is clear: the countries with more minimal winning single-party cabinets also tend to be the countries with greater executive dominance. The correlation coefficient is 0.78 (statistically significant at the 1 percent level).

Most of the countries are near the regression line. The main outliers are four of the presidential systems. The United States, Costa

7. Table 7.2 includes all cabinets that fall clearly into one of the five categories—which means that cabinets that have to be counted as, for instance, halfway between minimal winning and oversized or halfway between one-party and coalition cabinets had to be disregarded; moreover, cabinets that changed their coalitional status during the life of the cabinet also had to be put aside.

TABLE 7.2

Frequency and average cabinet duration (in years) of five types of cabinets in thirty parliamentary democracies, 1945–2010

Type of cabinet	Number of cabinets	Average cabinet duration (years)
Minimal winning, one-party	56	8.20
Minimal winning coalition	85	3.64
Minority, one-party	42	2.57
Minority coalition	62	1.52
Oversized coalition	106	2.27
All cabinets	351	3.45

Source: Based on data in Woldendorp, Keman, and Budge 2010; Bale and Caramani 2010 and earlier volumes of the "Political Data Yearbook"; Muller, Overstreet, Isacoff, and Lansford 2011 and earlier volumes of the *Political Handbook of the World;* and data provided by Krista Hoekstra, Jelle Koedam, and Linganaden Murday

Rica, and Uruguay have a much lower level of executive dominance than expected on the basis of their frequent majoritarian-type cabinets. Semipresidential France exhibits the opposite combination of characteristics. The explanation of the first three appears to be a feature of presidentialism: their cabinets are partly majoritarian—minimal winning and one-party—by definition, as argued in the previous chapter, but their separation of powers contributes to a modicum of executive-legislative balance. Before accepting this as a general explanation, however, we should note that it does not apply to the Argentine and Korean cases.

Of the parliamentary democracies, only five are in clearly deviant positions: Australia, Austria, Greece, New Zealand, and Spain. The reasons for the unexpectedly low figure for executive dominance in New Zealand were discussed above. In Greece, the

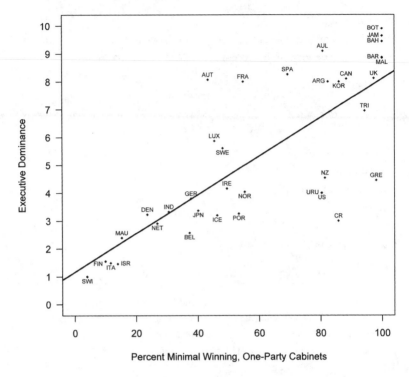

FIG. 7.2 The relationship between type of cabinet and executive dominance in thirty-six democracies, 1945–2010

turmoil caused by two indecisive parliamentary elections and three elections in less than ten months in 1990–91 is especially responsible for shortening the average cabinet duration. On the other side of the regression line, Austria has had many oversized coalitions that were unusually long-lived: one stretch of these lasted from 1947 to 1966. Spain has only had one-party cabinets, which have proved quite durable in spite of their frequent minority status. Australia has a high degree of executive dominance similar to that of most other former British dependencies but fewer one-party cabinets; the main reason is that the frequent Liberal-National cabinets have to be counted as half one-party and half coalition cabinets because of the "one-and-a-half parties" nature of Liberals and Nationals (see Chapter 5).

ADDENDUM: MONARCHS AND PRESIDENTS

The position of head of state has been mentioned repeatedly in this chapter, but the different kinds of heads of state and their relative powers have not been treated systematically. The most striking difference in this respect in our set of thirty-six democracies is that almost half are monarchies: Australia, the Bahamas, Barbados, Belgium, Canada, Denmark, Jamaica, Japan, Luxembourg, the Netherlands, New Zealand, Norway, Spain, Sweden, and the United Kingdom. The monarchs are mainly kings or queens—represented by a governor-general in Australia, the Bahamas, Barbados, Canada, Jamaica, and New Zealand—but Japan has an emperor and Luxembourg a grand duke as head of state. The exact number of monarchies as of the middle of 2010 was fifteen; in the early 1970s, exactly half were monarchies, but three Commonwealth countries later became republics: Malta in 1974, Trinidad in 1976, and Mauritius in 1992. It is rather surprising that so many of our democracies are or were monarchies, a constitutional form that appears to be less democratic than republican government. The explanation is that they are constitutional monarchies in which the monarch's power is severely limited. As Richard Rose and Dennis Kavanagh (1976, 568) write, "Monarchs have remained in power where the reigning family has been willing to withdraw from a politically active rule. Reciprocally, monarchies have fallen when the monarch has sought to continue to assert political power."

The advantage that the monarchy is frequently claimed to have for a democratic regime is that it provides a head of state who is an apolitical and impartial symbol of unity. This is generally true, although it is also possible for monarchs to become a divisive force. For instance, the behavior of King Leopold III during the Second World War became a major political issue in postwar Belgium. In the 1950 referendum on whether the king should be retained, a majority of Flemings and Catholics supported the king, and most Walloons, Socialists, and Liberals wanted him removed. Leopold III won the referendum with an overall majority of 58 percent—

not a landslide victory for a king!—but he soon abdicated in favor of his son Baudouin.

In terms of basic democratic principles, a disadvantage is that monarchs are not entirely powerless. In parliamentary systems, they generally retain the right to appoint the prime minister. This is not a significant function when there is a unanimous preference for a prime ministerial candidate, but when there is a sudden death or resignation, or when the parties in a multiparty parliament are unable to reach an agreement, the monarch's influence on the eventual choice of a prime minister may be far from negligible. In order to reduce the monarch's rule to a purely ceremonial one, Sweden's 1974 constitution transferred the function of appointing a prime minister from the monarch to the speaker of parliament.

Even though monarchs may have residual powers, the general assumption, accepted by the monarch himself or herself, is that the monarch is purely a head of state and not a head of government. The temptation to intrude on the powers of the head of government and of the cabinet is greater when parliamentary democracies have a president as head of state—generally someone who has had a former political career. One method that parliamentary systems use to minimize this risk is to not allow the president the democratic prestige and implicit power of being popularly elected. Instead, the usual procedure is to have parliament (or a special electoral college of members of national and state parliaments, as in Germany and India) elect the president. Another solution is not to have a separate president at all but to give the title and function of the president to the prime minister, as in Botswana. Switzerland uses a similar method by having the head of government—the rotating chair of the Federal Council—serve simultaneously as president. However, the special characteristic of semipresidential democracies that function mainly as parliamentary systems—Austria, Finland, Iceland, Ireland, and Portugal—is that they do have a popularly elected president. The danger here is that popular election may provide the head of state with a democratically legitimate justification to encroach upon or take over leadership of the government, thereby changing the nature of the parliamentary system.

Finally, for those who consider parliamentary systems to be preferable to presidential systems, an important advantage of a constitutional monarchy is that it is generally regarded as incompatible with presidentialism. As I argued earlier in this chapter, this view is not correct: in theory, it is quite possible to institute a presidential system with a president who serves as head of government and a monarch who is head of state. But there are no empirical examples of such a system, and the view that presidentialism and monarchy cannot be combined, however mistaken, may save democratizing countries with a monarch as head of state, like Spain in the late 1970s, from seriously considering the adoption of a presidential form of government.

CHAPTER 8

ELECTORAL SYSTEMS: MAJORITY AND PLURALITY METHODS VERSUS PROPORTIONAL REPRESENTATION

T he fourth difference between the majoritarian and consensus models of democracy is clear-cut. The typical electoral system of majoritarian democracy is the single-member district plurality or majority system; consensus democracy typically uses proportional representation (PR). The plurality and majority single-member district methods are winner-take-all methods—the candidate supported by the largest number of voters wins, and all other voters remain unrepresented—and hence a perfect reflection of majoritarian philosophy. Moreover, the party gaining a nationwide majority or plurality of the votes will tend to be overrepresented in terms of parliamentary seats. In sharp contrast, the basic aim of proportional representation is to represent both majorities and minorities and, instead of overrepresenting or underrepresenting any parties, to translate votes into seats proportionally.

The gap between the two types of electoral systems is also wide in the sense that changes within each type are common but that very few democracies change from PR to plurality or majority methods or vice versa (Nohlen 1984). Each group of countries appears to be strongly attached to its own electoral system. In a comment on his withdrawal of the nomination of Lani Guinier to the position of assistant attorney general for civil rights in 1993, President Bill Clinton—the head of a country that uses mainly plurality elections—stated that he objected to her advocacy of PR, which he called "very difficult to defend" and even "anti-democratic" (*New York Times,* June 4, 1993, A18).

In this chapter I present a more detailed classification of the electoral systems used in our thirty-six democracies in terms of seven basic aspects of these systems, emphasizing the electoral formula, district magnitude, and electoral thresholds. The scholarly literature on electoral systems focuses on the degree of proportionality or disproportionality in their translation of votes into seats and on their effects on the numbers of parties in party systems. This is also the focus of the remainder of this chapter. After discussing the question of how degrees of disproportionality can be measured most accurately, I show that, although there is a great deal of variation within the PR family and although no PR system is perfectly proportional, PR systems do tend to be considerably less disproportional than plurality and majority systems, except in presidential democracies. Electoral systems are also a crucial determinant, though by no means the sole determinant, of party systems. Last, I explore the relationship between electoral disproportionality and the effective number of parliamentary parties in the thirty-six democracies.

ELECTORAL FORMULAS

Although the dichotomy of PR versus single-member district plurality and majority systems is the most fundamental dividing line in the classification of electoral systems, it is necessary to make some additional important distinctions and to develop a more refined typology.[1] Electoral systems may be described in terms of

1. For thorough treatments of the various aspects of electoral systems, see Colomer (2004), Diamond and Plattner (2006), Farrell (2011), Gallagher and Mitchell (2005), Klingemann (2009), Lundell (2010), Norris (2004), and Reynolds, Reilly, and Ellis (2005).

seven attributes: electoral formula, district magnitude, electoral threshold, the total membership of the body to be elected, the influence of presidential elections on legislative elections, malapportionment, and interparty links.

Figure 8.1 presents a classification according to the first of these dimensions, the electoral formula, and it shows to which categories the thirty-six democracies or, in a few cases, particular periods in these countries belong. The first category of plurality and majority formulas can be subdivided into three more specific classes. The plurality rule—usually termed "first past the post" in Britain—is by far the simplest one: the candidate who receives the most votes, whether a majority or a plurality, is elected. It is obviously a popular formula: eleven of the thirty-six democracies used it in the period 1945–2010. It is also used for presidential elections in Korea and Iceland, and it was used in Uruguay in its three presidential elections between 1984 and 1994.[2]

Majority formulas require an absolute majority for election. One way to fulfill this requirement is to conduct a runoff second ballot between the top two candidates if none of the candidates in the first round of voting has received a majority of the votes. This method is frequently used for presidential elections—in France, Austria, Portugal, Finland (since 1994), and Uruguay (since 1999), as well as in the direct election of the Israeli prime minister (1996–2003). Argentina (since 1995) and Costa Rica use a combination of plurality and majority runoff: a plurality is sufficient if it is above, respectively, 45 and 40 percent; if this minimum is not reached, a majority runoff is necessary.[3] The majority-runoff

2. Uruguay used the plurality rule together with the "double simultaneous vote," which was a unique system of combining intraparty primaries and the interparty contest in one election. The double simultaneous vote continues to be used in conjunction with PR for lower-house elections.

3. An additional rule in Argentina is that the minimum of 45 percent can be lowered to 40 percent if there is at least a 10 percent difference between the plurality winner and the runner-up. This system was first used in 1995; until then, a presidential electoral college was used. Before its

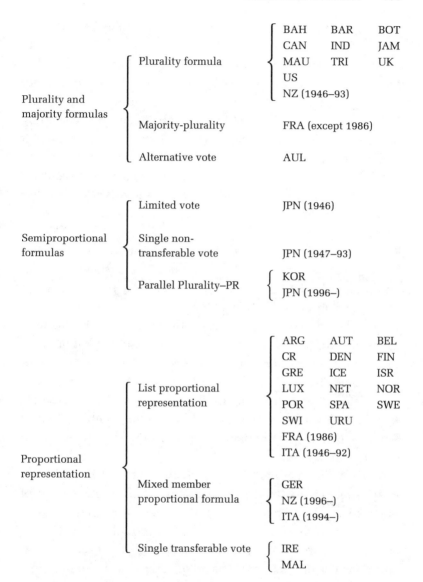

FIG. 8.1 A classification of the electoral formulas for the election of the first or only chambers of legislatures in thirty-six democracies, 1945–2010

method is not used for legislative elections in any of our countries, but a closely related method is used in France for elections to the National Assembly. It is elected by a mixed majority-plurality formula in single-member districts: on the first ballot an absolute majority is required for elections, but if no candidate wins a majority, a plurality suffices on the second ballot; candidates failing to win a minimum percentage of the vote on the first ballot—12.5 percent of the registered voters since 1976—are barred from the second ballot. The second-ballot contest is usually between two principal candidates so that, in practice, there is no big difference between the majority-plurality formula and the majority runoff.

The alternative vote, used in Australia, is a true majority formula. The voters are asked to indicate their first preference, second preference, and so on among the candidates. If a candidate receives an absolute majority of the first preferences, he or she is elected. If there is no such majority, the candidate with the lowest number of first preferences is dropped, and the ballots with this candidate as the first preference are transferred to the second preferences. This procedure is repeated by excluding the weakest candidate and redistributing the ballots in question to the next highest preferences in each stage of the counting, until a majority winner emerges. The alternative vote is also used for presidential elections in Ireland.

Three main types of PR must be distinguished. The most common form is the list PR system, used in half—eighteen out of thirty-six—of our democracies during most of the period 1945–2010. There are minor variations in list formulas, but they all basically entail that the parties nominate lists of candidates in multimember districts, that the voters cast their ballots for one

---

first majority-runoff election in 1994, Finland also used a presidential electoral college. Both countries abolished their electoral colleges in the 1990s, and the United States is now the only country still using an electoral college for electing its presidents.

party or another (although they are sometimes allowed to split their votes among several lists), and that the seats are allocated to the party lists in proportion to the number of votes they have collected. List PR systems may be subdivided further according to the mathematical formula used to translate votes into seats. The most frequently applied method is the d'Hondt formula, which has a slight bias in favor of large parties and against small parties compared with several other methods.[4]

The second form of PR is the "mixed member proportional" (MMP) formula—a term coined in New Zealand for its version of the system but now generally applied to the entire category. About half of the legislators in Germany and New Zealand are elected by plurality in single-member districts and the others are elected by list PR. Each voter has two votes, one for a district candidate and one for a party list. The reason why this combination of methods qualifies as a PR system is that the list PR seats compensate for any disproportionality produced by the district seat results. The exact degree of the overall results depends on how many list PR seats are available for the purpose of compensation; the Italian results have been considerably less proportional than those in the other two countries. Alan Siaroff (2009, 180) rightly calls the German and New Zealand MMP systems "fully compensatory" but Italian MMP only "semi-compensatory."

4. For a more detailed description, see Lijphart 1994, 153–59. Another difference among list PR formulas is whether their lists are open, partly open, or closed. In closed-list systems, voters can vote only for the list as a whole and cannot express a preference for any specific candidates on the list; candidates are elected strictly according to the order in which the party has nominated them. Examples are Argentina, Costa, Rica, Israel, Spain, and Uruguay. In a completely open-list system, of which Finland is the best example, the voters vote for individual candidates on the list, and the order in which the candidates are elected is determined by the votes they individually receive. In Belgium, the Netherlands, and several other countries, the lists are partly open: although voters can express preferences for individual candidates, the list order as presented by the parties tends to prevail.

The third main type of PR is the single transferable vote (STV). It differs from list PR in that the voters vote for individual candidates instead of for party lists. The ballot is similar to that of the alternative vote system: it contains the names of the candidates, and the voters are asked to rank-order these. The procedure for determining the winning candidates is slightly more complicated than with the alternative vote. Two kinds of transfers take place: first, any surplus votes not needed by candidates who already have the minimum quota of votes required for election are transferred to the next most preferred candidates on the ballots in question; second, the weakest candidate is eliminated and his or her ballots are transferred in the same way. If necessary, these steps are repeated until all of the available seats are filled. STV is often praised because it combines the advantages of permitting votes for individual candidates and of yielding proportional results, but it is not used very frequently. The only instances in Figure 8.1 are Ireland and Malta. The other major example of its use is for Senate elections in Australia.

Most electoral formulas fit the two large categories of PR and plurality-majority, but a few fall in between. These semiproportional formulas are rarely used, and the only examples in our set of countries are Korea and the three systems that have been used in Japan. The limited vote, used in Japan's 1946 election, and the single nontransferable vote (SNTV), used in all subsequent elections through 1993, are closely related. Voters cast their votes for individual candidates, and as in plurality systems, the candidates with the most votes win. However, unlike in plurality systems, the voters do not have as many votes as there are seats in the district, and districts have to have at least two seats. The more limited the number of votes each voter has, and the larger the number of seats at stake, the more the limited vote tends to deviate from plurality and the more it resembles PR. In the 1946 election, each voter had two or three votes in districts ranging from four to fourteen seats. SNTV is the special case of the limited vote where the number of votes cast by each voter is reduced to one. In the Japanese version of it, it was applied in districts with an average of about four seats.

In the parallel plurality-PR systems, introduced by the Japanese in 1996, 300 legislators were elected by plurality in single-member districts and 200 (reduced to 180 in 2000) by list PR; each voter has both a district vote and a PR vote. These features make it resemble MMP, but the crucial difference is that the PR seats are not compensatory. The plurality and PR components are "parallel" to each other—that is, they are kept entirely separate. Hence, unlike MMP, this system is only partly proportional instead of a form of PR. Korea has also used this parallel system for all of its six legislative elections since 1988, but with a much smaller PR component.

Most countries did not change their electoral formulas during the period 1945–2010. The one-time use of the limited vote in Japan in 1946 and of list PR in France in 1986 are minor exceptions. The more important changes that did occur all took place in the 1990s—in New Zealand, Italy, and Japan—and two of these countries switched to MMP.

DISTRICT MAGNITUDE

The magnitude of an electoral district denotes the number of candidates to be elected in the district. It should not be confused with the geographical size of the district or with the number of voters in it. Plurality and majority formulas may be applied in both single-member and multimember districts. PR and SNTV require multimember districts, ranging from two-member districts to a single nationwide district from which all members of parliament are elected. That district magnitude has a strong effect on the degree of disproportionality and on the number of parties has long been known. George Horwill (1925, 53) already called it "the all-important factor," and in Rein Taagepera and Matthew S. Shugart's (1989, 112) analysis, it was again found to be "the decisive factor."

District magnitude is of great importance in two respects. First, it has a strong influence in both plurality-majority systems and PR (and SNTV) systems, but in opposite directions: increasing the district magnitude in plurality and majority systems entails greater disproportionality and greater advantages for large parties, whereas under PR it results in greater proportionality and more favorable conditions for small parties. With regard to plurality, assume, for instance, that the election contest is between parties A and B and that party A is slightly stronger in a particular area. If this area is a three-member district, party A is likely to win all three seats; however, if the area is divided into three single-member districts, party B may well be able to win in one of the districts and hence one of the three seats. When the district magnitude is increased further, disproportionality also increases; in the hypothetical case of a nationwide plurality district, and assuming that all voters cast strictly partisan votes, the party winning a nationwide plurality of the votes would win all of the seats.

In the Australian alternative vote system and in the French majority-plurality system, only single-member districts have been used. In plurality systems, there are quite a few instances of the use of two-member and even larger districts, but larger than single-member districts are increasingly rare. The United Kingdom used several two-member districts in 1945, and both the United States and Canada had a few in the period 1945–68. In the 1952 and 1957 Indian elections, about a third of the legislators were elected from two-member districts, and Barbados elected its entire legislature from two-member districts in 1966. By 1970, however, all these two-member districts had been abolished.

The only plurality country in which larger than single-member districts survive is Mauritius, where sixty-two legislators are elected from twenty three-member districts and one two-member district.[5] An important reason why multimember districts have be-

5. Large multimember districts also survive in the American system for electing the presidential electoral college in which the fifty states and the District of Columbia serve as the election districts: the average magnitude is 10.5 seats per district.

come rare is that, as explained above, they lead to even greater disproportionality than the already high disproportional single-member districts. In the case of Mauritius, it should be noted, however, that the three-member districts have facilitated a different kind of proportionality: they encourage the parties and party alliances to nominate ethnically and religiously balanced slates, which has resulted in better ethnic and religious minority representation than would have been achieved through single-member district elections. Moreover, in addition to the sixty-two elected legislators, eight seats are allocated to the so-called best losers to further ensure fair minority representation (Mathur 1991, 54–71; 1997). Three other plurality countries have made special provisions for ethnic and communal minority representation by earmarking specific districts for this purpose: the Maori districts in New Zealand, discussed in Chapter 2; about a fifth of the districts in India that are set aside for the "scheduled castes" (untouchables) and "scheduled tribes"; and "affirmatively" gerrymandered districts in the United States.

The second reason why district magnitude is so important is that—unlike in plurality and majority systems—it varies greatly in PR systems and, hence, that it has a strong impact on the degree of proportionality that the different PR systems attain. For instance, a party representing a 10 percent minority is unlikely to win a seat in a five-member district but will be successful in a ten-member district. Two-member districts can therefore hardly be regarded as compatible with the principle of proportionality; conversely, a nationwide district is, all other factors being equal, optimal for a proportional translation of votes into seats. Israel and the Netherlands are examples of PR systems with such nationwide districts.

Many list PR countries use two levels of districts in order to combine the advantage of closer voter-representative contact in small districts and the higher proportionality of large, especially nationwide districts. As in MMP systems, the larger district compensates for any disproportionalities in the smaller districts, although these are likely to be much less pronounced in the small multimember list PR districts than in the MMP single-member districts. Examples of two-tiered list PR systems with a nation-wide district at the higher level are Denmark, Sweden since 1970, and Norway since 1989.

ELECTORAL THRESHOLDS

High-magnitude PR districts tend to maximize proportionality and to facilitate the representation of even very small parties. This is especially true for the Dutch and Israeli nationwide districts as well as for all systems that use upper-level nationwide districts. In order not to make it too easy for small parties to win election, all countries that use large or nationwide districts have instituted minimum thresholds for representation, defined in terms of a minimum number of seats won in the lower-tier districts and/or a minimum percentage of the total national vote. These percentages may be relatively low and hence innocuous, as the 0.67 percent threshold in the Netherlands since 1956 and the 1 percent threshold in Israel (increased to 1.5 percent for the 1992 and 2 percent for the 2006 election). But when they reach 4 percent, as in Sweden and Norway, or 5 percent, as in the German and post-1996 New Zealand MMP systems, they constitute significant barriers to small parties.

District magnitudes and electoral thresholds can be seen as two sides of the same coin: the *explicit* barrier against small parties imposed by a threshold has essentially the same function as the barrier *implied* by district magnitude. A reasonable approximation of their relationship is

$$T = \frac{75\%}{M + 1}$$

in which T is the threshold and M the average district magnitude (Taagepera 2007, 246–47). According to this equation, the median four-member district in Ireland (which uses districts with three, four, and five seats) has an implied threshold of 15 percent.

And the average district with a magnitude of 6.7 seats in the Spanish single-tier list PR system has an implied threshold of 9.7 percent. Conversely, the German 5 percent and Swedish 4 percent thresholds have roughly the same effect as district magnitudes of 14.0 and 17.8 seats.

OTHER ELECTORAL SYSTEM ATTRIBUTES

Another factor that can affect the proportionality of election outcomes and the number of parties is the size of the body to be elected. At first glance, this may appear to be a property that is not really part of the electoral system; however, because electoral systems are methods for translating votes into seats, the number of seats available for this translation is clearly an integral part of the system of translation. This number is important for two reasons. First, assume that three parties win 43, 31, and 26 percent of the national vote in a PR election. If the election is to a mini-legislature with only five seats, there is obviously no way in which the allocation of seats can be handled with a high degree of proportionality; the chances of a proportional allocation improve considerably for a ten-member legislature; and perfect proportionality could be achieved, at least in principle, for a hundred-member legislative body. For legislatures with a hundred or more members, size becomes relatively unimportant, but it is far from negligible for the lower or only legislative chambers of Mauritius (normally 70 members, although only 69 after the 2010 election because one "best loser" seat was not allocated), Malta (69), Iceland (63), Jamaica and Luxembourg (60 each), Botswana and Costa Rica (57 each), the Bahamas and Trinidad (41 each), and Barbados (30).

Second, the general pattern is that populous countries have large legislatures, that countries with small populations have smaller legislatures, and that the size of the legislature tends to be roughly the cube root of the population. Plurality elections always tend to be disproportional, but this tendency is reinforced when the membership of the legislature is significantly below the cube root of the population (Taagepera and Shugart 1989, 156–67).[6] Barbados is a case in point: on the basis of its population of 256,000 (see Table 4.3), its House of Assembly "should" have 63 instead of 30 members. Similarly, Trinidad should have a lower house with 110 instead of 41 members, and the Bahamas, Botswana, Jamaica, and Mauritius are also well below the number predicted by the cube root law—and can therefore be expected, all other factors being equal, to have abnormally high disproportionality in their election results. Small legislative size is not a characteristic of all plurality systems: for instance, the British House of Commons is quite a bit larger than predicted by the cube root law.

Presidential systems can have an indirect but strong effect on the effective number of parliamentary parties. Because the presidency is the biggest political prize to be won and because only the largest parties have a chance to win it, these large parties have a considerable advantage over smaller parties that tends to carry over into legislative elections, even when these are PR elections, as in Costa Rica, Uruguay, and Argentina. This tendency is especially strong when the presidential election is decided by plurality instead of majority runoff (where small parties may want to try their luck in the first round) and when the legislative elections are held at the same time or shortly after the presidential elections (Shugart and Carey 1992, 206–58; Jones 1995, 88–118). Even in France, where presidential and legislative elections have usually not coincided and where presidential elections are by majority runoff, presidentialism has reduced multipartism.

---

6. The cube law holds that if, in two-party systems and plurality single-member district elections, the votes received by the two parties are divided in a ratio of a:b, the seats that they win will be in the ratio of a^3:b^3. However, the exponent of 3 applies only when the size of the legislative body is in accordance with the cube root law, and the exponent goes up—and hence disproportionality also increases—as the size of the legislature decreases and/or the population increases (Taagepera and Shugart 1989, 158–67).

Maurice Duverger (1986, 81–82) compares the presidential Fifth Republic with the parliamentary Third Republic, both of which used the two-ballot system for legislative elections, and asks "why the same electoral system coincided with a dozen parties in the Third Republic but ended up with only four [parties in a two-bloc format] in the Fifth Republic." His main explanation is "the direct popular election of the president, which has transformed the political regime."

Malapportionment may also contribute to electoral disproportionality. In single-member districts, malapportionment means that the districts have substantially unequal voting populations; malapportioned multimember districts have magnitudes that are not commensurate with their voting populations. It is especially hard to avoid in plurality and majority systems with single-member districts, because equal apportionment requires that relatively many small districts be drawn with exactly equal electorates or populations. It is much less of a problem in PR systems that use relatively large districts of varying magnitudes, because seats can be proportionally allocated to preexisting geographical units like provinces or cantons. And malapportionment is entirely eliminated as a problem when elections are conducted in one large nationwide district as in Israel and the Netherlands or with a nationwide upper tier as in Germany and Sweden.

The main cases of malapportionment have had to do with rural overrepresentation: for instance, the United States (until the reapportionment revolution of the 1960s), Australia and France (until about 1980), Japan under the SNTV system, Norway until 1985, Iceland from 1946 to 1959, and Spain. However, malapportionment in favor of rural areas leads to increased disproportionality in partisan representation only if the larger parties benefit from it; this has clearly been the case for the Liberal Democrats in Japan, the Progressive party in Iceland, and the National party (formerly the Country party) in Australia to the extent that this relatively small party can be treated as part of the larger party formation with the Liberals.

Finally, some list PR systems allow parties to have separate lists on the ballot but to formally "link" these lists, which means that their combined vote total will be used in the initial allocation of seats; because PR systems are never perfectly proportional, the combined total may well be good for an extra seat compared with the sum of the seats that the parties would win separately. The next step is the proportional distribution of seats won by the linked parties to each of the parties. A set of such interparty connected lists is usually referred to by the French term *apparentement*. Examples of list PR systems with this special feature are Switzerland, Israel, and, since 1977, the Netherlands. Because apparentement is of some help to the smaller parties, which tend to be underrepresented, it tends to reduce disproportionality and to increase somewhat the effective number of parties. Moreover, the formation of mutually beneficial interparty electoral links is allowed not only by apparentement in some list PR systems but also as a logical consequence of three other electoral systems. Both the alternative vote and STV permit parties to link up for maximum electoral gain by simply agreeing to ask their respective voters to cast first preferences for their own candidates but the next preferences for the candidates of the linked party—an advantage of which Australian and Irish parties, but not the Maltese, often avail themselves. Similarly, the French two-ballot system implies the possibility for parties to link for the purpose of reciprocal withdrawal from the second ballot in different districts; both the parties of the left and those of the right regularly use this opportunity.

DEGREES OF DISPROPORTIONALITY

As we have seen, many attributes of electoral systems influence the degree of disproportionality and indirectly the number of parties in the party system. How can the overall disproportionality of elections be measured? It is easy to determine the disproportionality for each party in a particular election: this is simply the difference between its vote share and its seat share. The more

difficult question is how to aggregate the vote-seat share deviations of all of the parties. Summing the (absolute) differences is
not satisfactory because it does not distinguish between a few
large and serious deviations and a lot of small and relatively insignificant deviations.[7] The index of disproportionality proposed
by Michael Gallagher (1991), which is used in this study, solves
this problem by weighting the deviations by their own values—
thus making large deviations account for a great deal more in the
summary index than small ones. The computation of the Gallagher index (G) is as follows: the differences between the vote percentages (v_i) and seat percentages (s_i) for each party are squared
and then added; this total is divided by 2; and finally the square
root of this value is taken:[8]

$$G = \sqrt{\tfrac{1}{2} \Sigma \, (v_i - s_i)^2}$$

In a few electoral systems, two sets of votes can be used for
the purpose of calculating vote-seat share differences; which of the
two should be used? In MMP systems, the choice is between the
party list votes and the district votes, and the scholarly consensus is that the party list votes express the party preferences of
the electorate most accurately. In alternative vote and STV systems, the choice is between first preference votes and final-count
votes—that is, the votes after the transfer of preferences has been
completed; only first preference votes are usually reported, and
scholars agree that the differences between the two are of minor
importance. The one case where the difference is substantial is

7. One of the consequences of this problem is that the Loosemore-Hanby
(1971) index, which uses the additive approach, tends to understate the
proportionality of PR systems. An obvious alternative, offered by the Rae
(1967) index, is to average the absolute vote-seat share differences. It errs
in the other direction by overstating the proportionality of PR systems (see
Lijphart 1994, 58–60).

8. In the calculation of the Gallagher index, any small parties that are
lumped together as "other" parties in election statistics have to be disregarded.

between the first and second ballot results in France. On the first ballot, the votes tend to be divided among many candidates, and the real choice is made on the second ballot. The best solution is to count the *decisive* votes: mainly second-ballot votes, but first-ballot votes in districts where candidates were elected on the first ballot (Goldey and Williams 1983, 79).[9]

ELECTORAL DISPROPORTIONALITY IN PRESIDENTIAL DEMOCRACIES

The discussion of electoral systems has focused so far almost entirely on legislative elections. In presidential democracies, however, the election of the president is at least as important as the legislative election: of roughly the same importance in systems with executive-legislative balance and of greater importance in systems with executive dominance. In fact, even in balanced executive-legislative systems, the voters consider the presidential election to be the more important one, as indicated by their lower turnout levels in legislative elections when these are not held simultaneously with presidential elections; for instance, voter turnout in off-year congressional elections in the United States tends to be only about two-thirds of turnout in presidential election years.

Presidential elections are inherently disproportional as a result of two of the electoral system properties discussed above:

9. Several smaller methodological issues concerning the calculation of the index of disproportionality also need to be clarified. First, as in the calculation of the effective number of parliamentary parties, the seats are those in the lower or only houses of parliaments. Second, unlike in the calculation of the effective number of parties, the seats won by parties in the election are used and not those gained from legislators who join parties after the election, as in Japan. Third, any uncontested seats, mainly occurring but increasingly rare in plurality systems, are excluded (if it is possible to do so). Fourth, the two boycotted elections in Trinidad in 1971 and Jamaica in 1983 are disregarded. Fifth, factionalized and closely allied parties are again counted as one-and-a-half parties—a procedure that, however, has only a minimal impact on the index of disproportionality.

the electoral formula, which for the election of a single official is necessarily one of the plurality or majority formulas (or the majoritarian election by an electoral college), and the "size of the body to be elected," which is the absolute minimum of one. The party that wins the presidency wins "all" of the seats—that is, the one seat that is available—and the losing parties win no seats at all. This is also another respect in which presidential systems tend to be inherently majoritarian, in addition to their inherent tendency to have majoritarian cabinets and their reductive effects on the number of parties.

Table 8.1 presents the indexes of disproportionality for legislative and presidential elections in seven presidential systems. As expected, the disproportionality in presidential elections is higher than in legislative elections: on average, between 43 and 49 percent in the seven countries. If there are only two candidates, the index equals the vote percentage of the losing candidate. For instance, in the 2009 presidential election runoff in Uruguay, José Mujica won with 54.63 percent of the valid vote, and Luis Alberto Lacalle lost with 45.37 percent of the vote—yielding a disproportionality index of 45.37 percent. Moreover, the disproportionality in presidential elections is not just higher than in legislative elections, but a great deal higher: four of the seven presidential systems have average indexes of legislative disproportionality that are even below 5 percent. If both disproportionalities are relevant and should be counted, how can we best combine them? If the arithmetic average were used, the disproportionality in presidential elections would overwhelm that in legislative elections. It is therefore better to use the geometric mean—which is also generally more appropriate when values of greatly different magnitudes are averaged.[10] These geometric means are shown in the last column of Table 8.1.

10. The geometric mean of two numbers, like the two percentages in Table 8.1, is simply the square root of the product of these two numbers.

TABLE 8.1

Average disproportionalities in legislative and in presidential elections, the numbers of elections on which these averages are based, and the geometric means of the two disproportionalities in seven presidential systems, 1946–2010

	Legislative disproportionality (%)	Legislative elections (N)	Presidential disproportionality (%)	Presidential elections (N)	Geometric mean (%)
Argentina	7.35	13	43.94	4	17.98
Costa Rica	4.55	15	45.49	15	14.38
France[a]	12.08	10	43.53	8	22.93
Israel[b]	1.88	2	43.68	3	9.06
Korea	10.03	6	48.14	4	21.97
United States	4.43	32	46.03	16	14.28
Uruguay	0.75	6	48.81	6	6.05

Notes: a. Not including the 1986, 1993, and 1997 elections, which led to parliamentary phases

b. Only the 1996 and 1999 parliamentary elections and the 1996, 1999, and 2001 direct prime ministerial elections

Source: Based on data in Mackie and Rose 1991; Bale and Caramani 2010 and earlier volumes of the "Political Data Yearbook"; Nohlen 2005; Nohlen, Grotz, and Hartmann 2001; Nohlen and Stöver 2010; official election websites; and data provided by Royce Carroll, Mark P. Jones, and Dieter Nohlen

DEGREES OF DISPROPORTIONALITY IN
THIRTY-SIX DEMOCRACIES

The average electoral disproportionalities in all thirty-six countries are presented in ascending order in Table 8.2 together with
the types of electoral systems used in their legislative elections
(see the typology of Figure 8.1) and an asterisk indicating whether
the country is presidential or usually presidential (that is, including France but not Israel). The indexes span a wide range from
1.21 percent in the Netherlands to 21.97 in Korea; the mean is
8.55 and the median 7.14 percent.

There is a strikingly clear line dividing the top twenty countries from the sixteen countries at the lower end of the table: the
contrast is between mainly proportional and mainly majoritarian
systems. Of the top twenty, eighteen are parliamentary PR systems; the other two are Uruguay, which uses PR combined with
presidentialism, and Japan, which has used three different semiproportional systems. Greece and Spain are just below Uruguay
and Japan, and they are often regarded as only barely belonging
to the PR family. Spain's PR system is not very proportional
mainly because of its low-magnitude districts but also as a result
of the overrepresentation of the smaller provinces. The Greek PR
system has changed frequently, but the usual system is "reinforced
PR"—a deceptive label because what is being reinforced is the
large parties rather than proportionality. Nevertheless, even these
two impure PR systems have lower disproportionalities than any
of the plurality and majority systems. Most of the PR countries
have average disproportionalities between 1 and 5 percent; the
exemplar cases of Belgium and Switzerland are approximately in
the middle of this range.

On the plurality and majority side of the dividing line, the
only countries with disproportionalities below 10 percent are
New Zealand, Australia, and India. New Zealand's relatively low
overall percentage is partly based on its PR election results since
1966. Most of the plurality countries have disproportionalities
between 10 and 20 percent. The five parliamentary systems with

TABLE 8.2

Average electoral disproportionality and type of electoral system (used in legislative elections) in thirty-six democracies, 1945–2010

	Disproportionality (%)	Electoral system
Netherlands	1.21	List PR
Denmark	1.71	List PR
Sweden	2.04	List PR
Malta	2.07	PR-STV
Austria	2.51	List PR
Switzerland	2.55	List PR
Israel	2.60	List PR
Germany	2.67	PR-MMP
Finland	2.96	List PR
Belgium	3.35	List PR
Luxembourg	3.43	List PR
Italy	3.61	List PR (1946–92), PR-MMP (1994–)
Iceland	3.85	List PR
Ireland	3.93	PR-STV
Portugal	4.43	List PR
Norway	4.53	List PR
Uruguay	6.05	List PR*
Japan	7.00	Limited vote (1946), SNTV (1947–93), Parallel plurality-PR (1996–)
Spain	7.28	List PR
Greece	7.88	List PR
New Zealand	9.25	Plurality (1946–93), PR-MMP (1996–)
Australia	9.44	Majority: alternative vote
India	9.60	Plurality
Trinidad	11.33	Plurality

TABLE 8.2 *continued*

	Disproportionality (%)	Electoral system
Canada	11.56	Plurality
United Kingdom	11.70	Plurality
United States	14.28	Plurality*
Costa Rica	14.38	List PR*
Botswana	14.61	Plurality
Mauritius	15.61	Plurality
Jamaica	15.66	Plurality
Bahamas	16.48	Plurality
Barbados	17.27	Plurality
Argentina	17.98	List PR*
France	20.88	Majority-plurality (1958–81, 1988–), List PR (1986)*
Korea	21.97	Parallel plurality-PR*

*Presidential systems

Note: The number of elections on which these averages are based may be found in Table 5.2

   Source: Based on data in Mackie and Rose 1991; Bale and Caramani 2010 and earlier volumes of the "Political Data Yearbook"; Nohlen 2005; Nohlen, Grotz, and Hartmann 2001; Nohlen, Krennerich, and Thibaut 1999; Nohlen and Stöver 2010; official election websites; and data provided by Royce Carroll, Mark P. Jones, Dieter Nohlen, Ralph Premdas, and Nadarajen Sivaramen

the highest disproportionalities—Botswana, Mauritius, Jamaica, the Bahamas, and Barbados—are all small countries with plurality systems and unusually small legislatures; moreover, Mauritius uses mainly three-member districts. The United Kingdom is actually among the least disproportional of the plurality systems. The only exceptional cases of PR systems that are highly disproportional are two presidential democracies: Costa Rica and Argentina. A glance back at Table 8.1 reveals, however, that their legislative disproportionalities are only 4.55 and 7.35 percent, on the

high side but not completely abnormal for PR systems—similar
to those of, respectively, Norway and Spain. The presidentialism
of these countries is responsible for giving them their high overall disproportionality. Uruguay is exceptional in having a relatively low overall disproportionality—6.05 percent—in spite of
its presidential system of government and its high presidential
disproportionality. The explanation is that its legislative elections have been extremely proportional, even more so than those
in the Netherlands, which is at the top of Table 8.2: the respective
percentages are 0.75 and 1.21.

Legislative disproportionality is also relatively low in the United
States in spite of the plurality method for congressional elections. The main explanation of this unusual phenomenon is the
existence of primary elections in the United States. In most plurality systems, a major portion of the disproportionality of elections is caused by small parties that remain unrepresented or are
severely underrepresented; there are very few of these in the United
States because primary elections give strong incentives for dis-
sidents to try their luck in one of the major party primaries instead of establishing separate small parties; in addition, state laws
tend to discriminate against small parties. Yet the presidential
elections give the United States a high overall level of disproportionality after all. Korea has the highest disproportionality of our
thirty-six countries, produced not only by its presidentialism but
also—at first glance a bit surprisingly, because it has a semiproportional system for electing its legislature—by its high legislative disproportionality of 10.03 percent (see Table 8.1). The main
explanation is that fewer than 20 percent of the seats in its parallel plurality-PR system are PR seats.

Examining the effects of changes in the electoral systems and
shifts from presidential to parliamentary government in individual countries provides additional insight into the causes of electoral disproportionality. France's percentage is lower in Table 8.2
than in Table 8.1, because the three elections that triggered parliamentary phases were somewhat more proportional than under

presidentialism, especially in 1986, when PR was used and the degree of disproportionality dropped to 7.23 percent. Israel's already low overall disproportionality of 2.60 percent was even lower in the purely parliamentary elections before and after the years with the directly elected prime minister: 1.78 percent. The most dramatic change took place in New Zealand when PR replaced plurality elections: average disproportionality decreased from 11.11 to 2.92 percent. In contrast, the electoral system changes in Italy and Japan produced substantial increases in disproportionality even though these changes were within rather than between the three broad categories of electoral formulas shown in Figure 8.1. Italy's shift from list PR to PR-MMP more than doubled its disproportionality, from 2.47 to 6.34 percent. Both are PR formulas, but, as mentioned earlier, the PR component of Italy's PR-MMP—in contrast with Germany's and New Zealand's—is only partly compensatory. Japan's old limited vote and SNTV systems yielded relatively proportional results—their average disproportionality was only 5.03 percent. Although the new parallel plurality-PR system has about twice as many PR seats available as Korea's similar system, Japan's percentage of disproportionality increased dramatically to 14.48—a percentage typical of plurality and majority systems and one that does not appear to justify Japan's "semiproportional" label.

ELECTORAL SYSTEMS AND PARTY SYSTEMS

A well-known proposition in comparative politics is that the plurality method favors two-party systems; Duverger (1964, 217, 226) calls this proposition one that approximates "a true sociological law." Conversely, PR and two-ballot systems (like the French majority-plurality method) encourage multipartism. Duverger explains the differential effects of the electoral systems in terms of "mechanical" and "psychological" factors. The mechanical effect of the plurality rule is that all but the two strongest parties are severely underrepresented because they tend to lose in each district; the British Liberals and Liberal Democrats, continually the disadvantaged third party in the postwar era, are a good example. The psychological factor reinforces the mechanical one: "The electors soon realize that their votes are wasted if they continue to give them to the third party: whence their natural tendency to transfer their vote to the less evil of its two adversaries." In addition, the psychological factor operates at the level of the politicians, whose natural tendency is not to waste their energy by running as third-party candidates but instead to join one of the large parties.

Douglas W. Rae (1967, 67–129) has contributed a number of significant refinements to the study of the links between electoral and party systems. Different electoral systems have varying impacts on party systems, but, Rae emphasizes, they also have important effects in common. In particular, all electoral systems, not just the plurality and majority ones, tend to overrepresent the larger parties and underrepresent the smaller ones. Three important aspects of this tendency must be distinguished: (1) all electoral systems tend to yield disproportional results; (2) all electoral systems tend to reduce the effective number of parliamentary parties compared with the effective number of electoral parties; and (3) all electoral systems can manufacture a parliamentary majority for parties that have not received majority support from the voters. On the other hand, all three tendencies are much stronger in plurality and majority than in PR systems.

Rae's first proposition is clearly shown in Table 8.2: even the most proportional system, that of the Netherlands, still has a disproportionality of 1.21 percent instead of zero percent. But, as highlighted earlier, the disproportionality of PR systems generally is much lower than that of plurality and majority systems. Rae's second and third propositions are based on the fact that the disproportionalities of electoral systems are not random but systematic: they systematically advantage the larger parties and disadvantage the smaller parties—and again especially so in plurality and majority systems. That is why elections generally, but plurality and majority elections in particular, reduce the effective number of parties.

The systematic advantage that electoral systems give to large parties becomes especially important when parties that fail to get a majority of the votes are awarded a majority of the seats. This makes it possible to form single-party majority cabinets—one of the hallmarks of majoritarian democracy. Rae (1967, 74–77) calls such majorities "manufactured"—that is, artificially created by the electoral system. Manufactured majorities may be contrasted with earned majorities, when a party wins majorities of both votes and seats, and natural minorities, when no party wins a majority or either votes or seats. The clearest examples of manufactured majorities can be found in our prototypical cases of Great Britain and New Zealand, but many such majorities have also occurred in Australia and Canada; a recent Canadian example is the clear seat majority won by the Conservatives with merely 39.6 percent of the popular vote in the May 2011 election. Earned majorities are common in plurality systems with strict two-party competition: the Bahamas, Botswana, Jamaica, Trinidad, and the United States. In contrast, PR can also produce manufactured or earned majorities, but it rarely does so. Moreover, any manufactured majorities in PR systems tend to be produced from popular votes that are closer to 50 percent instead of the popular votes closer to 40 percent that are typical in plurality countries. These infrequent results have occurred mainly in countries that, in spite of PR, have relatively few parties (Austria and Malta), in countries with relatively impure PR (Spain and Greece), and in presidential systems that use PR for legislative elections (Argentina, Costa Rica, and Uruguay).

We can also expect a strong negative relationship between the disproportionality of the electoral system and the effective number of parliamentary parties. Figure 8.2 shows this relationship in our thirty-six democracies. The correlation coefficient is −0.57, which is statistically significant at the 1 percent level. As disproportionality increases, the effective number of parties decreases.

The figure shows considerable scattering and quite a few outliers, however. Other factors clearly also strongly affect the number of parties. One is the degree of pluralism and the number of

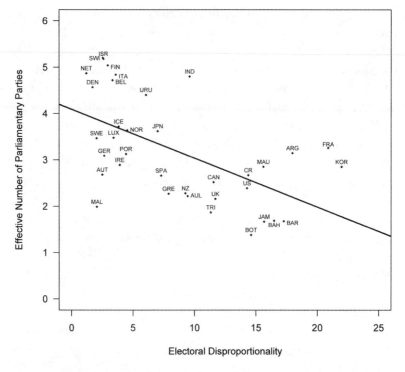

FIG. 8.2 The relationship between electoral disproportionality and the effective number of parliamentary parties in thirty-six democracies, 1945–2010

groups into which a society is divided, which can explain India's multipartism in spite of the reductive effects of its disproportional electoral system. Similarly, the seven countries grouped together in the top left corner of the figure—Switzerland, Israel, the Netherlands, Finland, Italy, Belgium, and Denmark—have even more multipartism than could be expected from their proportional election systems, and with the exception of Denmark, they are all plural or semiplural societies. The opposite effect can be seen in Austria, whose plural and later semiplural society has consisted mainly of two large "camps," and in Malta, where the electorate has long tended to line up in two groups of almost equal size: in these two countries, two-party and two-and-a-half party systems have coexisted with highly proportional PR systems. Three of the presidential democracies—Argentina, France, and Korea—are also relatively deviant, with considerably more parties than expected on the basis of their electoral disproportionalities. Botswana, on the other side of the regression line, has even fewer parties than could be expected from its highly disproportional plurality system.

The overall relationship between the two variables depends to a great extent on the sizable difference between two groups of countries, largely but not entirely coinciding with the difference between PR and plurality systems: most of the PR countries with relatively many parties on one hand, and most of the plurality and majority countries, the impure PR systems of Greece and Spain, and, although not as clearly, most of the presidential systems with relatively few parties on the other.

Chapter 9

Interest Groups: Pluralism Versus Corporatism

The fifth difference between majoritarian and consensus democracy—and the last of the five that together constitute the executives-parties dimension—concerns the interest group system. The typical interest group system of majoritarian democracy is a competitive and uncoordinated pluralism of independent groups in contrast with the coordinated and compromise-oriented system of corporatism that is typical of the consensus model. Corporatism is often also termed "democratic corporatism," "societal corporatism," or "neocorporatism" to distinguish it from authoritarian forms of corporatism in which interest groups are entirely controlled by the state. I shall use the short term "corporatism" but always as a synonym of democratic corporatism.

Corporatism has two conceptually distinct meanings. The first refers to an interest group system in which groups are organized into national, specialized, hierarchical, and monopolistic peak organizations. The second refers to the incorporation of interest groups into the process of policy formation. Philippe C. Schmitter (1982, 263–64) argues that the second type of corporatism ought to be labeled "concertation." Empirically, however, the two tend to occur together because corporatism in the narrow sense is almost a necessary condition for concertation. As Schmitter states, there appears to be a "structural compatibility . . . between corporatism and concertation," and he suggests that "elements of centralization, monopoly representation, etc., have historically emerged first and have, so to speak, prepared the way for initial policy concertation, which in turn encouraged further corporatization of interest associations."

Each of the two elements can be subdivided to arrive at the four key components by which corporatism can be readily recognized. Corporatism in Schmitter's narrow sense means that (1) interest groups are relatively large in size and relatively small in number, and (2) they are further coordinated into national peak organizations. Concertation means (3) regular consultation by the leaders of these peak organizations, especially those representing labor and management, both with each other and with government representatives to (4) arrive at comprehensive agreements that are binding on all three partners in the negotiations—so-called tripartite pacts. Interest group pluralism can be recognized by the opposite characteristics: a multiplicity of small interest groups, the absence or weakness of peak organizations, little or no tripartite consultation, and the absence of tripartite pacts. Katzenstein (1985, 32, 157) adds another distinctive trait of corporatism: "an ideology of social partnership" and the absence of "a winner-take-all mentality"—a characteristic that links corporatism to the other characteristics of consensus democracy. Of course, pure pluralism and pure corporatism are rare, and most democracies can be found somewhere on the continuum between the pure types.

In this chapter, I discuss the continuing relevance of the pluralism-corporatist distinction for the description and analysis of interest groups and then turn to the question of how degrees of pluralism and corporatism can be measured, both in the industrialized and in the developing countries. After presenting the index of interest group pluralism for all thirty-six democracies, I analyze the relationship of this variable with the types of cabinet in the thirty-six countries and with their effective number of political parties.

THE DECLINE OF CORPORATISM?

Since the 1970s the subject of corporatism and its contrast with pluralism have been the major focus in the scholarly study of interest groups (Almond 1983, Wilson 1990). The general verdict of this literature has tended to be highly favorable to corporatism. In particular, its macroeconomic performance measured in terms of high growth, low unemployment, and low inflation rates was found to be superior to that of pluralist interest group systems: it appeared to produce "a superior economic system" (Pekkarinen, Pohjola, and Rowthorn 1992). In the 1990s, however, scholars began to dissent from this sanguine interpretation, and corporatism was often claimed to be "in decline" (Gobeyn 1993), even in the once most strongly corporatist countries such as Austria (Gerlich 1992) and Sweden (Lewin 1994).

These judgments, however, must not be taken to mean that the distinction between corporatist and pluralist interest groups systems should be abandoned. First of all, what the "decline of corporatism" usually means is that the efficacy of corporatist structures and the frequency of their use have decreased, not that these structures themselves have disappeared or are being dismantled. Second, to the extent that there has been a decline in some countries, it has been merely a matter of degree. For instance, when Peter Gerlich (1992, 145) says "farewell to corporatism" in Austria—to cite the title of his article—his main point is that Austria is no longer the exceptionally pure example of corporatism it was for several decades, not that it is turning into its pluralist opposite; instead, he predicts that Austria will simply become more like "other European nations," which tend to be more moderately corporatist.

Third, in his painstaking quantitative study of changes in corporatism from the 1960s through the 1990s, Alan Siaroff (1999,

198) found no major shifts in the level of corporatism in twenty-one countries. Moreover, the minor changes were more often increases rather than decreases in corporatism. Only four countries experienced a change of more than 10 percent on the spectrum from pure pluralism to pure corporatism in their interest group systems: Australia, Finland, and Italy became more and Israel less corporatist. Eleven other countries underwent smaller changes: seven became slightly more and four slightly less corporatist.

Fourth, Howard J. Wiarda (1997, 175) argues that corporatism, instead of declining, is simply developing into new areas: "It is not so much corporatism that is under attack or disappearing [but] just one particular arena (labor-management relationships) that is now being restructured and taking new directions." He speculates that although the "*industrial* phase of corporatist tripartite relationships is fading, new *postindustrial* issues (education, health care, welfare, the environment, others) are coming to the fore," and these new issues are frequently negotiated in the familiar corporatist manner among the relevant interest groups—representing teachers, doctors, nurses, retired persons, and environmentalists—and the government. He concludes that "the policy process is still corporatist."

Fifth, a major and often used explanation for the supposed decline of traditional corporatism is economic globalization, which limits the capacity of national actors in steering the economy; it is "everyone's favorite suspect these days" (Schmitter 2008, 202). What should be noted here is that Katzenstein (1985, 9) uses precisely the same factor to explain not the decline but the *growth* of corporatism and why it developed, especially in the smaller European countries: "because of their open economies," these small countries "have been vulnerable to shifts in the world economy during the twentieth century," and they adopted corporatism as a protective device. Katzenstein's analysis suggests that the negative influence of globalization on corporatism is not inescapable and that, in the longer run, it may well reverse course. Markus M. L. Crepaz and Jürg Steiner (2011, 165) argue that such a reverse was triggered by the financial and economic crisis of 2008: it "has given corporatism a new lease on life as the 'laissez-faire' American model disintegrated, shattering the very assumptions of the free-market philosophy."

Sixth, another reason given for the decline of corporatism is the "eroding . . . level of integration of individuals with interest organizations and political parties" (Armingeon 1997, 165). In particular, this development weakens the ability of labor unions to act on behalf of large numbers of workers and hence also weakens their influence in tripartite negotiations. Katzenstein's (1985, 104–23) distinction between liberal corporatism, in which business is the stronger force, and social corporatism, in which labor dominates, is relevant here. It suggests that the decline in the strength of labor unions does not necessarily mean an overall decline in corporatism but merely a shift from social to liberal corporatism.

Schmitter's (1989, 72) long-term view—stated in his provocatively titled article "Corporatism Is Dead! Long Live Corporatism!"—is eminently sensible: interest group corporatism has a kind of "dynastic continuity punctuated by periodic demise and subsequent resurrection." The clamor about the decline of corporatism in the late 1980s and 1990s is reminiscent of the concern about what Alfred Grosser (1964, 242) called "the indisputable decline of . . . legislatures," which were "definitely in a state of crisis" in the 1960s. Contrary to Grosser's dire prediction, legislatures are still a sufficiently important institution in the early twenty-first century for me to devote a chapter to them (Chapter 11) as well as one on executive-legislative relations in which one of the forms of this relationship is a balance of power between the two branches of government (Chapter 7)!

DEGREES OF PLURALISM AND CORPORATISM IN THIRTY-SIX DEMOCRACIES

Although many comparative analyses of interest groups have attempted to measure the degree of pluralism or corporatism in relatively large number of countries, these measurements are of limited utility for the purposes of this study. For one thing, they tend to focus on different aspects of corporatism: some are based more on the presence and strength of peak organizations, whereas others emphasize the process of concertation; some studies focus on how centralized wage bargaining tends to be; others emphasize the strength and historical orientation—reformist versus revolutionary—of labor unions; yet others try to measure the success, or rather the failure, of concertation in terms of the levels of strikes and lockouts in different countries. These different emphases account for the fact that, although the measures used in different studies are in reasonable agreement with one another, there is far from perfect agreement (Kenworthy 2003). Other weaknesses of these measures are that most of them are rough trichotomous classifications—high versus medium versus low pluralism or corporatism—that they usually cover short periods and only from fifteen to eighteen countries, and that their focus is entirely on the industrialized democracies.

Most of these problems are solved by Siaroff's (1999) comparative study of as many a twenty-four industrialized democracies. He takes eight basic aspects of the pluralism-corporatism contrast—aggregating the foci of previous studies, mentioned in the previous paragraph—and rates his twenty-four democracies on each of these, using a five-point scale. He then averages these ratings to arrive at a comprehensive score for each country. Moreover, he does so for four periods: the 1960s and 1970s for twenty-one countries and the 1980s and 1990s for the same twenty-one plus Spain, Portugal, and Greece. Siaroff's measures have been well received and are used widely by other researchers (Armingeon 2002, 154). His scores for the 1960s can be regarded as roughly representative for the prior years since the late 1940s as well. For the first decade of the twenty-first century, Siaroff's scores for the 1990s can be used with minor adjustments suggested by Jaap Woldendorp's (2011) careful assessment of the evolution of corporatism in several European countries: small decreases in Belgium and Sweden and a small increase in Ireland (Bulsara and Kissane 2009, 179–80). Two-thirds of Table 9.1 is therefore almost entirely based on Siaroff's figures for the industrialized democracies.[1] The scores are pluralism scores: high scores reflect a high degree of pluralism, and low scores indicate strong corporatism.

The one industrialized country not covered by Siaroff is Korea, but it is not difficult to rate it on the index of pluralism. In response to the financial crisis that began at the end of 1997, President Kim Dae Jung's government established a tripartite commission that quickly reached an agreement on labor market flexibility in February 1998, but this effort to establish corporatism in Korea was short-lived. There was a great deal of tension among the labor union representatives and only weak participation by the employers' organizations. Taekyoon Kim (2008) contrasts this Korean "corporatism without capital" with what is often called "corporatism without labor"—that is, corporatism with a relatively weak input by organized labor—in Japan. The tripartite commission soon ceased to play a significant policy-making role. Korea's interest group system can therefore be placed among those at the pluralist end of the scale in Table 9.1.

Siaroff's study does not cover any developing countries, and these are generally neglected in comparative studies of interest group systems. One reason for this neglect is that the necessary data are often not available for the less developed countries. Another is that scholars of interest group systems have been particularly interested in corporatist instead of pluralist systems and that, broadly speaking, the developing countries tend to be more pluralist than corporatist. Stephan Haggard and Robert R. Kauf-

1. Another indication that there was little change from the 1990s to the years after 2000 can be found in the data on degrees of corporatism, based on a different set of indicators, collected by Adrian Vatter and Julian Bernauer (2010). Their corporatism data cover more than thirty countries (including twenty-three of our democracies) for each year from 1997 to 2006. Their impression was one of great stability in all of their countries, and accordingly, they present no year-to-year changes at all.

TABLE 9.1

Interest group pluralism in thirty-six democracies, 1945–2010

	Index of interest group pluralism
Sweden	0.35
Austria	0.38
Norway	0.38
Denmark	0.78
Finland	0.85
Germany	0.88
Luxembourg	0.88
Switzerland	0.88
Netherlands	0.98
Belgium	1.15
Israel	1.15
Mauritius	1.30
Japan	1.48
Uruguay	1.70
Australia	2.12
India	2.15
Barbados	2.20
Costa Rica	2.20
Iceland	2.20
Italy	2.42
Ireland	2.55
Botswana	2.60
Portugal	2.62
New Zealand	2.68
Argentina	2.70
France	2.90
Korea	2.90
Bahamas	3.00

continued

TABLE 9.1 *continued*

	Index of interest group pluralism
Jamaica	3.00
Malta	3.00
Trinidad	3.00
United Kingdom	3.02
United States	3.02
Spain	3.04
Greece	3.12
Canada	3.25

Source: Based on data in Siaroff 1999 for the twenty-four industrial democracies and the author's estimates for the other democracies

man (1995, 341) point out that the most important reason for this
is "the organizational weakness of the relevant players, including both interest groups and parties," which makes tripartite concertation very difficult. Nevertheless, the interest group systems
of the developing countries are not uniformly and purely pluralist, and the degree to which they are pluralist or, to some extent,
corporatist is measurable on the basis of judgments expressed by
country and area experts.

Of the eleven developing democracies included in this study,
the country with the most corporatist interest group system is
Mauritius. Deborah Bräutigam (1997, 54–55) writes that Mauritius cannot be called highly corporatist but that it does have
"institutional mechanisms [that] ensure that labor, business, and
government meet periodically to negotiate wage rates and other
economic parameters." Mauritian political scientist Hansraj Mathur
(personal communication, March 31, 1997) adds the following
more detailed description: "Most of the trade unions are members of federations which are in turn members of large confedera-

tions. These large confederations, along with the Mauritius Employers Federation (a strong group uniting all the employers) and the government hold tripartite meetings to discuss the annual quantum of compensation to be paid to meet any rise in the cost of living. The quantum once decided is applied to all the workers of the various industries."

Toward the other end of the scale we find four of the small Commonwealth democracies that are mainly pluralist. The ruling party in Trinidad organized a tripartite conference in 1964, shortly after independence, which led to the appointment of several tripartite committees to study and make recommendations on labor utilization and economic development. This incipient corporatism failed mainly because of the hostility of the labor unions, which saw it as a ploy by the government and the employers to weaken labor (MacDonald 1986, 150). Botswana is less pluralist and even, in the opinion of Botswana expert John D. Holm and the two Botswanan social scientists Patrick P. Molutsi and Gloria Somolekae (1996, 58), in the process of "developing toward the democratic corporatism so evident in Western Europe. . . . Groups organize on a bottom up basis and work with government officials to formulate a comprehensive policy regarding a particular sector of society or the economy." However, Zibani Maundeni (2004, 70–71) points out that the partners in Botswana's tripartism have been far from equal: the government has been dominant, the employers have been compliant, and labor has been extremely weak.

Barbados is a surprising exception to the steady pluralism of the small Commonwealth countries. From independence in 1966 until 1993, it was about as pluralist as its Caribbean neighbors. Following the economic crisis of 1991–93, however, a comprehensive tripartite pact was negotiated by the government and the peak organizations of labor and business, formally called the Protocol for the Implementation of a Prices and Incomes Policy. Sir Lloyd Erskine Sandiford (2004, 87), who was prime minister at the time of its signing, writes that "under that Protocol, the Social Partners acknowledged that Barbados' national success was largely due to its peaceful and harmonious labour-management relations [and] that the tripartite approach was the most effective strategy for achieving national development and cooperation." The protocol was extended several times—the fourth and fifth were called Protocol of the Social Partnership—and lasted for more than a decade and a half (Downes and Nurse 2004).

India is also in the top half of Table 9.1. Its interest group system has traditionally been largely pluralist. The field of agriculture is the one exception—but a significant one because India has long been a mainly rural and agricultural country. The "institutional centerpiece of agricultural policy" is the Commission on Agricultural Costs and Prices, composed of technocrats representing the government and farmers' representatives (Varshney 1995, 147).

Our three Latin American democracies are at a considerable distance apart from one another. Although it is generally true that "Latin America's deepest tendencies are corporatist" rather than pluralist (Murillo and Schrank 2010, 268), there are significant differences in the degree of corporatism in Argentina, Costa Rica, and Uruguay as well as major changes within two of the three countries. Costa Rica's position has changed little over the years and is roughly in the middle between pluralism and "a surprising amount of corporatism" (Wiarda 2004, 294). Uruguay has a long history of democratic tripartism, although mainly at the sectoral rather than the national level—and with many ups and downs. Tripartite "wage councils" were established in 1943 for different occupational categories. They were disbanded by the military regime that came to power in 1973; all unions and union-related activities were also banned. The wage councils were restored on the return to democracy in 1985, but weakened considerably when the government withdrew its participation in most of them in the 1990s and early years of the twenty-first century. But from 2005 on, under the government of two successive leftist Broad Front presidents, they have flourished again. Uruguay also has an overarching Superior Tripartite Council with an important coordinating and advisory function (Buchanan 2008, Meyer 2010).

Argentina has a long history of authoritarian or state corporatism but very little corporatism of any kind in the two decades since redemocratization in 1984. During the presidency of Nestor Kirchner, however, there was a resurgence of both union power and democratic neocorporatism. Sebastián Etchemendy and Ruth Berins Collier (2007, 264) write that "the first two months of 2006 and 2007 witnessed a general round of peak-level centralized wage bargaining in most industrial and service sectors. In neocorporatist fashion, national union leaders, business associations, and the government concluded agreements on sectorwide wage increases and on the minimum wage." They emphasize that this tripartism was limited to the unionized and formal sector, about 60 percent of wage earners, and therefore less inclusive than in European-style neocorporatism. This pattern has continued since then. In Etchemendy's words (personal communication, November 19, 2010), "The main wage pacts are in the large sectors of the economy between business and labor national associations, but the government informally negotiates a 'reference' percentage of wage increases—which basically serves as a minimum— for all sectors, and enforces it through the strongest unions allied with the government."[2]

The scores in Table 9.1 are pluralism scores ranging from a theoretical high of 4.00 to a theoretical low of zero but having a somewhat narrower empirical range from 3.25 for the most pluralist country—Canada—to 0.35 for the most corporatist country— Sweden. The countries are listed in ascending order of plural-

2. The pluralism scores for the twelve countries not included in Siaroff's study are based on my reading of the descriptions of their interest group systems by the various country experts cited in the text, on additional advice from almost all of them, and on my reading of the criteria used by Siaroff. They remain largely impressionistic, however, and clearly lack the precision of the scores for the other twenty-four countries.

ism. The mean score is 2.02 and the median 2.20, only slightly higher than the theoretical midpoint of 2.00 between pluralism and corporatism—indicating that the thirty-six democracies as a group are only slightly more pluralist than corporatist. The United Kingdom and Switzerland are respectively near the pluralist and corporatist ends of the spectrum; New Zealand and Belgium are in the expected halves of the pluralism-corporatism range; but, as already highlighted, prototypically majoritarian Barbados appears rather surprisingly in the middle of the range on the strength of its tripartite protocols since 1993.

INTEREST GROUP SYSTEMS, PARTY SYSTEMS, AND CABINET TYPES

The interest group system differs from the other basic variables of the executives-parties dimension in that there is no clear causal connection that links it to the other variables, whereas these other four do have such causal links: electoral systems shape party systems, which in turn have a strong causal effect on the formation of cabinets, and types of cabinet are further causally related to cabinet duration. Therefore, the hypothesis that interest group systems are related to these other variables rests entirely on the conceptual correspondence between the corporatism-pluralism distinction and the broad consensus-majoritarian difference.

Figures 9.1 and 9.2 show the relationships between the interest group systems in the thirty-six democracies and their types of cabinets and party systems. As hypothesized, democracies that have more minimal winning one-party cabinets are also the countries that have more pluralist interest groups systems; and countries with greater multipartism tend to be less pluralist. The correlation coefficient is stronger for the link between cabinets and interest groups than for the link between parties and interest groups (0. 71 and −0.61, respectively), but both are statistically significant at the 1 percent level. The main deviant cases in Figure 9.1 are the three most corporatist systems—Austria, Norway, and Sweden—which are much more consensus-oriented in this

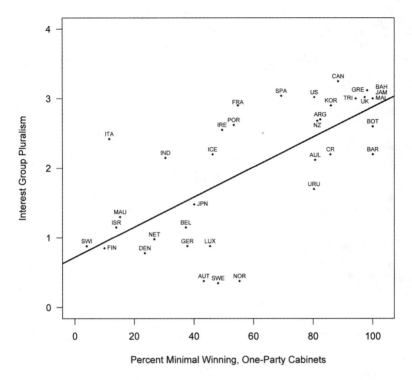

FIG. 9.1 The relationship between type of cabinet and interest group pluralism in thirty-six democracies, 1945–2010

respect than with regard to their usual cabinets. By contrast, Italy
is considerably less corporatist than expected on the basis of its
infrequent minimal winning one-party cabinets.

Figure 9.2 shows a roughly similar pattern: corporatist Austria, Norway, and Sweden are outliers again, and so is Italy. Joseph LaPalombara (1987, 213–220) offers an intriguing explanation for Italy's unusual position. He describes Italy, before the
reforms of 1994, as a *partitocrazia* with broad participation of all
parties in policy-making and a strong inclination to seek consensus: the party leaders had "a deep psychological aversion to divisive confrontations." The consensus produced by partitocrazia
was so strong, in LaPalombara's opinion, that there was simply

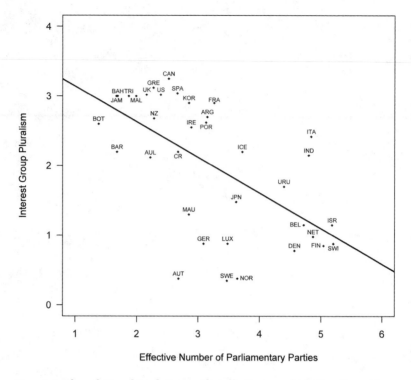

FIG. 9.2 The relationships between the effective number of parliamentary parties and interest group pluralism in thirty-six democracies, 1945–2010

no need for any further consensus to be produced by corporatism. This view is certainly plausible: broad political coalitions and interest group corporatism are both methods of achieving consensus and, in principle, can be seen as alternative methods. Strong interparty cooperation can therefore compensate for weaknesses in interest group coordination. This appears to have been the case in Italy, but it is clearly not a general pattern in most democracies; if it were, we would find a negative relationship between multipartism and broad coalition cabinets on one hand and corporatism on the other—instead of the strong positive relationships that are shown in Figure 9.1 and 9.2.

Several other authors have questioned the link between multipartism and interest group corporatism. Rein Taagepera (2003, 7) writes that "it feels odd that two-party systems would go with a profusion of interest groups, while multi-party systems require a two-group interest pattern." John Gerring and Strom C. Thacker (2008, 190) ask: "It would seem that the multiplication of groups in civil society should be classified in much the same way as the multiplication of groups in government: if multiparty systems are a feature of consensus, why not multi-interest group systems?" And Liam Anderson (2001, 444–45) also suggests that one can make at least as good a case for expecting a connection between consensus democracy and pluralism as for expecting a consensus-corporatism link. There is an undeniable logic to these arguments, but I still believe that the latter connection, most clearly and explicitly articulated by Katzenstein, cited in the beginning of this chapter, is far more plausible theoretically. Moreover, when there are two completely opposite hypotheses, and one of these fits the facts and the other does not, we can and should discard the disproved hypothesis.

The type of interest group system is also correlated with the electoral system and, though less strongly, with executive dominance. The correlations among all five variables involved in the executives-parties dimension are presented in Chapter 14. First, however, I turn in the next four chapters to a discussion of the variables belonging to the federal-unitary dimension.

CHAPTER 10

DIVISION OF POWER: THE FEDERAL-UNITARY AND CENTRALIZED-DECENTRALIZED CONTRASTS

The prime characteristic of the majoritarian model of democracy, as I have emphasized in previous chapters, is concentration of power in the hands of the majority. The consensus model is characterized by *non*-concentration of power, which can take the two basic forms of sharing of power and division of power. These two forms provide the theoretical underpinnings of the two dimensions of the majoritarian-consensus contrast. The crucial distinction is whether in consensus democracy power is dispersed to political actors operating together *within* the same political institutions or dispersed to *separate* political institutions (see Chapter 1). In the previous five chapters I discussed the five variables of the executives-parties (joint-power) dimension; in this chapter I deal with the first variable of the federal-unitary (divided-power) dimension: federalism and decentralization versus unitary and centralized government. It is appropriate to give this first-place honor to the subject of federalism because it can be considered the most typical and drastic method of dividing power: it divides power between entire levels of government. In fact, as a term in political science, "division of power" is normally used as a synonym for federalism.

In all democracies, power is necessarily divided to some extent between central and noncentral governments, but it is a highly one-sided division in majoritarian democracy. To maintain majority rule in the pure majoritarian model, the central government must control not only the central government apparatus but also all noncentral, potentially competing, governments. Majoritarian government is therefore both unitary (nonfederal) and centralized. The consensus model is inspired by the opposite aim. Its methods are federalism and decentralization—that is, not only a guaranteed division of power between the central and noncentral levels of government but also, in practice, strong noncentral governments that exercise a substantial portion of the total power available at both levels.

In this chapter I discuss the concept of federalism and its primary and secondary characteristics. On the basis of the primary traits, I develop a five-point scale of federalism and decentralization and assign each of the thirty-six democracies a place on this scale. This scale will be compared with four alternative methods of measuring division of power. Last, I discuss the potential advantages of federalism for two purposes: providing autonomy for minority groups in plural societies and permitting institutional experimentation.

FEDERALISM AND DECENTRALIZATION

A variety of definitions of federalism may be found in the literature on this subject, but there is broad agreement on its most basic characteristic: a guaranteed division of power between central and regional governments. William H. Riker's (1975, 101) authoritative definition reads as follows: "Federalism is a political organization in which the activities of government are divided between regional governments and a central government in such a way that each kind of government has some activities on which it makes final decisions." One aspect of this definition that deserves emphasis and to which I return later in this chapter is that the component units are called "regional" governments. This is in accordance with the conventional view: federalism is usually described as a spatial or territorial division of power in which the component units are geographically defined. These units are variously called states (in the United States, India, and Australia), provinces (Argentina and Canada), *Länder* (Germany and Austria), cantons (Switzerland), and regions (Belgium).

Instead of Riker's definition in terms of a guaranteed division of power, the description preferred by Daniel J. Elazar (1997, 239) focuses on "noncentralization" of power: he sees federalism as "the fundamental distribution of power among multiple centers . . . , not the devolution of powers from a single center or down a pyramid." None of these multiple centers in the federal system "is 'higher' or 'lower' in importance than any other, unlike in an organizational pyramid where levels are distinguished as higher or lower as a matter of constitutional design."

Both Elazar's and Riker's definitions allow for a wide range of actual power exercised by the different levels of government. Riker (1975, 101) states that each level "has some activities on which it makes final decisions" but does not specify any particular ratio of such activities between the central and regional governments. Likewise, Elazar (1997, 239) states that "the powers assigned to each [of the] multiple centers" in federalism may be large or small. Both of these federalism experts assume, however, that the fundamental purpose of guaranteeing a division of power is to ensure that a substantial portion of power will be exercised at the regional level or, to put it more succinctly, that the purpose of noncentralization of power is decentralization of power. These two elements are conceptually distinct, but they should both be regarded as primary characteristics of federalism.

In addition to these primary characteristics, federalist theorists often identify several secondary characteristics of federalism: in particular, a bicameral legislature with a strong federal chamber to represent the constituent regions, a written constitution that is difficult to amend, and a supreme court or special constitutional court that can protect the constitution by means of its power of judicial review. These are among the most important of what Ivo D. Duchacek (1970, 188–275) calls the "yardsticks of federalism." Their connection with federalism is that they can all serve to ensure that the basic federal division of power will be preserved. Unlike the primary characteristics, they are guarantors of federalism rather than components of federalism itself. I discuss these variables in more detail in the next two chapters.

The primary federal characteristics of noncentralization and decentralization are the building blocks for the construction of the fivefold classification in Table 10.1. The first criterion is whether states have formally federal constitutions. As Elazar (1987, 42) argues, "The first test of the existence of federalism is the desire or will to be federal on the part of the polity involved. Adopting and maintaining a federal constitution is . . . the first and foremost means of expressing that will." This criterion yields an initial distinction between federal and unitary systems. Each of these categories can then be divided into centralized and decentralized subclasses; centralization and decentralization are obviously matters of degree, but it is not difficult in practice to classify most countries according to the simple centralized-decentralized dichotomy. Finally, an intermediate category of semifederal systems is needed for a few democracies that cannot be unambiguously classified as either federal or unitary.

Table 10.1 also assigns a score to each category so that the classification can serve as a quantitative index of federalism, and it shows in which category—or, in some cases, between which categories—each of the thirty-six democracies belongs. The table is organized so that the easy cases that clearly fit a particular category are listed in the left and middle columns and the column to the right contains the more complex cases that fall between categories or changed their status during the period under consideration. The same convention is used for similar tables in the next two chapters.

Two striking features of the classification in Table 10.1 are, first, that federalism is relatively rare: there are more than twice

TABLE 10.1

Degrees of federalism and decentralization in thirty-six democracies, 1945–2010

Federal and decentralized [5.0]

Australia	Switzerland	(Belgium after 1993)
Canada	United States	
Germany		

Federal and centralized [4.0]

		Argentina [4.5]
		Austria [4.5]
		India [4.5]

Semifederal [3.0]

Israel	Spain	Belgium [3.5]
Netherlands		(Belgium before 1993)

Unitary and decentralized [2.0]

Denmark	Norway	(United Kingdom after 1998)
Finland	Sweden	
Japan		

Unitary and centralized [1.0]

Bahamas	Jamaica	France [1.3]
Barbados	Luxembourg	Italy [1.3]
Botswana	Malta	Korea [1.5]
Costa Rica	Mauritius	Trinidad [1.3]
Greece	New Zealand	United Kingdom [1.2]
Iceland	Portugal	(United Kingdom before 1998)
Ireland	Uruguay	

Note: The indexes of federalism are in square brackets

as many unitary as federal states. Second, the federal-unitary and centralized-decentralized differences are closely related: most federal systems are decentralized—in fact, there are no cases in the pure "federal and centralized" category at all—and most unitary systems are centralized. As a result, more than half of the democracies can be classified in one of the two extreme categories. The mean score is 2.3 and the median is 1.4—both much closer to the 1.0 score of the most unitary and centralized countries than to the 5.0 score at the other end of the scale.

Six of the nine federal systems—Australia, Canada, Germany, Switzerland, the United States, and, from 1993 on, Belgium—are also clearly decentralized systems of government. Austria and India are roughly in between these two types of federalism: not as decentralized as the other six federations but not centralized either. K. C. Wheare's (1964, 28) conclusion that both India's constitution and its governmental practices are only "quasi-federal" instead of fully federal is often cited. In particular, until the mid-1990s, the frequent use of so-called President's Rule for partisan purposes detracted from strong federalism: the constitution gives the central government the right to dismiss state governments and to replace them with direct rule from the center for the purpose of dealing with grave emergencies, but in practice President's Rule was used mainly by the central government to remove state governments controlled by other parties and to call new state elections in the hope of winning these (Tummala 1996, 378–82). President's Rule has been used rarely since the mid-1990s, partly as a result of the Supreme Court's 1994 ruling that arbitrary dismissal of state governments was unconstitutional, and partly because since 1996 all federal cabinets have been coalitions—which have had to rely on state-level parties to stay in power. Federal Argentina cannot be placed in the highest category either, but it fits the same intermediate category together with Austria and India on the strength of the important role played by the provincial "party bosses." The provincial governors are usually the undisputed bosses of the provincial-level parties, and, often acting collectively, they "have constituted a more relevant counterweight to the presidential authority" than the national legislature and judiciary (Spiller and Tommasi 2008). Instead of shoehorning these three countries into one or the other category, it is more realistic to give them an intermediate position and the intermediate score of 4.5.

Of the many unitary democracies, only the four Nordic countries and Japan can be classified as decentralized. Many of the others are very small countries, which hardly need a great deal of decentralization, but the unitary and centralized category also includes several larger countries like the United Kingdom, France, and Italy. These three countries, as well as Trinidad, are given a slightly higher score than the minimum of 1.0 because they became slightly less centralized—to a point roughly halfway between the centralized and decentralized categories—during the period under consideration. This process started in Italy around 1970, in France after the election of President Mitterrand in 1981 (Loughlin and Mazey 1995), and in the United Kingdom after the Labour party's election victory in 1997 (see Chapter 2). The other large country that is unitary and centralized, Korea, can also be given a slightly higher score. In Trinidad and Tobago, the smaller island of Tobago was granted a measure of self-government and its own House of Assembly in 1980 (Payne 1993, 61). The scores of the four countries that became less centralized represent averages for the entire period.

The semifederal category includes three democracies that Robert A. Dahl has called "sociologically federal" (cited in Verba 1967, 126): Belgium, the Netherlands, and Israel. The central governments of these countries have long recognized, heavily subsidized, and delegated power to private associations with important semipublic functions, especially in the fields of education, culture, and health care, established by the major religious and ideological groups in these societies. Because these groups are not geographically concentrated, sociological federalism deviates from Riker's criterion that the component units of a federation should be *regional* in nature. Belgium moved from this sociological federalism to a more formal semifederalism from 1970 on and finally to full federalism in 1993—which, however, still includes the nongeographically defined cultural communities among the constituent units of the federation. Belgium's score of 3.5 is the average over the whole 1946–2010 period.

The country that is the most difficult to classify is Spain. The extensive autonomy that Spain has granted to several regions—first to Catalonia, the Basque Country, and Galicia, and later to other regions—has convinced a number of scholarly experts that it should be considered a federal system, although there is far from full agreement on this point. Alfred Stepan (2001, 346) calls Spain "clearly federal," and Jan Erk and Edward Koning (2010) concur. Other authors are more cautious. Siaroff (2009, 167) includes Spain among his federal systems but adds that it is a "borderline case." Spain has also been called a case of "incomplete federalism" (Grau i Creus 2000) and "imperfect federalism" (Moreno 1994). The crucial missing factor is that Spain is not formally federal and does not call itself a federation. Section 2 of the Spanish constitution proclaims "the indissoluble unity of the Spanish Nation [and] recognizes and guarantees the right to self-government of the nationalities and regions of which it is composed," but studiously avoids any mention of federalism—thereby failing Elazar's "first test of the existence of federalism," cited earlier in this chapter. Ronald L. Watts (2008, 42) writes that "Spain is a federation in all but name"—but it is that formal name that is a critical issue. Similarly, Thomas O. Hueglin and Alan Fenna (2006, 19) call Spain "a *de facto* federal system"—not the de jure federation required by Elazar's criterion. Because Spain is neither undeniably federal nor clearly unitary, the best solution is to place it in the semifederal category in the middle of Table 10.1.

OTHER INDICATORS OF FEDERALISM AND DECENTRALIZATION

Does the index of federalism express the properties of federalism and decentralization accurately and reliably? Confidence in the

index can be strengthened by comparing it with a few other indicators that scholars have proposed. They cannot be used as alternative measures in this study, however, because most of them focus
on either the federal-unitary or the centralization-decentralization
contrast—unlike our index of federalism and decentralization that
includes both of these characteristics—and/or because they are not
available for all of our thirty-six democracies.

A widely used measure of centralization is the central government's share of a country's total tax receipts. It is based on the
reasonable assumptions that the relative powers of the central
and noncentral governments can be measured in terms of their
resources, especially tax revenues. Noncentral taxes are the taxes
collected by the noncentral governments for themselves plus those
shares of taxes collected by the central government that accrue
automatically to noncentral governments. Government centralization can then be measured as the central governments' share
of total central and noncentral tax receipts. However, there are
major problems concerning the degree of discretion that noncentral governments truly possess. For instance, do "automatic"
transfers exclude any influence by the central government on the
purposes for which these funds can be spent? Jonathan Rodden
(2004, 484–85) suggests that all transfers and grants be excluded
and that only "own-source revenues" be used as an indicator of
noncentral government autonomy. Even so, he cautions, own-
source revenues can still severely overestimate the extent of noncentral revenue autonomy: "While subnational governments
may collect the revenues labeled as own-source, the central government may nevertheless maintain the power to set the rate and
the base, leaving the subnational governments as mere collectors
of centrally determined taxes."

In spite of these problems, it is useful to compare fiscal centralization data, available for twenty-eight of our countries, with
the index of federalism and decentralization (Woldendorp, Keman,
and Budge 2000, 34–35). The correlation coefficient is a strong
−0.56. An alternative indicator is Siaroff's (2009, 218–21) mea-

sure of "relevant regional governments" for a large number of countries, including our thirty-six democracies. It is a simple three-point index based on the author's impressionistic but plausible judgments. Here the correlation coefficient is an extremely strong 0.89. A measure that is based exclusively on the federalism-unitary contrast is Gerring and Thacker's (2008) "nonfederalism" index, also on a three-point scale and available for all of our countries. The correlation coefficient is −0.73. Finally, Woldendorp, Keman, and Budge's (2000, 34–36) "autonomy" index does take both decentralization and federalism into account. It is a nine-point scale with data for twenty-eight of our countries; the correlation is again strong, with a coefficient of 0.83. All of the strong correlations mentioned in this paragraph are statistically significant at the 1 percent level.

FEDERALISM AND ETHNIC AUTONOMY

Federalism tends to be used in two kinds of countries: relatively large countries and plural societies. The largest countries in terms of population included in this study, India and the United States, are both federations; the least populous federation is Switzerland, which is approximately in the middle of our thirty-six democracies ranked by population. Four of the nine federal systems are plural societies: Belgium, Canada, India, and Switzerland. These are also among the largest of the eight plural societies listed in Table 4.3. In these plural societies, federalism performs the special function of giving autonomy to ethnic minorities.

To analyze this function of federalism it is useful to distinguish between congruent and incongruent federalism, as suggested by Charles D. Tarlton (1965, 979). Congruent federations are composed of territorial units with a social and cultural character that is similar in each of the units and in the federation as a whole. In a perfectly congruent federal system, the component units are "miniature reflections of the important aspects of the whole federal system." Conversely, incongruent federations have units with social and cultural compositions that differ from one another and from the country as a whole.[1] Another way of expressing this difference is to compare the political boundaries between the component units of the federation and the social boundaries among groups like ethnic minorities. In incongruent federations these boundaries tend to coincide, but they tend to cut across each other in congruent federal systems.

If the political boundaries are drawn so as to approximate the social boundaries, the heterogeneity in the federation as a whole is transformed into a high degree of homogeneity at the level of the component units. In other words, incongruent federalism can make a plural society less plural by creating relatively homogeneous smaller areas. This is the pattern in all four of the federal systems that are also plural societies, although their political and ethnic boundaries generally do not coincide perfectly. In Switzerland, there is considerably less linguistic diversity in the cantons than at the national level. The Swiss federation has four official languages, but twenty-two of the twenty-six cantons and half-cantons are officially unilingual; only three—Bern, Fribourg, and Valais—are bilingual, and just one—Graubünden—has three official languages (McRae 1983, 172–79). In Canada, the Francophone minority is concentrated mainly in Quebec, and the Quebec government has served as the principal mouthpiece for the interests of the French-speaking community in Canada, but Ontario and New Brunswick also contain substantial numbers of French-speakers.

The British colonial rulers of India drew the administrative divisions of the country with little regard for linguistic differ-

1. Tarlton uses the terms "symmetry" and "asymmetry" instead of "congruence" and "incongruence." Because the former pair of terms is most often used to describe different distributions of power—for instance, between the two chambers of bicameral legislatures—it is less confusing to use the latter pair of terms to characterize different compositions of two or more entities. Congruence and incongruence in federalism have a meaning that is analogous to congruence and incongruence in bicameralism (see Chapter 11).

ences; the imposition of federalism on these divisions led to a mainly congruent type of federalism in the early years of independent India. However, a complete transformation to an incongruent federal system based on linguistic divisions took place in the 1950s. After the state of Madras was divided into the separate Tamil-speaking and Telugu-speaking states of Tamil Nadu and Andhra Pradesh in 1953, the States Reorganization Commission embraced the linguistic principle and recommended drastic revisions in state boundaries along linguistic lines in 1955. These were quickly implemented in 1956, and several additional linguistic states were created in later years (Brass 1990, 146–56). Because of India's extreme linguistic diversity, the incongruent linguistic federalism has not managed to accommodate all of the smaller minorities, but on the whole it has, in Indian political scientist Rajni Kothari's (1970, 115) words, succeeded in making language "a cementing and integrating influence" instead of a "force for division."

Finally, the new Belgian federalism is the result of a determined effort to set up a federation that is as incongruent as possible. The three geographically defined regions are already highly incongruent: the two largest, Flanders and Wallonia, are unilingual, and only Brussels is bilingual. In order to perfect this linguistic incongruence, three nongeographically defined cultural communities are superimposed on the regions; here the political and linguistic boundaries coincide completely—making the federal system a purely incongruent one (see Chapter 3).

FEDERALISM AND INSTITUTIONAL EXPERIMENTATION

One aspect of the autonomy of the constituent units of federations is that they have their own constitutions, which they can amend freely within certain limits set by the federal constitution. In theory, this gives them the opportunity to experiment with different forms of government. Such experimentation, if successful, can be beneficial both for the other members of the federation and for the central government. In practice, however, we find al-

most complete isomorphism both between the central and component units' governmental forms and among those of the component units in each country.

With regard to the choice of presidential or parliamentary systems, for instance, the United States is solidly presidential, with
governors serving as "presidents" at the state level. However, there
has been more experimentation with the electoral system in the
United States than in other federations. The principal example at
the state level is Illinois, which used a semiproportional system—
cumulative voting—for electing its lower house from 1870 to
1980. Another example is Louisiana's use of the majority-runoff
method (where the first stage of the election is termed the "nonpartisan primary") instead of the plurality rule for electing its
members of the US House of Representatives.

The Australian House of Representatives and the lower houses
of the Australian states are all elected by the alternative vote,
except one: Tasmania uses the STV form of PR. PR is the norm
both at the national and cantonal levels in Switzerland, but a few,
mainly small, cantons use majority methods. The other federations
are even more isomorphic with regard to their electoral systems:
Canada and India are solidly wedded to the plurality rule, and
Argentina, Austria, Belgium, and Germany to PR. The same isomorphism is apparent with regard to the choice of presidential
and parliamentary systems, as already noted for the American
case. The only slight exceptions can be found in Germany and
Switzerland. All of the German Länder have parliamentary systems, but in Bavaria the prime minister cannot be dismissed by a
vote of no confidence. In Switzerland, the cantons deviate in one
respect from the hybrid parliamentary-presidential system at the
federal level—their collegial executives are popularly elected—
but they are similar to each other in this respect. It is symptom-
atic that the drafters of the constitution of the new canton of Jura,
which formally came into being in 1979, discussed the British
and German examples of parliamentary systems but that in the
end they stuck to "accepted Swiss norms" (Tschaeni 1982, 116).

CHAPTER 11

PARLIAMENTS AND CONGRESSES: CONCENTRATION VERSUS DIVISION OF LEGISLATIVE POWER

The second component of the federal-unitary dimension is the distribution—concentration versus division—of power in the legislature. The pure majoritarian model calls for the concentration of legislative power in a single chamber; the pure consensus model is characterized by a bicameral legislature in which power is divided equally between two differently constituted chambers. In practice, we find a variety of intermediate arrangements. In Chapters 2 and 3 we saw that the New Zealand parliament (after 1950) and the Swiss parliament are, in this respect, perfect prototypes of majoritarian and consensus democracy, respectively, but that the other three main examples deviate from the pure models to some extent. The British parliament is bicameral, but because the House of Lords has little power, it can be described as asymmetrically bicameral. The same description fits the Barbadian legislature because its appointed Senate has delaying but no veto power. The prefederal bicameral Belgian parliament was characterized by a balance of power between the two chambers, but these chambers hardly differed in composition; in the new federal legislature, elected for the first time in 1995, the Senate is still not very differently composed from the

Chamber of Representatives, and it has also lost some of its former powers.

The first topic of this chapter is the simple dichotomous classification of parliaments as bicameral or unicameral. Next, I discuss the differences between the two chambers of bicameral legislatures, especially with regard to their respective powers and composition. On the basis of these two key differences, I develop a quantitative index of bicameralism. Last, I explore the relationship between the strength of bicameralism, as measured by this index, and the degree of federalism and decentralization discussed in the previous chapter.

Two additional introductory comments are in order. First, legislative chambers have a variety of proper names (among them House of Commons, House of Representatives, Chamber of Deputies, Bundestag, and Senate), and in order to avoid confusion the following generic terms will be used in the discussion of bicameral parliaments: first chamber (or lower house) and second chamber (or upper house). The first chamber is always the more important one or, in federal systems, the house that is elected on the basis of population.[1] Second, the bicameral legislature as a whole is usually called Congress in presidential systems—but not, of course, in France, where the term "parliament" originated—and Parliament in parliamentary systems of government. However, the term "parliament" is also often used generally as a synonym for "legislature," and I shall follow this conventional usage here.

UNICAMERALISM AND BICAMERALISM

A dichotomous classification of parliaments as unicameral or bicameral appears to be simple and straightforward, but two legislatures do not fit either category: those of Norway until 2009

1. The only potential difficulty of this terminology is that the first chamber of the Dutch parliament is formally called the Second Chamber, and the second chamber is called the First Chamber. Similarly, the first and second chambers of the pre-1970 bicameral legislature of Sweden were called the Second and First Chamber, respectively.

and Iceland until 1991. Until 2009, Norwegian legislators were elected as one body, but after the election they divided themselves into two chambers by choosing one-fourth of their members to form a second chamber. The two chambers, however, had joint legislative committees, and any disagreements between the chambers were resolved by a plenary session of all members of the legislature. Roughly the same description fits the Icelandic case as well, except that the second chamber in Iceland was formed from one-third of the elected legislators. These legislatures therefore had some features of unicameralism and some of bicameralism; the resolution of disagreements by means of a joint session does not necessarily point to unicameralism because it is not an uncommon method for unambiguously bicameral legislatures either. If one were forced to make a purely dichotomous choice, these legislatures should probably be regarded as somewhat closer to unicameralism than to bicameralism. But there is no need for such a difficult choice, and the classification of all legislatures presented later in this chapter simply places these two cases in a special one-and-a-half chambers category.

In their broad comparative study of bicameralism, George Tsebelis and Jeannette Money (1997, 1) report that about one-third of the countries in the world have bicameral and about two-thirds have unicameral legislatures. The ratio for our thirty-six democracies is quite different: bicameralism is much more common than unicameralism. In 2010, only fourteen of the thirty-six democracies, slightly more than one-third, had unicameral parliaments. Five countries shifted to unicameralism during the period under consideration: New Zealand in 1950, Denmark in 1953, Sweden in 1970, Iceland in 1991, and Norway in 2009. At the beginning of the period in which each of the thirty-six democracies is covered, only nine—exactly one-fourth—had unicameral legislatures: Costa Rica, Finland, Greece, Israel, Korea, Luxembourg, Malta, Mauritius, and Portugal. There were no shifts in the opposite direction, from a unicameral to a bicameral parliament (Longley and Olson 1991).

Most of the fourteen democracies with unicameral parliaments listed in the previous paragraph are the smaller countries, with the exception of Korea with its population of almost fifty million. The next largest, Greece, has a population of only about eleven million. An even more striking characteristic is that none of them is a federal system. To put it slightly differently, the nine formally federal systems among the thirty-six democracies all have bicameral legislatures, whereas, as of 2010, the twenty-seven formally unitary systems (including those labeled semifederal in the previous chapter) are almost evenly divided between unicameralism and bicameralism: fourteen have unicameral and thirteen bicameral legislatures. This is already a strong indicator of the relationship between cameral structure and the federal-unitary distinction. This relationship is analyzed in more detail at the end of this chapter, after the discussion of the different forms that bicameralism can assume.

VARIETIES OF BICAMERALISM

The two chambers of bicameral legislatures tend to differ in several ways. Originally, the most important function of second chambers, or "upper" houses, elected on the basis of a limited franchise, was to serve as a conservative brake on the more democratically elected "lower" houses. With the advent of universal franchise for all elections in our set of fully democratic regimes, this function has become obsolete. However, the British House of Lords and the House of Chiefs in Botswana are borderline cases: membership in the House of Lords is still partly based on hereditary principles, and in Botswana, although the chiefs are now subject to formal election, heredity still prevails in practice. Of the remaining six differences between first and second chambers, three are especially important in the sense that they determine whether bicameralism is a significant institution. Let us first take a brief look at the three less important differences.

First, second chambers tend to be smaller than first chambers. In fact, this would be an absolute rule for the bicameral legislatures in our set of democracies if it were not for the British House of Lords, which used to have almost twice as many members as the House of Commons; the numbers after the 2010 election were 650 members of the Commons and about 800 Lords—still a larger number in the latter, but not as lopsided as earlier. Among all of the other second chambers that are smaller than the first chambers, there is still a great variety in how much smaller they are. A few second chambers are relatively close to the sizes of the respective first chambers: for instance, in Trinidad the respective numbers are 31 and 43, and in Spain 264 and 350. At the other extreme, Germany has a very large first chamber with 622 members after the 2009 election—almost as many as the House of Commons—and one of the smaller second chambers consisting of just 69 members.

Second, legislative terms of office tend to be longer in second than in first chambers. The first chamber terms range from two to five years compared with a second chamber range of four to nine years (and, in Britain and Canada, respectively, life membership and membership until retirement). Switzerland is the only, relatively minor exception: a few of its second-chamber members are elected for terms that are shorter than the four-year term of the first chamber. In all the other bicameral legislatures, the members of second chambers have terms of office that are either longer than or equal to those of the first-chamber members.[2]

Third, a common feature of second chambers is their staggered election. One-half of the membership of the Australian and Japanese second chambers is renewed every three years. One-third of

---

2. The US House of Representatives is exceptional in that it has a short term of office of only two years. The Australian lower house and the New Zealand unicameral legislature are elected for three years. In Sweden, the term was four years until 1970, when both unicameralism and three-year terms were adopted, but four-year terms were restored from 1994 on. In all other countries, the members of first or only chambers may serve as long as four or five years, but in most parliamentary systems premature dissolutions may shorten these maximum terms.

the American, Argentine, and Indian second chambers is elected every second year, and one-third of the French second chamber is renewed every three years. Similarly, the members of the Austrian, German, and Swiss federal chambers are selected in a staggered manner but at irregular intervals. The first chamber in Argentina is unique in also have staggered terms: one-half is elected every other year.

These three differences do affect how the two chambers of the several legislatures operate. In particular, the smaller second chambers can conduct their business in a more informal and relaxed manner than the usually much larger first chambers. But they do not affect the question of whether a country's bicameralism is a truly strong and meaningful institution.

STRONG VERSUS WEAK BICAMERALISM

Three features of bicameral parliaments determine the strength or weakness of bicameralism. The first important aspect is the formal constitutional powers that the two chambers have. The general pattern is that second chambers tend to be subordinate to first chambers. For instance, their negative votes on proposed legislation can frequently be overridden by the first chambers, and in most parliamentary systems the cabinet is responsible exclusively to the first chamber. The only examples of bicameral legislatures with formally equal power in our set of democracies are the legislatures of Argentina, Italy, Switzerland, the United States, and Uruguay; three countries used to have formally equal chambers—Belgium, Denmark, and Sweden—but the Belgian Senate's power was severely reduced when it was elected in its new federal form in 1995, and Denmark and Sweden abolished their second chambers in 1953 and 1970, respectively.

Second, the actual political importance of second chambers depends not only on their formal powers but also on their method of selection. All first chambers are directly elected by the voters, but the members of most second chambers are elected indirectly (usually by legislatures at levels below that of the national government, as in India, the Netherlands, and, until 1970, in Sweden) or, more frequently, appointed (like the senators in Canada and in the four Commonwealth Caribbean countries, some of the Irish senators, and life peers in the British House of Lords). Second chambers that are not directly elected lack the democratic legitimacy, and hence the real political influence, that popular election confers. Conversely, the direct election of a second chamber may compensate to some extent for its limited formal power.

On the basis of the above two criteria—the relative formal powers of the two chambers and the democratic legitimacy of the second chambers—bicameral legislatures can be classified as either *symmetrical* or *asymmetrical.* Symmetrical chambers are those with equal or only moderately unequal constitutional powers and democratic legitimacy. Asymmetrical chambers are highly unequal in these respects. The symmetrical category includes the five legislatures, noted above, that still have chambers with formally equal powers. Four of these legislatures also have directly elected second chambers—Argentina, Italy, the United States, and Uruguay—and most of the members of the Swiss second chamber are popularly elected. In addition, the chambers of four bicameral legislatures are not completely equal but can still be classified as symmetrical according to the above definition: those in Australia, Germany, Japan, and the Netherlands. The entire Australian and Japanese parliaments are elected directly. The Dutch parliament belongs in this category in spite of the second chamber's indirect election by the provincial legislatures, because this chamber has an absolute veto power over all proposed legislation that cannot be overridden by the first chamber. The German Bundesrat owes its strength neither to popular election nor an absolute legislative veto but to the fact that it is a unique federal chamber composed of representatives of the *executives* of the member states of the federation—usually ministers in the member state cabinets. It can thus be described as "one of the strongest second chambers in the world" (Edinger 1986, 16). The power relation-ship between the two houses in the remaining bicameral parliaments is asymmetrical.

The third crucial difference between the two chambers of bicameral legislatures is that second chambers may be elected by different methods or designed so as to overrepresent certain minorities. If this is the case, the two chambers differ in their composition and may be called *incongruent*. The most striking examples are most of the second chambers that serve as federal chambers and that overrepresent the smaller component units of the federation. The greatest degree of overrepresentation occurs when there is equality of state, provincial, or cantonal representation regardless of the populations of these federal units. Such parity can be found in the federal chambers of Switzerland and the United States (two representatives per canton or state), Argentina (three members per province), and Australia (twelve from each state).[3] The German Bundesrat and the Canadian Senate are examples of federal chambers in which the component units are not equally represented but in which the smaller units are overrepresented and the larger ones underrepresented. The Austrian Bundesrat is an exception, as its membership is roughly proportional to the population of the Länder rather than giving special representation to the smaller Länder. Similarly, the new Belgian Senate gives only slight overrepresentation to the French-speaking and German-speaking linguistic minorities. India is an intermediate case.

Table 11.1 presents the degree of overrepresentation of the smaller units in the nine federations and in the Spanish and Dutch semifederal systems in a more precise way—in terms of the degree of inequality of representation caused by the favorable treatment of the small units. The first column shows the percentage of

3. Partial exceptions to parity are the half cantons in Switzerland, which have only one representative each in the federal chamber, and the Australian Capital Territory and Northern Territory, which have two senators each.

TABLE 11.1

Inequality of representation in eleven federal and semifederal chambers, ca. 2000

	Percentages of seats held by the 10 percent best represented voters	Gini Index of Inequality	Samuels-Snyder Index of Malapportionment
Argentina	44.8	0.61	0.49
United States	39.7	0.49	0.36
Switzerland	38.4	0.46	0.34
Canada	33.4	0.34	—
Australia	28.7	0.36	0.30
Germany	24.0	0.32	0.24
Spain	23.7	0.31	0.29
India	15.4	0.10	0.07
Austria	11.9	0.05	0.03
Belgium	10.8	0.01	—
Netherlands	10.0	0.00	0.00

Source: Based on data in the Stepan-Swenden Federal Databank, All Souls College, Oxford University, and in Samuels and Snyder (2001, 662)

the membership of the federal chamber that represents the most favorably represented 10 percent of the population. The best represented citizens are those in the smallest component units of the federation. The following example illustrates how these percentages are calculated. Assume that the smallest and best represented state in a federation has 6 percent of the population and ten of the one hundred seats in the federal chamber, and that the second smallest and second best represented state has 8 percent of the population and also ten of the one hundred federal chamber seats. Then the best represented 10 percent of the population are the 6 percent in the smallest state plus half of the people in the second smallest state. Together, these 10 percent of the people have 15 percent of the seats in the federal chamber.

The inequality in the above illustration is minor compared with the actual inequalities that we find in most of the federal chambers. Argentina is the most extreme case: the most favorably represented 10 percent of the people, living in the smallest provinces, have almost 45 percent of the representation in the Senate. The percentages for the United States and Switzerland—almost 40 percent—are close to Argentina's, and the US Senate and the Swiss Council of State can therefore be said to be almost as malapportioned as the Argentine Senate. In Canada, Australia, Germany, and Spain, the inequalities are less extreme but still substantial: the most favorably represented 10 percent of the people can elect between 23 and 34 percent of the legislators in the federal chambers. The Austrian Bundesrat and the Belgian Senate are the only federal chambers in which the degree of overrepresentation is so slight that they can almost be regarded as proportionally apportioned chambers—in fact, almost like the perfectly proportional upper house of the Netherlands (which is classified as semifederal because of its sociological federalism rather than a territorial federal system). The composition of the Indian federal chamber appears to be closer to the Austrian and Belgian pattern than to that of the other seven federal systems; however, because the Indian second chamber is also elected by a different method—the STV form of PR instead of the plurality rule used for lower house elections—it should be classified as incongruent.

Table 11.1 also shows two summary measures of the degree of inequality. The Gini index is often used for the measurement of inequalities of income and wealth, but it can be used to measure any kind of inequality. The Index of Malapportionment, devised by David Samuels and Richard Snyder (2001) and available for nine of the democracies in the table, is similar to one of the indexes of electoral disproportionality: just as differences between percentages of votes and seats won by political parties can be added up to arrive at an overall measure of disproportionality, so can differences between percentages of state or province popula- tions and percentages of the seats allocated to them be used for a summary measure of legislative malapportionment.[4] Both indexes can range from zero when there is complete proportionality—the Belgian Gini index of 0.01 is close to this point and both Dutch indexes are exactly zero—to a theoretical maximum approximat- ing 1.00 when the tiniest state or province has all of the seats in the federal chamber and the others get none. The values of the Samuels-Snyder index are lower than those of the Gini index, but their rank ordering of the federal chambers is the same and also virtually the same as the rank ordering of the percentages in the first column. All three show the federal chamber of Argentina to be the most malapportioned, closely followed by those of the United States and Switzerland. Although the malapportionment of the next five countries is less extreme, their legislatures should also be classified as incongruent.

One nonfederal second chamber must be similarly classified: the French Senate. It is elected by an electoral college in which the small communes, with less than a third of the population, have more than half of the votes; on account of this rural and small-town overrepresentation, Duverger once characterized the Senate as the Chamber of Agriculture (cited in Ambler 1971, 165). Many of the other bicameral legislatures are congruent be- cause their chambers are elected by similar methods: list PR in Italy (until 1992), the Netherlands, and prefederal Belgium; MMP in Italy since 1994; and SNTV in Japan until 1996 (although partly

4. The measure of disproportionality on which the Samuels-Snyder Index of Malapportionment is based is the Loosemore-Hanby (1971) index, mentioned in Chapter 8 (note 7). Samuels and Snyder (2001, 660– 61) also analyze the malapportionment in first chambers and find that it is generally much lower than in upper houses. However, Argentina and Spain have significantly malapportioned lower houses, too: values on the index of 0.14 and 0.10, respectively. Even more malapportioned are the unicameral parliaments of Korea (0.21) and Iceland (0.17).

list PR for upper house elections since 1983). In the Bahamas, Barbados, and Jamaica, the upper houses are appointed by the governor-general, and in Trinidad by the president, according to various criteria, but always in such a way that the prime minister nominates the majority; thus the majority party in the first chamber also becomes the majority party in the second chamber. Ireland's Senate appears to be incongruent, because a large number of senators have to be elected from candidates nominated by vocational and cultural interest groups, but in the electoral college, composed of national and local legislators, party politics predominates. Hence the Irish Senate "is composed largely of party politicians not very different from their colleagues in the [first chamber] and, in the case of many of them, with only tenuous connections with the interests they affect to represent" (Chubb 1982, 212).

THE CAMERAL STRUCTURES OF THIRTY-SIX
DEMOCRATIC LEGISLATURES

Table 11.2 uses the distinctions between bicameralism and unicameralism, between symmetrical and asymmetrical bicameralism, and between congruent and incongruent bicameralism to construct a classification of the cameral structures of thirty-six democracies as well as an index of bicameralism ranging from 4.0 to 1.0 points. There are four principal categories: strong, medium-strength, and weak bicameralism, and unicameralism. Strong bicameralism is characterized by both symmetry and incongruence. In medium-strength bicameralism, one of these two elements is missing; this category is split into two subclasses according to whether symmetry or incongruence is the missing feature, but both are ranked equally and have the same index of bicameralism (3.0 points). The third category is weak bicameralism in which the chambers are both asymmetrical and congruent. And the fourth category is that of unicameral legislatures. A plausible case can be made for the merger of the last two categories: Does a bicameral legislature with two or more identical houses

TABLE 11.2

Cameral structure of legislatures in thirty-six democracies, 1945–2010

Strong bicameralism: symmetrical and incongruent chambers [4.0]

Argentina	Switzerland
Australia	United States
Germany	

Medium-strength bicameralism: symmetrical and congruent chambers [3.0]

Italy	Netherlands	Belgium [2.8]
Japan	Uruguay	(Belgium before 1995)
		(Denmark before 1953)
		(Sweden before 1970)

Medium-strength bicameralism: asymmetrical and incongruent chambers [3.0]

Canada	India
France	Spain

Between medium-strength and weak bicameralism [2.5]

Botswana	United Kingdom

Weak bicameralism: asymmetrical and congruent chambers [2.0]

Austria	Ireland	Sweden [1.7]
Bahamas	Jamaica	(Belgium after 1995)
Barbados	Trinidad	(New Zealand before 1950)

One-and-a-half chambers [1.5]

Iceland [1.4]
Norway [1.5]
(Iceland before 1991)
(Norway before 2009)

continued

TABLE 11.2 *continued*

Unicameralism [1.0]

Costa Rica	Luxembourg	Denmark [1.2]
Finland	Malta	New Zealand [1.1]
Greece	Mauritius	(Denmark after 1953)
Israel	Portugal	(Iceland after 1991)
Korea		(New Zealand after 1950)
		(Norway after 2009)
		(Sweden after 1970)

Note: The indexes of bicameralism are in square brackets

and one house that is much more powerful than the other differ in any significant way from a unicameral legislature? Tsebelis and Money (1997, 211) give an emphatically affirmative answer to this question: "All second chambers exercise influence even if they are considered weak or insignificant." Therefore, for the purpose of measuring the division of legislative power, weak bicameralism still represents a degree of division, whereas unicameralism means complete concentration of power.

As in Table 10.1, which showed the degrees of federalism and decentralization in the previous chapter, Table 11.2 places several countries in intermediate positions between the four principal categories. This is necessary, first, because several countries changed their cameral structure during the period under consideration; for these countries, both their type of cameral structure in each period and their average scores for the entire period are shown.[5] Second, British and Botswanan bicameralism, although technically incongruent, is "demoted" by half a point because

5. Somewhat confusingly, Sweden's average score of 1.7 points places it in the weak bicameralism category, although it actually never had this kind of parliament; the explanation is that 1.7 represents the average of its relatively long period of unicameralism (1.0 point) and the shorter period of symmetrical and congruent chambers (3.0 points).

the upper houses are relics of a predemocratic era. Third, as discussed earlier, the in-between legislatures of Iceland (until 1991) and Norway (until 2009) should be classified as one-and-a-half cameralism and assigned the commensurate index of 1.5 points. The mean index of bicameralism for all thirty-six countries is 2.2 and the median 2.0 points—both well below the theoretical midpoint of 2.5 points between strong bicameralism on one hand and unicameralism on the other.[6]

CAMERAL STRUCTURE AND DEGREES OF FEDERALISM AND DECENTRALIZATION

As pointed out earlier, there is a strong empirical relationship between the bicameral-unicameral and federal-unitary dichotomies: all formally federal systems have bicameral legislatures, whereas some nonfederal systems have bicameral and others unicameral parliaments. The same strong link appears when the two indexes of federalism and bicameralism are correlated, as Figure 11.1 shows. As the degree of federalism and decentralization increases, first a shift from unicameralism to bicameralism takes place and then the strength of bicameralism increases. The correlation coefficient is 0.70 (significant at the 1 percent level).

Federal Austria is, not unexpectedly, one of the deviant cases as a result of its weakly bicameral legislature. Finland—one of the four Nordic countries that were classified as unitary and decentralized—has a low bicameralism score that is more typical of unitary and centralized systems. Similarly, Israel has a unicameral parliament that is at odds with its classification as a semifederal system. On the other side of the regression line, a cluster of

6. In the previous chapter, I compared the index of federalism and decentralization with indexes developed by other scholars. Similarly, the index of bicameralism can be compared with the Siaroff (2009, 218) and Woldendorp-Keman-Budge (2000, 40) indexes of bicameralism and the Gerring-Thacker (2008) index of non-bicameralism, all of which use a three-point scale. The correlation coefficients are, respectively, 0.91, 0.81, and −0.68—all three statistically significant at the 1 percent level.

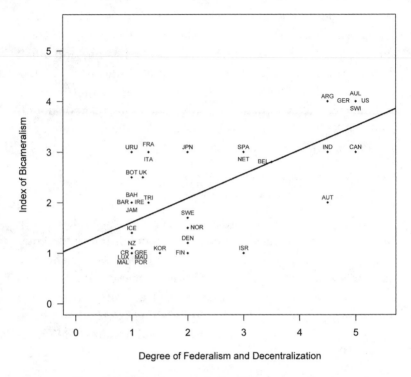

FIG. 11.1 The relationship between federalism-decentralization and cameral structure in thirty-six democracies, 1945–2010

four unitary and largely centralized systems—France, Italy, Uruguay, and Japan—have a much stronger bicameralism than expected. One explanation for these deviant cases appears to be population size. The smaller countries—Austria (which is the second
smallest of the nine federal systems), Israel, and Finland—tend
to have unicameral or weakly bicameral legislatures in spite of
their federal, semifederal, or decentralized status. By contrast,
large countries like France, Italy, and Japan have a relatively
strong bicameralism in spite of their unitary systems. I noted in
the previous chapter that population size was also related to federalism: the federal systems tend to be the larger countries. The
three variables are clearly far from perfectly correlated; Uruguay

with its small population and unitary government but medium-strength bicameralism is a notable exception. However, in Chapter 14 I show that population size is closely linked to the entire federal-unitary dimension of which the indexes of federalism and bicameralism are two of the five components.

CHAPTER 12

CONSTITUTIONS: AMENDMENT PROCEDURES AND JUDICIAL REVIEW

In this chapter I discuss two variables, both belonging to the federal-unitary dimension, that have to do with the presence or absence of explicit restraints on the legislative power of parliamentary majorities. Is there a constitution serving as a "higher law" that is binding on parliament and that cannot be changed by a regular parliamentary majority, or is parliament—that is, the majority in parliament—the supreme and sovereign lawmaker? The first variable is the ease or difficulty of amending the constitution: the conventional distinction is between *flexible* constitutions that can be changed by regular majorities and *rigid* constitutions that require supermajorities in order to be amended. The second variable concerns the presence or absence of judicial review; when the constitution and an ordinary law conflict, who interprets the constitution: parliament itself—again meaning the majority in parliament— or a body such as a court or a special constitutional council outside and independent of parliament? In the pure consensus model, the constitution is rigid and protected by judicial review; the pure majoritarian model is characterized by a flexible constitution and the absence of judicial review.

In practice, the two differences are not dichotomies: there are

degrees of flexibility or rigidity of constitutions and, when judicial review is present, degrees to which it is actively used. I propose four-point scales to measure both constitutional rigidity and
judicial review. I also analyze the relations between the two variables: rigid constitutions tend to have more judicial review protection than more flexible constitutions. In a brief addendum I
discuss the role of referendums, which are frequently required in
the process of constitutional amendment: Should they be seen
mainly as majoritarian instruments or rather as incentives for
seeking consensus? A second addendum takes a look inside powerful and activist high courts, characteristic of consensus democracy, in order to discover to what extent their internal organization
and operation are also in accordance with the consensus model.

WRITTEN AND UNWRITTEN CONSTITUTIONS

The distinction between written and unwritten constitutions
appears to be relatively unimportant for two reasons. One is that
almost all of the constitutions in the world are written; unwritten
ones are extremely rare. In our set of thirty-six democracies, only
three have unwritten constitutions: the United Kingdom and
New Zealand, the two prime examples of majoritarian democracy discussed in Chapter 2, as well as Israel. The absence of a
written constitution in Britain and New Zealand is usually explained in terms of their strong consensus on fundamental political norms, which renders a formal constitution superfluous.
The opposite explanation applies to the Israeli case. Israel has
tried but failed to adopt a written constitution because on a number of key questions, especially the role of religion in the state
and in the legal system, agreement could simply not be reached
(Gutmann 1988). This dissensus has been solved by an agreement
to disagree, while on other fundamental matters the consensus
has been strong enough to allow the country to be run without a
formal constitution, as in Britain and New Zealand. Second, from
the perspective of the fundamental contrast between the majoritarian and consensus models of democracy, it is more relevant to

determine whether the constitution, written or unwritten, im-
poses significant restraints on the majority than to ask whether it
is written or not. Written constitutions may be as easily amend-
able and as free from judicial review as unwritten constitutions.

There are two strong counterarguments, however. First, if the
written constitution is a single document, explicitly designated
as the country's highest law, the parliamentary majority is likely
to feel morally bound to respect it to a greater degree than if it is
merely a more or less amorphous collection of basic laws and
customs without even a clear agreement on what exactly is and
what is not part of the unwritten constitution. Second, even more
significant is the fact that unwritten constitutions by their very
nature—because they do not have a formal status superior to that
of other laws—logically entail both complete flexibility and the
absence of judicial review. The use of "entrenched clauses" and
"basic laws" in New Zealand and Israel are only apparent exceptions because the entrenchment can be removed or superseded
relatively easily.[1] In contrast, written constitutions may be both
completely flexible and completely unprotected by judicial review, but in practice this combination is rare; in our set of thirty-
three democracies with written constitutions, France between
1958 and approximately 1974 is the only example.

FLEXIBLE AND RIGID CONSTITUTIONS

Democracies use a bewildering array of devices to give their
constitutions different degrees of rigidity: special legislative ma-

1. In the important *Bergman* case in 1969, the Israeli Supreme Court
for the first time declared an act of the Knesset (parliament) void for vio-
lating a basic law; however, this basic law provided for its own amendment by an absolute majority of all members of the Knesset, enabling the
Knesset to pass a modified version of the invalidated law with the required
absolute majority, but not a supermajority. Presumably the Knesset could
also first have amended the absolute-majority requirement of the basic
law (by an absolute majority) and then re-passed the invalidated act in
its original form (and even without an absolute majority).

jorities, approval by both houses of bicameral legislatures (even when these are asymmetrical as far as ordinary legislation is concerned), approval by ordinary or special majorities of state or provincial legislatures, approval by referendum, and approval by special majorities in a referendum. Further complications are that some constitutions stipulate different methods of amendment for different provisions in the constitution or alternative methods that may be used for amending any part of the constitution (Maddex 2008). Nevertheless, this great variety of constitutional provisions can be reduced to four basic types, as shown in Table 12.1. These four types are based, first, on the distinction between approval by ordinary majorities—indicating complete flexibility—and by larger than ordinary majorities. Next, three categories of rigidity can be distinguished: (1) approval by two-thirds majorities—a very common rule, based on the idea that supporters of a constitutional change have to outnumber their opponents by a ratio of at least two to one; (2) approval by *less* than a two-thirds majority (but more than an ordinary majority)—for instance, a three-fifths parliamentary majority or an ordinary majority plus a referendum; and (3) approval by *more* than a two-thirds majority, such as a three-fourths majority or a two-thirds majority plus approval by state legislatures.

The only major adjustment that needs to be made concerns the classification of special majorities—also called extraordinary majorities or supermajorities—when these are special parliamentary majorities in parliaments elected by plurality. In such legislatures, large majorities often represent much smaller popular majorities and sometimes merely a popular plurality; moreover, these large majorities are often single-party majorities. For instance, shortly after the assassination of Indira Gandhi, India's prime minister and leader of the Congress party, her party won a huge majority of 76.5 percent of the seats in the 1984 election—many more than the two-thirds majority needed for amending the constitution—with a mere 48.1 percent of the popular vote. Two-thirds majorities are also required for amending the consti-

TABLE 12.1

Majorities or supermajorities required for constitutional amendment in thirty-six democracies, 1945–2010

Supermajorities greater than two-thirds [4.0]

Argentina	Korea	Germany [3.5]
Australia	Switzerland	
Canada	United States	
Japan		

Two-thirds majorities or equivalent [3.0]

Austria	Malta
Bahamas	Mauritius
Belgium	Netherlands
Costa Rica	Norway
Finland	Portugal
India	Spain
Jamaica	Trinidad
Luxembourg	

Between two-thirds and ordinary majorities [2.0]

Barbados	Greece	France [1.7]
Botswana	Ireland	Sweden [1.5]
Denmark	Italy	(France after 1974)
		(Sweden after 1980)

Ordinary majorities [1.0]

Iceland	United Kingdom	(France before 1974)
Israel	Uruguay	(Sweden before 1980)
New Zealand		

Note: The indexes of constitutional rigidity are in square brackets tution of Barbados, but in five of the ten elections since 1966 such large one-party majorities were manufactured from between 50 and 60 percent of the popular votes, and in one from a 48.8 percent plurality.

Supermajorities in plurality systems are clearly much less constraining than the same supermajorities in PR systems; to take this difference into account, plurality systems are classified in Table 12.1 in the category below the one to which they technically belong. The need for this adjustment appears to be recognized by plurality countries themselves: the only countries that require three-fourths parliamentary majorities for constitutional amendment are the Bahamas, Jamaica, Mauritius, and Trinidad—all plurality countries. These four democracies are classified in the second category of Table 12.1 as the substantive equivalents of countries with two-thirds majority rules. For the same reason, Barbados and Botswana are placed in the third category even though their formal requirements for constitutional amendment are two-thirds majorities.

The problem of different rules for constitutional amendment in the same constitution can be solved relatively easily. First, when alternative methods can be used, the least restraining method should be counted. For instance, the Italian constitution can be amended either by two-thirds majorities in the two chambers or by absolute majorities—that is, majorities of all members of the two chambers, but no supermajorities—followed by a referendum. The latter method is more flexible in terms of the criteria of Table 12.1, and Italy is therefore classified in the third instead of the second category. Second, when different rules apply to different parts of constitutions, the rule pertaining to amendments of the most basic articles of the constitution should be counted. For instance, some provisions of India's lengthy constitution can be changed by regular majorities in both houses, others by absolute majorities of all members of the two houses, and yet others only by two-thirds majorities plus approval by the legislatures of half of the states. The last group contains key provisions like the division of the power between the central and state governments, and it is the rule for amending these that is decisive for the classification of India in the second category of Table 12.1: the two-thirds majorities in a plurality system would only be good for a place in the third category, but the additional requirement of approval by half of the states puts India back in the second.

Rules for constitutional amendments tend to be quite stable, and any changes that do occur tend not to be far-reaching. Only two such changes are indicated in Table 12.1. The change in Sweden merely entailed the addition of a referendum requirement. The last article of the French constitution stipulates that amendments require either majority approval by the two legislative chambers followed by a referendum or a three-fifths majority in a joint session of the legislature; both methods qualify for the third category of Table 12.1. In addition, President Charles de Gaulle's decision in 1962 to circumvent parliament and to submit a proposed amendment directly to a referendum, overwhelmingly approved by the voters, established a purely majoritarian third procedure for constitutional amendment. However, by about 1974, when the first non-Gaullist president was elected, this extraconstitutional method was no longer regarded as a viable option.

Most countries fit the two middle categories of Table 12.1: they require more than ordinary majorities for constitutional amendment but not more than two-thirds majorities or their equivalent. The mean index of constitutional rigidity is 2.7 and the median is 3.0 points. Seven countries have or had more flexible constitutions: the three democracies with unwritten constitutions, but also four with written constitutions: France and Sweden (before 1974 and 1980, respectively), Iceland, and Uruguay. The most flexible is Uruguay's constitution: one of the alternative procedures is for two-fifths of all members of the legislature—that is, fewer than a majority—to propose an amendment to be submitted to the voters, who can approve it as long as (1) the "yes" votes exceed the "no" votes and any abstentions and (2) the "yes" voters represent at least 35 percent of all registered voters—again, less than a requirement of a full majority (Maddex 2008, 485).

Seven countries receive the highest value on the index of constitutional rigidity. The United States is the least flexible because amendments require two-thirds majorities in both the Senate and the House of Representatives as well as approval by three-fourths of the states. The Argentine constitution requires the same two-thirds majorities plus approval by a special constitutional convention. In Canada, several key provisions can only be amended with the approval of every province. In Australia and Switzerland, amendments require the approval in a popular referendum of not just majorities of the voters but also majorities in a majority of the states or cantons; this enables the smallest of the states and cantons with less than 20 percent of the population to block constitutional changes. The Japanese constitution requires two-thirds majorities in both houses of parliament as well as a referendum. Korea has the same rule except that it has a unicameral legislature. A good case can be made for including the German constitution in the same category because two-thirds majorities are required in both chambers and because the Bundesrat's composition differs from that of the Bundestag in several important respects; however, Table 12.1 places it more conservatively between the top two categories. All of these rigid constitutions are also difficult to amend in practice: the Japanese constitution has never been amended in the more than sixty years of its existence, and Korea's more recent 1987 constitution has never been amended either.[2]

2. The index of constitutional rigidity in Table 12.1 compares well with Siaroff's (2009, 218) similar three-point index—the correlation coefficient is 0.80—but less well with Donald S. Lutz's (2006, 170) "index of difficulty," that is, the difficulty of adopting constitutional amendments, and with Astrid Lorenz's (2005, 358–59) rigidity index—the correlation coefficients are only 0.46 and 0.59, respectively. The index of judicial review in Table 12.2 is also closely correlated with Siaroff's similar index, which is again on a three-point scale: the coefficient is 0.78. The three strongest correlations are statistically significant at the 1 percent level, and the correlation with Lutz's is significant at the 5 percent level.

JUDICIAL REVIEW

One can argue that a written and rigid constitution is still not a sufficient restraint on parliamentary majorities, unless there is an independent body that decides whether laws are in conformity with the constitution. If parliament itself is the judge of the constitutionality of its own laws, it can easily be tempted to resolve any doubts in its favor. The remedy that is usually advocated is to give the courts or a special judicial tribunal the power of judicial review—that is, the power to test the constitutionality of laws passed by the national legislature.

In the famous *Marbury v. Madison* decision (1803), which established judicial review in the United States, Chief Justice John Marshall argued that the presence of a written constitution and an independent judiciary logically implied the Supreme Court's power of judicial review: the court, faced with an incompatibility between the Constitution and an ordinary law, had no choice but to apply the higher law and therefore to invalidate the law with a lower status. The logic of this reasoning is incontrovertible: even if the constitution does not explicitly prescribe judicial review, it is implied by the higher status of the constitution. Many constitutions, however, do specifically grant this power to the courts. For instance, the Greek constitution states that "the courts shall be bound not to apply laws, the contents of which are contrary to the Constitution" (Brewer-Carías 1989, 169). Article 2 of the Trinidad constitution asserts: "This Constitution is the supreme law of Trinidad and Tobago, and any other law that is inconsistent with this Constitution is void to the extent of the inconsistency." Very similar language is used in the constitutions of the three other Caribbean countries.[3]

3. These constitutions, as well as the constitution of Mauritius, also stipulate that the highest court for the purpose of judicial review is the Judicial Committee of the Privy Council in London. Partly because of dissatisfaction among Caribbean countries with the liberal rulings of the Judicial Committee in death-penalty cases, they established the Caribbean Court of Justice, based in Port of Spain (Trinidad) as an alternative in 2001. Barbados joined the new court in 2005 together with Guyana; Belize joined in 2010.

Several constitutions explicitly deny the power of judicial review to their courts. Article 120 of the Dutch constitution, for instance, states: "The constitutionality of acts of parliament and treaties shall not be reviewed by the courts." A noteworthy attempt to exclude part of a written constitution from judicial review can be found in the proposed balanced budget amendment to the US Constitution, twice defeated by the Senate in 1995 and 1997, which contained the following clause: "The judicial power of the United States shall not extend to any case or controversy arising under this [amendment] except as may be specifically authorized by legislation" (*New York Times,* March 1, 1995, A16). Not only in countries without written constitutions but also in those that do have written constitutions but do not have judicial review, parliaments are the ultimate guarantors of the constitution. The logic on which this alternative is based is that of democratic principle: such vital decisions as the conformity of law to the constitution should be made by the elected representatives of the people rather than by an appointed and frequently quite unrepresentative judicial body.

Mainly as a compromise between these two contradictory logics, several countries entrust judicial review to special constitutional courts instead of to the regular court systems. The ordinary courts may submit questions of constitutionality to the special constitutional court, but they may not decide such questions themselves. This type is called the centralized system of judicial review. It was proposed by the famous Austrian jurist Hans Kelsen and first adopted by Austria in 1920. It is now also used in Belgium, Costa Rica, Germany, Italy, Korea, Portugal, and Spain. The alternative, decentralized judicial review, in which all courts may consider the constitutionality of laws, is still the more common system.

France was long considered the prime example of a country in which the principle of popular sovereignty was said to prevent any application of judicial review. The constitution of the Fifth Republic did set up a constitutional council, but at first this body served mainly to protect executive power against legislative encroachment; only the president, the prime minister, and the presidents of the two chambers were permitted to submit questions of constitutionality to the council. However, a constitutional amendment passed in 1974 also gave relatively small minorities in the legislature—sixty members of either chamber—the right to appeal to the constitutional council, and the council itself has strongly asserted its power of judicial review (Stone 1992). Although the courts still cannot turn to the constitutional council, parliament is no longer the ultimate interpreter of the constitutionality of its own laws; hence France must now also be counted among the countries with judicial review of the centralized kind.

JUDICIAL REVIEW AND JUDICIAL ACTIVISM

The impact of judicial review depends only partly on its formal existence and much more vitally on the vigor and frequency of its use by the courts, especially supreme and constitutional courts. Table 12.2 presents a fourfold classification of the strength of judicial review based, first, on the distinction between the presence and absence of judicial review, and, second, on three degrees of activism in the assertion of this power by the courts. There are only six countries where judicial review is very strong: the United States, Germany, India, and, in recent years, Canada, Costa Rica, and Argentina. The activist American courts and the Supreme Court in particular have been accused of forming an "imperial judiciary" (Franck 1996), but the German Constitutional Court has been at least as activist: "Next to the U.S. Supreme Court, the German [Constitutional Court] is widely considered to be one of the most powerful and influential constitutional courts in the world. It almost certainly ranks as the most important high court in Europe" (Vanberg 2005, 17). India's courts were not very assertive before the return to democracy in 1977, but Carl Baar (1992) argues that from 1977 on they have become "the world's most active judiciary." The Indian Supreme Court has gone so far as to declare that its power of judicial review is "an inseparable

TABLE 12.2

The strength of judicial review in thirty-six democracies, 1945–2010

Strong judicial review [4.0]

Germany*	United States	Canada [3.4]
India		(Argentina after 2003)
		(Canada after 1982)
		(Costa Rica after 1989*)

Medium-strength judicial review [3.0]

Australia	Mauritius	Argentina [2.7]
Austria*	Spain*	Costa Rica [2.7]
Korea*		(Argentina before 1989)
		(Belgium after 1984*)
		(Canada before 1982)
		(France after 1974*)
		(Italy after 1996*)

Weak judicial review [2.0]

Bahamas	Jamaica	Belgium [1.8]
Barbados	Japan	France [2.4]
Botswana	Malta	Italy [2.1]
Denmark	Norway	Uruguay [2.5]
Greece	Portugal*	(Argentina 1989–2003)
Iceland	Trinidad	(Costa Rica before 1989)
Ireland		(Italy 1956–96*)

No judicial review [1.0]

Finland	New Zealand	(Belgium before 1984)
Israel	Sweden	(France before 1974)
Luxembourg	Switzerland	(Italy before 1956)
Netherlands	United Kingdom	

*Centralized judicial review by special constitutional courts

Note: The indexes of judicial review are in square brackets

part of the Constitution" that can never be taken away—not "even by a constitutional amendment" (Jain 2000, 15).

In Canada, the adoption of the Charter of Rights and Freedoms in 1982 began "an era of judicial activism" (Baar 1991, 53); it moved Canada from medium-strength to strong judicial review. A bigger change occurred in Costa Rica; Bruce M. Wilson (2009, 70, 73) calls it "a significant shift from judicial passivity to judicial activism," especially with regard to civil rights. Before 1989, the Supreme Court did have the right of judicial review but could only invalidate laws with a two-thirds majority—and in practice rarely exercised this power. The new constitutional chamber of the Supreme Court, created in 1989, was given an explicit mandate to be the guardian of the constitution, and "within months of its creation, [the constitutional chamber] made it clear that it would no longer be blindly deferential to the popular branches of government." The former two-thirds rule was also abandoned, and the chamber can now declare laws unconstitutional by a simple majority. In Argentina, during the much shorter period since redemocratization in 1984, even bigger changes have occurred. Under President Raúl Alfonsín, the Supreme Court became gradually more independent and activist, but this trend was reversed with the election of Carlos Menem, who forced the court into subservience during his two terms of office. After Menem's departure, the court came to life again as a highly independent constitutional arbiter (Carnota 2010, Tuozzo 2009). Gretchen Helmke (2005, 162) concludes that after its years of abject deference to the government, the court's stance was "profoundly reversed."

Medium-strength judicial review characterizes five countries during their entire periods under consideration: Australia, Austria, Korea, Mauritius, and Spain. The activism of the Korean Constitutional Court is especially noteworthy because, although it was modeled closely on its German counterpart, it was not expected to play an important role. However, the court "served notice with its very first decision that it would be willing to strike legislation and government action that it found to interfere with the Constitution" (Lim 2004, 19). The formal requirement of a two-thirds majority to declare laws unconstitutional has not proved a significant limitation. Dae-Kyu Yoon (2010, 145) gives the court great credit for its "contribution to the stabilization and consolidation of [Korea's] newly established democracy." Five other countries fit the medium-strength category during parts of their democratic history covered in this book. The Argentine, Canadian, and Costa Rican cases were discussed above, and the shift to activist judicial review in Belgium was treated in Chapter 3. The fifth country is Italy, which developed toward medium-strength judicial review in two steps. There was essentially no judicial review until 1956, when the constitutional court provided for in the postwar constitution was finally established. The new court proved to be activist with regard to fascist-era laws but avoided intervening in other political matters, following a "policy of rigorous self-restraint and almost subservient deference to parliament" (Volcansek 1994, 507). In tandem with other major changes in Italian politics in the 1990s—such as the far-reaching electoral reform, discussed in Chapter 8—the court has abandoned much of its former restraint and has "stepped more boldly into the spotlight" (Volcansek 2000, 157).

Among the countries with weak judicial review, the Scandinavian countries are regarded as the weakest. Their courts can invalidate laws but have been extremely reluctant to do so. The Swedish constitution formally limits judicial review to cases where the unconstitutionality of a law is "manifest," and M. Steven Fish and Matthew Kroenig (2009, 633) argue that in practice "the legislature's laws are supreme and not subject to judicial review." I have therefore placed Sweden in the bottom category of Table 12.2 but kept Denmark and Norway in the higher category. A few of the others—like Portugal and, after 1982, Malta (Agius and Grosselfinger 1995)—can be rated as slightly stronger, but the differences are not great. An exception is Uruguay, which can be placed between the weak and medium-strength categories. Its courts are widely regarded as among the most independent and impartial in Latin America (Brinks 2008, 196), but they have only a modest record with regard to exercising judicial review.

The general pattern shown in Table 12.2 is one of relatively weak judicial review. The mean score is 2.2 and the median 2.0 points, well below the midpoint of 2.5 on the four-point scale. However, there appears to be a trend toward more and stronger judicial review: the six countries that are classified in different categories in the table during different periods all moved from lower to higher degrees of strength of judicial review. Moreover, the five countries with written constitutions but still no judicial review are older European democracies; the newer democracies, without exception, do have judicial review. Finally, like the United Kingdom (see Chapter 2), these five older European democracies have accepted the supranational judicial review of the European Court of Justice and/or the European Court of Human Rights. These trends confirm, to cite the title of C. Neal Tate and Torbjörn Vallinder's (1995) book, "the global expansion of judicial power."

Table 12.2 also shows that countries with centralized judicial review tend to have stronger judicial review than countries with decentralized systems: eight of the nine centralized systems are in the top two categories as of 1996 (when Italy's constitutional court became more activist). This is a rather surprising conclusion because centralized review was originally developed as a compromise between not having judicial review at all and the decentralized type of it. The explanation must be that, if a special body is created for the express and exclusive purpose of reviewing the constitutionality of legislation, it is very likely to carry out this task with some vigor.

CONSTITUTIONAL RIGIDITY AND JUDICIAL REVIEW

There are two reasons to expect that the variables of constitutional rigidity versus flexibility and the strength of judicial review will be correlated. One is that both rigidity and judicial review are antimajoritarian devices and that completely flexible constitutions and the absence of judicial review permit unrestricted majority rule. Second, they are also logically linked in that judicial review can work effectively only if it is backed up by constitutional rigidity and vice versa. If there is strong judicial review but the constitution is flexible, the majority in the legislature can easily respond to a declaration of unconstitutionality by amending the constitution. Similarly, if the constitution is rigid but not protected by judicial review, the parliamentary majority can interpret any constitutionally questionable law it wants to pass as simply not being in violation of the constitution.

Figure 12.1 shows the empirical relationship between the two variables for the thirty-six democracies. The correlation coefficient is 0.46—not exceptionally strong but still statistically significant at the 1 percent level. One prominent outlier is Switzerland, where, as emphasized in Chapter 3, the absence of judicial review is the only majoritarian characteristic in an otherwise solidly consensual democracy. The other main deviant cases are Finland, the Netherlands, and Luxembourg—countries with two-thirds majority rules for constitutional amendment but no judicial review—and India and Germany—where very strong judicial review is combined with rigid but not maximally rigid constitutions. Both judicial review and rigid constitutions are linked with federalism as well as with the other two variables of the federal-unitary dimension: bicameralism and independent central banks. Central banks are the subject of the next chapter, and the links among all five federal-unitary variables are discussed in Chapter 14.

FIRST ADDENDUM: REFERENDUMS AND CONSENSUS DEMOCRACY

A striking feature of the amendment procedures specified by written constitutions is their frequent use of the referendum either as an absolute requirement or as an optional alternative: in fourteen of the thirty-three written constitutions (as of 2010). If majority approval in a referendum is the only procedure required

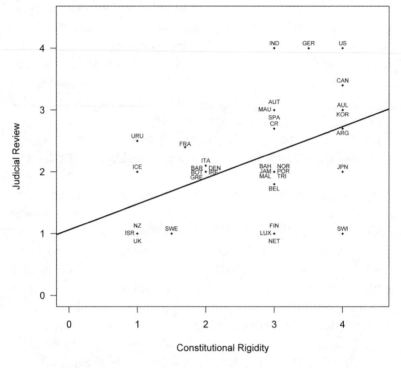

FIG. 12.1 The relationship between constitutional rigidity and judicial review in thirty-six democracies, 1945–2010

for constitutional amendment, the referendum serves as a majoritarian device; however, the only example of this kind of referendum in our set of democracies was President de Gaulle's extraconstitutional use of it in France. Arguably, one of the alternative methods for constitutional amendment in Uruguay—approval by referendum of a proposal initiated by a legislative minority instead of a majority—should also be seen as majoritarian. In all of the other cases, the referendum is prescribed in addition to legislative approval by ordinary or extraordinary majorities, making amendments harder to adopt and constitutions more rigid—and hence serving as an antimajoritarian device (Gallagher 1995).

This function of the referendum conflicts with the conventional view that the referendum is the most extreme majoritarian method of decision-making, that is, even more majoritarian than representative majoritarian democracy, since elected legislatures offer at least some opportunities for minorities to present their case in unhurried discussion and to engage in bargaining and log-rolling. In their classic study of referendums, David Butler and Austin Ranney (1978, 36) state: "Because they cannot measure intensities of beliefs or work things out through discussion and discovery, referendums are bound to be more dangerous than representative assemblies to minority rights." Although Butler and Ranney's argument has considerable force in most situations, it clearly requires modification. Its use in the process of consti-tutional amendment, as a requirement in addition to legislative approval, is more antimajoritarian than majoritarian: in particu-lar, it offers dissatisfied minorities the opportunity to launch a campaign against the proposed amendment.

There is an additional important way in which referendums differ from the blunt majoritarian character that the conventional wisdom attributes to them. In fact, this happens when they as-sume their strongest form: in combination with the popular ini-tiative. Switzerland and Uruguay are the prime examples. In these countries, the referendum and initiative give even very small mi-norities a chance to challenge any laws passed by the majority of the elected representatives. Even if this effort does not succeed, it forces the majority to pay the cost of a referendum campaign. Hence the potential calling of a referendum by a minority is a strong stimulus for the majority to be heedful of minority views. Franz Lehner (1984, 30) convincingly argues that in Switzerland "any coalition with a predictable and safe chance of winning has to include all parties and organizations that may be capable of calling for a successful referendum." The referendum-plus-initiative has thus reinforced two Swiss traditions: the broad four-party coalitions in the executive Federal Council and the search for legislative majorities on particular bills that are as close to una-nimity as possible.

Uruguay's similar system, inspired by the Swiss example, has had the same result.[4] David Altman (2011, 330) conducted interviews with almost all of the members of the House of Representatives and found that more than 70 percent of them answered in the affirmative to the question: "Is the presence of a potential referendum a sufficient reason to look for a broader consensus among political parties?" Italy is the third country where this option is available but where it has not had the same effect as in Switzerland and Uruguay. The main reason is that for a referendum to be successful not only majority approval but also a minimum turnout of 50 percent are required. The second requirement has made it much easier for referendums to be defeated by counseling nonvoting instead of casting a "no" vote, and many referendums have failed because of the turnout rule (Altman 2011, 21–25; Uleri 2002).

Both the logic of the referendum-plus-initiative and the examples of how it has worked in Switzerland and Uruguay support the conclusion that it can be seen as a strong consensus-inducing mechanism and the very opposite of a blunt majoritarian instrument. Other types of referendums clearly do have a majoritarian character, of course (Vatter 2000, 2009). Because of these differences, the relative frequency of the use of referendums in different countries does not correlate well with either the executives-parties or the federal-unitary dimension—and should probably be seen as a separate third dimension.[5] It is also important to

4. Uruguay has been called the Switzerland of Latin America, partly because of its small size and democratic stability (although interrupted by a military dictatorship from 1973 to 1985) and also partly because it has been "tremendously influenced by Swiss political institutions" (Altman 2008, 483). Uruguay's mechanisms of direct democracy were borrowed from Switzerland, and its nine-member collegial presidency, which replaced the usual one-person executive in its otherwise purely presidential system during the 1952–67 period, was patterned after the Swiss seven-member Federal Council (Lijphart 1977, 212–16).

5. Adrian Vatter (2009) and Vatter in collaboration with Julian Bernauer (2009) have constructed a scale that takes these differences into

note that, while the use of referendums is increasingly popular, they are still a relatively rare occurrence except among a handful of countries.

SECOND ADDENDUM: A LOOK INSIDE POWERFUL SUPREME AND CONSTITUTIONAL COURTS

In this book I focus on the ten most important institutional differences among democracies. Some of the institutions can be explored in greater detail by examining their internal organization and operation. I do so in the Addendum to Chapter 6, where I look inside cabinets in order to discover the degree of majoritarianism or consensus in the relations between prime ministers and presidents on one hand and their cabinet members on the other. In Chapter 11, I analyze legislatures in terms of the bicameralism-unicameralism contrast, but they can be similarly "unpacked"— something that I do not do in this book—by looking at their committee organization, which can vary from majoritarian to consensual patterns: Are all of the committee chairs members of the majority party or majority coalition, or are the chair appointments proportionally distributed among all of the parties in the legislature?

Another opportunity for this kind of "unpacking" has to do with supreme and constitutional courts. In this chapter I have focused on whether they have the right of judicial review and their degree of activism in using this right. Additional characteristics that affect the majoritarian or consensual nature of these courts are the sizes of the courts, the methods of electing justices,

---

account—from citizen-initiated referendums on the consensus end to government-initiated referendums on the majoritarian end—but they, too, find that referendums form a separate third dimension. Rather surprisingly, their factor analysis reveals that the type of cabinet (which is part of the first dimension in this book) also belongs to the third dimension. Switzerland is a good example of a democracy where citizen-initiated referendums and oversized coalition cabinets occur together. Uruguay (not included in the Vatter-Bernauer studies), with its mainly one-party, minimal winning cabinets (see Table 6.3), clearly does not fit this pattern.

their terms of office, and the courts' internal decision rules.[6] Let us look at the most powerful high courts—those of the United States, Germany, and India—in terms of these variables. The American Supreme Court is highly majoritarian in all respects, while the German Constitutional Court and the Indian Supreme Court are examples of more consensual high courts. First, the Supreme Court of the United States has an unusually small membership of only nine justices, compared with sixteen in Germany (divided into two "senates") and twenty-nine in India. Obviously, larger court memberships offer better opportunities for broad representation of different parties and population groups. Second, election can be by majority vote, which is roughly the American pattern, or by supermajorities, like the two-thirds legislative majorities required in each of the German legislative chambers. Third, new justices can be chosen as vacancies occur, as in the United States—which means that majorities can keep electing their own favorites sequentially; or they can be elected simultaneously or in groups—which makes it more likely that members of minorities will be chosen. Fourth, terms of office can be longer or shorter, and long terms are an obstacle to broad representation. The American Supreme Court is at one extreme of this spectrum: no fixed terms and no mandatory retirement. In Germany, justices have twelve-year nonrenewable terms, and they have to retire at age sixty-eight; the mandatory retirement age in India is sixty-five. Finally, court decisions can be by regular or by extraordinary majorities. As emphasized earlier in this chapter, supermajority requirements make it harder to invalidate laws and thus reduce the courts' powers, but within the courts supermajorities make for more consensual decision-making. In the United States, a majority of five out of nine suffices, whereas in each of the German "senates," an absolute majority of five or, in some cases, a three-fourths majority of six votes out of eight are required.

What is especially worth noting here is that the US Supreme

6. I am indebted to Isaac Herzog for suggesting these differences among high courts.

Court presents a paradox: it clearly fits the consensus model as far as its strong exercise of judicial review is concerned, but it is highly majoritarian with regard to all five aspects of its selection, composition, and decision rules. The American presidency—and, in fact, all presidential systems—present a similar paradox: separation of powers fits the divided-power character of the second dimension of consensus democracy, but the concentration of executive power in the hands of one person is the very opposite majoritarian characteristic.

CHAPTER 13

CENTRAL BANKS: INDEPENDENCE VERSUS DEPENDENCE

T he fifth and last variable in the federal-unitary dimension concerns central banks and how much independence and power they enjoy. Central banks are key governmental institutions that, compared with the other main organs of government, tend to be neglected in political science. In single-country and comparative descriptions of democratic political systems, political scientists invariably cover the executive, the legislature, political parties, and elections, and often also interest groups, the court system, the constitutional amendment process, and central-noncentral government relations—but hardly ever the operation and power of the central bank.

When central banks are strong and independent, they play a critical role in the policy process. For instance, Robert B. Reich (1997, 80), secretary of labor in the first Clinton administration, described not President Clinton but Alan Greenspan, chairman of the Federal Reserve Board, as "the most powerful man in the world." Conversely, when central banks are dependent branches of the executive and hence relatively weak, this weakness is also a highly relevant attribute of the democratic system—just as the weakness of a legislature or the reluctance of a supreme court to use judicial review is a significant indicator of the kind of democracy to which these institutions belong. Giving central banks independent power is yet another way of dividing power and fits the cluster of divided-power characteristics (the second dimension) of the consensus model of democracy; central banks that are subservient to the executive fit the concentrated-power logic of majoritarian democracy.

Fortunately, economists have paid a great deal of attention to central banks and have developed precise measures of central bank autonomy that can be used for the purpose of this study. The best-known and most widely used measure is the Cukierman index: his "method yields the most nuanced and detailed index" of legal central bank independence (Sadeh 2006, 66). Alex Cukierman, Steven B. Webb, and Bilin Neyapti (1994) present the values on this index for seventy-two industrialized and developing countries, including thirty-three of our thirty-six democracies, for the long period from 1950 to 1989. Simone Polillo and Mauro F. Guillén (2005) have extended the Cukierman-Webb-Neyapti analysis to the 1990s, and Christopher Crowe and Ellen E. Meade (2007) extend it further to 2003. In addition, Cukierman, Webb, and Neyapti have proposed an alternative indicator, based on the turnover rate of the central bank governor, which is useful when the index of legal central bank independence is not available or to adjust the basic Cukierman index for countries that have unusually frequent turnovers. Finally, Vittorio Grilli, Donato Masciandaro, and Guido Tabellini (1991) have independently developed an index of the political and economic autonomy of central banks in eighteen countries for the pre-1990 period. These five measures are combined into a comprehensive measure of central bank independence of our thirty-six democracies—a much more precise measure of this fifth variable than the four-point and five-point scales used for the measurement of the other federal-unitary variables.

A cautionary note is in order concerning the discussion in the remainder of this chapter. Major changes in the position of central banks have taken place since the mid-1990s, especially the creation of the European Central Bank, which has become the central bank for seventeen countries in the so-called eurozone, including thirteen of our democracies. These countries have "outsourced" most of the functions of their own national central banks to an institution in the international system. Moreover, several other countries have changed the functions and powers of their central banks as a result of international pressures. These developments have important consequences for our analysis of central banks and their degrees of independence: from the mid-1990s on, they can no longer be treated as domestic institutions, and it makes little sense to expect the continuation of similarities between their characteristics and the characteristics of other domestic institutions like legislatures and supreme courts. There are two possible solutions: we can either remove central banks entirely from our analysis and focus exclusively on the other four variables in the federal-unitary dimension, or we can still include them but only up to the middle of the 1990s. I shall discuss this dilemma in more detail later in this chapter.

THE DUTIES AND POWERS OF CENTRAL BANKS

The most important task of central banks is the making of monetary policy—that is, the regulation of interest rates and the supply of money. Monetary policy has a direct effect on price stability and the control of inflation, and it indirectly, but also very strongly, affects levels of unemployment, economic growth, and fluctuations in the business cycle. Other duties that central banks frequently perform are managing the government's financial transactions; financing the government's budget deficits by buying government securities, making loans from their reserves, or printing money; financing development projects; regulating and supervising commercial banks; and, if necessary, bailing out insolvent banks and publicly owned enterprises. These other tasks may conflict with the task of controlling inflation, and the power of central banks over monetary policy can therefore be enhanced by not giving them these additional duties: "Although most governments recognize the long-term benefit of price stability, other goals often loom larger in the short run . . . Assuring price stability, therefore, usually requires ensuring that the central bank is not forced to perform these [other] functions, at least not when they would cause inflation" (Cukierman, Webb, and Neyapti 1994, 2).

Central banks and their role in monetary policy have become especially critical since 1971 when President Nixon devaluated the US dollar—breaking the fixed link of the dollar to gold and of nondollar currencies to the dollar, fashioned in the Bretton Woods agreement of 1944. In the much more uncertain situation of floating exchange rates, central bank independence became an even more important tool to limit price instability.

MEASURING THE INDEPENDENCE OF CENTRAL BANKS

The powers and functions of central banks are usually defined by bank charters that are statute laws and not by means of constitutional provisions; nevertheless, these charters have tended to harden into "conventions with quasi-constitutional force" (Elster 1994, 68). Cukierman, Webb, and Neyapti (1994, 5–12) analyze sixteen variables concerning the legal independence of central banks, each coded from zero to one—the lowest to the highest level of independence. Their overall index of legal independence is a weighted average of these sixteen ratings. There are four clusters of variables: the appointment and tenure of the bank's governor (chief executive officer), policy formulation, central bank objectives, and limitations on lending.

To give a few examples, the highest (most independent) ratings are given to a governor whose term of office is eight years or longer, who cannot be dismissed, and who may not simultaneously hold other offices in government. The lowest (least independent) ratings are given to governors who are appointed for fewer than four years, who can be dismissed at the discretion of the executive, and who are not barred from holding another government appointment. As far as policy formulation is concerned, the highest ratings go to banks that have exclusive responsibility to formulate monetary policy and play an active role in the government's budgetary process; central banks that have no influence on monetary and budgetary policy are given the lowest ratings.

With regard to objectives, the highest rating is accorded when "price stability is the major or only objective in the charter, and the central bank has the final word in case of conflict with other government objectives." Medium ratings are given when "price stability is one goal [together] with other compatible objectives, such as a stable banking system," and, slightly lower, "when price stability is one goal, with potentially conflicting objectives, such as full employment." The lowest rating is given when the goals stated in the charter do not include price stability. Finally, central banks are rated as independent when they are allowed to lend only to the central government and when they fully control the terms of lending; conversely, they are the least independent when they can lend to all levels of government, to public enterprises, and to the private sector and when the terms of lending are decided by the executive branch of government.

Cukierman, Webb, and Neyapti rate central banks in each of the four decades from the 1950s to the 1980s. In order to take advantage of additional expert judgments, I also use the index of political and economic independence of central banks designed by Grilli, Masciandaro, and Tabellini (1991, 366–71) and applied by them to the central banks of eighteen industrialized countries in roughly the same period. Although these three economists use the term "political and economic independence," they emphasize formal rules, and hence their index is, in principle, quite similar to the Cukierman-Webb-Neyapti index. They differ, however, with regard to several of the specific variables on which they focus and the weighting of these variables. For the eighteen countries that they rate, the index values can be converted to the Cukierman index and then averaged with the values of the latter index. Both indexes can also be assumed to cover the late

1940s for the older democracies. In the decades before 1990, legal central bank independence was remarkably stable in most countries.

For the 1990s, in which major changes occurred, we have precise figures provided in Polillo and Guillén's (2005) study: indexes for each year in the decade. Similar yearly indexes are not available for the first decade of the twenty-first century, but the indexes for 2000 in the Polillo-Guillén study and for 2003 in the analysis by Crowe and Meade (2007) can be assumed to be roughly representative for the whole decade. These two studies both use the Cukierman index, but it is worth noting that they treat the central bank independence of countries in the eurozone slightly differently. Crowe and Meade give each eurozone country the same high 0.83 score on the basis of the indeed very high degree of independence of the European Central Bank. Polillo and Guillén's numbers are also high for all of the eurozone countries but not identical. Most are in the even higher 0.88 to 0.92 range but, for instance, Finland and France have lower—although obviously still very high—scores of 0.75 and 0.78. There are two reasons for these differences. First, each country has retained its own central bank, which may perform other functions like the supervision of the local banks of deposit. Second, and more important, the head of each national bank is a member of the governing council—the most important decision-making body—of the European Central Bank. Therefore, questions such as who appoints the heads of each of the banks and whether they are free from political interference still matter to some extent.

Cukierman, Webb, and Neyapti (1994, 13–19) propose a second index based on a simple variable—the rate of turnover in the governorship of the central bank—which they found to be a better indicator of central bank independence and a better predictor of inflation rates for the less developed countries in the 1980s than their more complex legal measure: the greater the turnover rate of the central bank governor, the less the independence of the central bank and vice versa. This measure can be used for the three countries for which the principal Cukierman index is not available: Jamaica had the highest, Mauritius the lowest, and Trinidad an intermediate turnover rate. It should also be used to adjust the legal Cukierman indexes for those developing countries that have experienced high rates of turnover. Frequent turnovers are not typical of all of the less developed countries; for instance, Barbados and the Bahamas had only two turnovers in the more than twenty years prior to 1994. But Argentina had ten turnovers in the eleven years from 1984 to 1994, and Uruguay a more modest, but still relatively high, three turnovers from 1985 to 1994.[1]

CENTRAL BANKS: DOMESTIC OR INTERNATIONAL INSTITUTIONS?

The establishment of the European Central Bank in 1998 and the adoption of the euro as a common currency by the original eurozone members in 1999 transformed the central bank for the countries involved from a domestic institution to an element of the international system. Hence, it also cut the links that had existed between their national central banks and other domestic institutions. This change had been under way for several years before 1998: the 1992 Maastricht Treaty had already required a high degree of central bank independence as a condition for participating in the euro. The annual Cukierman indexes in Polillo and Guillén's (2005) study provide some good examples: the in-

---

1. The second Cukierman index, based on the turnover rates of central bank governors, can be converted to the same zero to one scale used for the legal Cukierman index. I converted a high turnover rate (more than 0.2 turnovers per year) to a 0.30 score on the Cukierman index and a low rate (less than 0.1 per year) to a 0.40 score. From the legal Cukierman scores of developing countries with very high turnover rates, I subtracted 0.10 points, and from those with medium turnover rates 0.05 points. For instance, Argentina's 0.49 score in 1984–94 was lowered to 0.39, and Uruguay's score in 1985–94 was reduced from an already low 0.24 to 0.19.

dependence of the Spanish central bank jumped from 0.23 to 0.86 in 1994; one year earlier, the French central bank increased its independence from 0.24 to 0.78; and in the same year, Italy's Cukierman index was boosted from 0.25 to 0.75. It is worth noting that all these high indexes exceed the indexes of the three countries—Germany, Switzerland, and the United States—that were long regarded as having the most independent central banks in the world (see Table 13.1). International pressures were also responsible for the dramatic increase in central bank independence in several other countries, especially in Latin America, in the 1990s. One such pressure was the globalization of finance, which made it important for developing countries to "signal their creditworthiness" to international investors (Maxfield 1997, 7–11). Another "international coercive pressure" was exerted by the International Monetary Fund, which "increasingly attached certain conditions, including an independent central bank, to its lending agreements" (Polillo and Guillén 2005, 1774). For instance, Argentina went from a Cukierman index of 0.40 to 0.74 in 1992, and Uruguay from 0.24 to 0.54 in 1995.

Most of the shifts toward greater central bank independence happened in 1995 or later, and 1994 can be considered the last year in which central banks were still mainly domestic institutions unaffected by the preparatory steps toward the adoption of the euro and other international developments. Accordingly, the average indexes from 1945 (or from the first year that each country is included in this study) until 1994 are used as the basic measures of central bank independence. They are shown in the first column of Table 13.1, in descending order of central bank independence. The decade and a half that is excluded is relatively brief compared with the much longer pre-1995 period for most countries. However, if I were to prepare a further update of this book in say 2025, the period of the internationalization of the central banks will have lasted so long that central bank independence should be dropped as a component of the federal-unitary

TABLE 13.1

Central bank independence in thirty-six democracies, 1945–94, 1945–2010, and 1995–2010

	1945–94	1945–2010	1995–2010
Germany	0.69	0.73	0.84
Switzerland	0.61	0.62	0.66
United States	0.56	0.56	0.56
Austria	0.55	0.61	0.77
Canada	0.52	0.51	0.50
Netherlands	0.48	0.55	0.79
Denmark	0.46	0.44	0.40
Malta	0.44	0.42	0.39
Australia	0.42	0.41	0.38
Bahamas	0.41	0.42	0.43
Ireland	0.41	0.50	0.75
Israel	0.41	0.46	0.62
Mauritius	0.40	0.35	0.35
Argentina	0.39	0.54	0.66
Barbados	0.38	0.38	0.39
Greece	0.38	0.54	0.77
Costa Rica	0.37	0.42	0.55
France	0.35	0.48	0.80
Trinidad	0.35	0.35	0.35
Iceland	0.34	0.37	0.47
India	0.34	0.33	0.32
Botswana	0.33	0.38	0.47
Luxembourg	0.33	0.44	0.76
Portugal	0.32	0.56	0.80
United Kingdom	0.31	0.33	0.38
Jamaica	0.30	0.30	0.35
Spain	0.29	0.57	0.85
Sweden	0.29	0.39	0.69

TABLE 13.1 *continued*

	1945–94	1945–2010	1995–2010
Finland	0.28	0.38	0.68
Italy	0.28	0.42	0.86
Belgium	0.27	0.40	0.77
Korea	0.27	0.36	0.41
Japan	0.25	0.29	0.41
New Zealand	0.21	0.24	0.33
Uruguay	0.19	0.35	0.45
Norway	0.17	0.18	0.22

Source: Based on data in Cukierman, Webb, and Neyapti 1994; Grilli, Masciandaro, and Tabellini 1991; Polillo and Guillén 2005; and Crowe and Meade 2007

dimension.[2] Table 13.1 also shows the indexes for the entire period from 1945 to 2010 in the second column and the indexes for 1995–2010, the years in which central banks became internationalized, in the third column.

The Cukierman index can theoretically range from one to zero, but the empirical range for the 1945–94 period in the first column is only about half as large. Only five countries have indexes that are greater than 0.50—the point that represents semi-independence. The midpoint of the empirical range is 0.43, but the mean and median are lower—0.37 and 0.35, respectively—indicating that

2. Conceivably, but probably at a later stage, the European Court of Justice could become the ultimate arbiter on all constitutional questions for all or most of the members of the European Union, which would mean that judicial review would also have to be removed from the federal-unitary dimension. And an even further update, perhaps in 2035, might still cover approximately the same number of countries, but the European Union might be one country—one of the largest, together with India and the United States—and some of the democracies listed in Table 4.2 might be added to the comparative analysis.

more countries are concentrated in the lower half of the empirical range. The German, Swiss, and American central banks head the list and were (until the middle of the 1990s) also generally regarded as the world's strongest, but even these banks do not have the highest possible scores.

The third column shows the major changes that have occurred from the mid-1990s on. Germany, an original member of the eurozone, still has a high index—increased from 0.69 to 0.84—but is now in third place, slightly below Italy and Spain. Switzerland is in a shared thirteenth place together with Argentina, and the United States is number seventeen. The empirical range has widened, from a high of 0.86 to a low of 0.22—almost two-thirds of the theoretical range. The mean and median are also considerably higher than in the pre-1995 years: the mean has gone up from 0.37 to 0.56, and the median from 0.35 to 0.52. Nevertheless, there are eight countries that have the same or lower scores in the post-1995 than in the pre-1994 periods, but all of these downward shifts are small; the largest change, in Denmark, is a mere 0.06 points. In sharp contrast, many upward shifts are very large—by 0.58 points in Italy, 0.56 in Spain, and 0.50 in Belgium— three original eurozone participants that used to have low scores for central bank independence before 1995. Substantial increases can be seen in non-eurozone members as well; for instance, in Sweden by 0.40 points, 0.27 in Argentina, 0.26 in Uruguay, and 0.21 in Israel. The numbers in the second column are generally closer to those in the first than the third column because for most countries the pre-1994 period was considerably longer than the decade and a half from 1995 on.

FEDERALISM AND CENTRAL BANK INDEPENDENCE

Central bank independence has been linked to several other institutional characteristics of democracies. Peter A. Hall (1994) argues that corporatist institutions facilitate central bank independence: they allow central banks to control inflation without having to pay the full price of higher unemployment, because

coordinated wage bargaining can counteract the tendency for unemployment to increase. In our set of thirty-six democracies, however, there is little or no systematic relationship between the two.
The correlation between the independence of the central bank
and interest group pluralism is a weak and insignificant –0.10.

John B. Goodman (1991, 346) argues that central bank independence is mainly a function of the time horizons of the politicians who are in power: "Politicians generally wish to maintain
a high degree of freedom in their actions. However, they will be
willing to change the status of the central bank to bind the hands
of their successors, a decision they make when they expect a
short tenure in office." Goodman's argument suggests that central

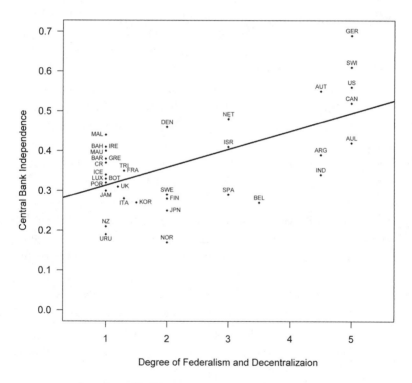

FIG. 13.1 The relationship between federalism-decentralization and central bank independence in thirty-six democracies, 1945–94

banks should have less autonomy in majoritarian democracies where executives are stronger and more durable than in consensus democracies. However, the correlation between executive dominance and central bank independence is an insignificant −0.06.

A third suggestion of an institutional connection—between central bank independence and federalism—is much more fruitful (Banaian, Laney, and Willett 1986). The correlation between our indexes of federalism and decentralization on one hand and central bank independence on the other is a strong 0.60 (significant at the 1 percent level). Further hypotheses are that, because of the internationalization of central banks, there should be little or no such relationship from 1995 on and that it should be weaker in the entire 1945–2010 period. Indeed, the correlation for the 1995–2010 period is a completely insignificant 0.20; for the 1945–2010 period it is still a relatively high 0.52 (and still significant at the 1 percent level)—mainly on the strength of the stronger correlation of 0.60 in the pre-1994 years.

The shape of the relationship between the index of central bank independence (1945–94) and the federalism-decentralization index is shown in Figure 13.1. The five central banks with the greatest independence in the 1945–94 period all operated in federal systems: Germany, Switzerland, the United States, Austria, and Canada. In the rank order of Table 13.1, Australia is in ninth and Argentina is in fourteenth place—still in the top half of the table—and India is just below the midpoint. The ninth federal system, Belgium, had one of the lowest indexes of bank independence, but Belgium did not become federal until 1993, and as discussed in Chapter 3, it made its central bank much more independent at about the same time. As shown in the next chapter, central bank independence is also strongly correlated with the other three variables of the federal-unitary dimension.

CHAPTER 14

THE TWO-DIMENSIONAL CONCEPTUAL
MAP OF DEMOCRACY

In this brief chapter I summarize the main findings of Chapters 5 through 13, which have dealt with each of the ten basic majoritarian versus consensus variables. I focus on two aspects of the "grand picture": the two-dimensional pattern formed by the relationships among the ten variables and the positions of each of the thirty-six democracies in this two-dimensional pattern. In addition, I explore the changes in these positions from the pre-1980 to the post-1981 period of twenty-seven of the thirty-six democracies for which a sufficiently long time span is available in the first period.

THE TWO DIMENSIONS

In Chapter 1, I previewed one of the most important general findings of this book: the clustering of the ten institutional variables along two clearly separate dimensions, which I have called the executives-parties and federal-unitary dimensions—although, as I explained in Chapter 1, it might be more accurate and theoretically more meaningful to call the two dimensions the joint-power and divided-power dimensions. In Chapters 5 through 13, too, I have repeatedly called attention to the close links among some of the variables within each cluster. Table 14.1 now presents the overall pattern by means of the correlation matrix for all ten variables. It shows strong relationships within each cluster and only weak connections between variables belonging to different clusters. All of the correlations within the two clusters are statistically significant: fifteen of the twenty at the 1 percent level and the remaining five at the 5 percent level; the correlation coefficients are shown in the two highlighted triangles in Table 14.1. In sharp contrast, only one of the twenty-five correlations between variables in the different clusters, shown in the bottom left of the table, is large enough to be statistically significant, and only at the 5 percent level.

The first cluster of variables has somewhat stronger interconnections than the second cluster: the averages of the absolute values of the correlation coefficients are 0.66 and 0.47, respectively. Within the first cluster, the percentage of minimal winning one-party cabinets is a particularly strong element: it has the highest correlations with the other variables. This finding is of great theoretical interest because, as argued earlier (in the beginning of Chapter 5), this variable can be seen as conceptually close to the essence of the distinction between concentration of power and the joint exercise of power. The effective number of parliamentary parties is a second key component in this cluster. In the second cluster, the federalism and decentralization variable emerges as the strongest element. This finding is theoretically significant, too, because this variable can be seen as conceptually at the heart of the federal-unitary dimension.

An even better and more succinct summary of the relationships among the ten variables can be achieved by means of factor analysis. The general purpose of factor analysis is to detect whether there are one or more common underlying dimensions among several variables. The factors that are found can then be seen as "averages" of the closely related variables. Table 14.2 presents the results of the factor analysis of our ten basic variables. The values that are shown for each variable are the factor loadings, which

TABLE 14.1

Correlation matrix of the ten variables distinguishing majoritarian from consensus democracy in thirty-six democracies, 1945–2010

Variable 1: Effective number of parliamentary parties
Variable 2: Minimal winning one-party cabinets
Variable 3: Executive dominance
Variable 4: Electoral disproportionality
Variable 5: Interest group pluralism
Variable 6: Federalism-decentralization
Variable 7: Bicameralism
Variable 8: Constitutional rigidity
Variable 9: Judicial review
Variable 10: Central bank independence

	[1]	[2]	[3]	[4]	[5]
[1]	1.00				
[2]	−0.85**	1.00			
[3]	−0.79**	0.78**	1.00		
[4]	−0.57**	0.58**	0.55**	1.00	
[5]	−0.61**	0.71**	0.51**	0.61**	1.00
[6]	0.26	−0.26	−0.08	−0.15	−0.23
[7]	0.09	−0.03	0.10	0.09	0.07
[8]	−0.08	0.00	0.11	0.17	0.01
[9]	−0.24	0.17	0.18	0.36*	0.26
[10]	−0.04	−0.15	−0.02	−0.12	−0.10

	[6]	[7]	[8]	[9]	[10]
[1]					
[2]					
[3]					
[4]					
[5]					
[6]	1.00				
[7]	0.70**	1.00			
[8]	0.56**	0.39*	1.00		
[9]	0.47**	0.41*	0.46**	1.00	
[10]	0.60**	0.38*	0.38*	0.34*	1.00

*Statistically significant at the 5 percent level (one-tailed test)

**Statistically significant at the 1 percent level (one-tailed test)

TABLE 14.2

Varimax orthogonal rotated matrix of the ten variables distinguishing majoritarian from consensus democracy in 36 democracies, 1945–2010

Variable	Factor I	Factor II
Effective number of parliamentary parties	−0.91	0.09
Minimal winning one-party cabinets	0.92	−0.09
Executive dominance	0.84	0.08
Electoral disproportionality	0.66	−0.03
Interest group pluralism	0.72	−0.10
Federalism-decentralization	−0.19	0.98
Bicameralism	0.03	0.72
Constitutional rigidity	0.10	0.60
Judicial review	0.28	0.53
Central bank independence	−0.03	0.61

Note: The factor analysis is a principal components analysis with eigenvalues over 1.0 extracted

may be interpreted as the correlation coefficients between the variable and the first and second factors detected by the factor analysis. The same two clusters emerge prominently from this analysis; they are also clearly separate clusters, because the factor analysis used an orthogonal rotation, which guarantees that the two factors are completely uncorrelated.

The factor loadings are very high within each of the two clusters and much lower—lower than 0.10 in seven of the ten cases— outside the clusters. The percentage of minimal winning one-party cabinets again turns out to be the strongest variable in the first dimension: its factor loading of 0.92 means that it almost coincides with the factor. The effective number of parties is an almost equally strong element with a factor loading of −0.91. And the federalism variable emerges once more as the strongest element in the second dimension with an extremely high factor loading of 0.98. The remaining factor loadings within the two clusters are lower but still strong: the lowest is still an impressive 0.53.

THE CONCEPTUAL MAP OF DEMOCRACY

The two-dimensional pattern formed by the ten basic variables allows us to summarize where the thirty-six individual countries are situated between majoritarian and consensus democracy. Their characteristics on each of the two sets of five variables can be averaged so as to form just two summary characteristics, and these can be used to place each of the democracies on the two-dimensional map of democracy shown in Figure 14.1.[1] The horizontal axis represents the executives-parties and the vertical axis the federal-unitary dimension. Each unit on these axes represents one standard deviation: high values indicate majoritarianism and low values consensus. On the executives-parties dimension, all countries are within two standard deviations from the middle; on the federal-unitary dimension, two countries— Germany and the United States—are at the greater distance of almost two and a half standard deviations below the middle. The exact scores of each of the thirty-six countries on the two dimensions can be found in the Appendix.[2]

1. In order for the five variables in each of the two clusters to be averaged, they first had to be standardized (so as to have a mean of 0 and a standard deviation of 1), because they were originally measured on quite different scales. Moreover, their signs had to be adjusted so that high values on each variable represented either majoritarianism or consensus and low values the opposite characteristic; for the purpose of constructing the conceptual map, I arbitrarily gave the high values to majoritarianism (which entailed reversing the signs of the effective number of parties and of all five variables in the federal-unitary dimension). After averaging these standardized variables, the final step was to standardize the averages so that each unit on the two axes represents one standard deviation.

2. Note, however, that in the Appendix all values on the two dimensions are expressed in terms of degrees of consensus democracy; these can be converted easily into degrees of majoritarian democracy by reversing the signs.

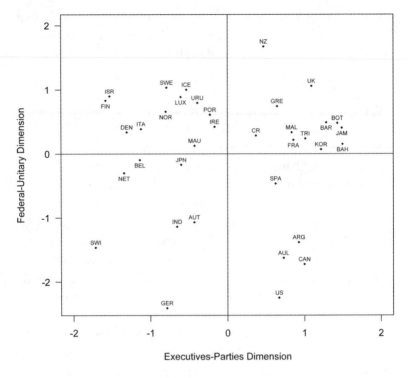

FIG. 14.1 The two-dimensional conceptual map of democracy

Most of the prototypical cases of majoritarian and consensus democracy discussed in Chapters 2 and 3 are in the expected positions on the map. The United Kingdom and New Zealand are in the top right corner. The United Kingdom is considerably more majoritarian on the executives-parties dimension, mainly because New Zealand, after a long period of being roughly equal in this respect, became considerably less majoritarian after its first PR election in 1996. But New Zealand is a great deal more majoritarian—that is, unitary—on the federal-unitary dimension. Until 1996, therefore, New Zealand's position was more extreme than that of the United Kingdom—in line with the proposition that it was the purer example of the Westminster model. Chapter 2 used Barbados as an exemplar of majoritarian democracy on the executives-parties dimension only and not as typically majoritarian on the federal-unitary dimension; its location below the United Kingdom and New Zealand but also somewhat farther to the right fits this description well. Switzerland is, as expected, in the bottom left corner but not quite as far down as several other federal democracies, mainly due to its one nonconsensual characteristic—the absence of judicial review. It is still the clearest consensual prototype, however, because it is more than one and a half standard deviations away from the center on both dimensions, whereas Germany—which the map suggests could also have served as the prototype—is located farther down but less than one standard deviation left of the center. Belgium is the one exemplar case not to be in an extreme position, but this is not unexpected either because it only became fully federal in 1993; it does, however, have a strong consensual position on the executives-parties dimension.

The two-dimensional map also reveals prototypes of the two combinations of consensus and majoritarian characteristics. In the top left corner, Israel represents the combination of consensus democracy on the executives-parties dimension (in particular, frequent oversized coalition cabinets, multipartism, highly proportional PR elections, and interest group corporatism) but, albeit somewhat less strongly, majoritarianism on the federal-unitary dimension (an unwritten constitution and a unicameral parliament, moderated, however, by intermediate characteristics with regard to federalism and central bank independence). In the bottom right-hand corner, Canada is the strongest candidate for the opposite prototype of majoritarianism on the executives-parties and consensus on the federal-unitary dimension: on one hand, dominant one-party cabinets, a roughly two-and-a-half party system, plurality elections, and interest group pluralism, but on the other hand, strong federalism and judicial review, a rigid constitution, an independent central bank, and bicameralism, albeit of only medium strength (Studlar and Christensen 2006). The United States is located in the same corner and is stronger on the federal-unitary dimension—but not exceptionally majoritarian on the executives-parties dimension, especially due to its lower degree of executive dominance in comparison with Canada.

EXPLANATIONS

Are any general patterns revealed by the distribution of the thirty-six democracies on the map? Is there, for instance, any correspondence between the conceptual and geographical maps? There does appear to be such a relationship as far as the consensus side of the executives-parties dimension is concerned: most continental European countries are located on the left side of the map, including the five Nordic countries, which have been called "the consensual democracies" with a "distinctively Scandinavian culture of consensus and . . . structures for conciliation and arbitration" (Elder, Thomas, and Arter 1988, 221). On the right-hand side, the four Caribbean countries are close together, but most of the other countries are geographically distant from one another. The striking feature that many countries on the right-hand side of the conceptual map do have in common is that they are former British colonies. In fact, it is the presence or absence of a British political heritage that appears to explain the distribution on the left and right side of the executives-parties dimension better than any geographical factor. Dag Anckar (2008) finds the same strong influence of the British model in his comparative study of democratic "microstates" with populations below one million— including five of our democracies with populations over a quarter of a million as well as twenty-four smaller countries.

There are several obvious exceptions to this twofold division based on the influence of a British heritage. Two of the Latin American democracies—Argentina and Costa Rica—form one exception. Other notable exceptions are Greece, Spain, and, farther to the right, Korea and France. France is an especially interesting exceptional case: in view of French president de Gaulle's deeply felt and frequently expressed antagonism toward *les anglo-saxons,* it is ironic that the republic he created is the most Anglo-Saxon of any of the continental European democracies. There are exceptions on the left side of this dimension, too: Ireland, India, Israel, and Mauritius all emerged from British colonial rule. Ireland is only slightly to the left of the dividing line, and what unites the other three countries is that they are plural societies—suggesting that the degree of pluralism is what explains why countries are consensual rather than majoritarian on the executives-parties dimension. Of the seventeen plural and semiplural societies listed in Table 4.3, eleven are located on the left side of the map.

Regression analysis confirms that both explanations are important but also that British political heritage is the stronger influence. The correlation between British heritage—a dummy variable with a value of one for Britain itself and for the fourteen countries it formerly ruled, and zero for the other twenty-one countries—and majoritarian democracy on the executives-parties dimension has a coefficient of 0.50 (significant at the 1 percent level); the correlation with degree of plural society—plural versus semiplural versus nonplural—is −0.30 (significant at the 5 percent level). When both of the independent variables are entered into the regression equation, the multiple correlation coefficient is 0.60 (significant at the same levels). Finally, in a stepwise regression analysis, British heritage explains 23 percent of the variance in majoritarian democracy, and the degree of pluralism adds another 9 percent for a total of 32 percent of the variance explained (measured in terms of the adjusted R-squared).[3]

3. It can be argued that three additional countries—Austria, Germany, and Japan—should also be coded as having had a strong degree of British, or rather Anglo-American, influence on their political systems. The postwar Japanese constitution was drafted by General Douglas MacArthur's staff and was largely inspired by the British model. American and British occupation authorities also oversaw the reestablishment of democracy in Germany and Austria, and they had an especially strong and direct hand in the shaping of the postwar German democratic system (Muravchik 1991, 91–114). However, assigning these three countries a code of 1 on the British heritage variable weakens all of the correlations; for instance, the total variance explained goes down from 32 to 21 percent.

The degree to which countries are plural societies also appears to explain the location of the thirty-six democracies on the federal-unitary dimension. Of the twelve countries situated below the middle, nine are plural or semiplural societies. An additional explanation suggested by the map is population size. The four largest countries—India, the United States, Japan, and Germany— are all located in the bottom part of the map, and of the sixteen countries with populations greater than ten million, ten are in the bottom part. This potential explanation is bolstered by Robert A. Dahl and Edward R. Tufte's (1973, 37) finding that size is related to federalism and decentralization, the key variable in the federal-unitary dimension: "the larger the country, the more decentralized its government, whether federal or not."

Regression analysis again confirms both of these impressions. The correlation coefficients are −0.53 for population size (logged) and −0.38 for degree of pluralism (significant at the 1 and 5 percent level, respectively). In the multiple regression, both remain significant explanatory variables (although pluralism only at the 10 percent level), and the multiple correlation coefficient is 0.58. Population size by itself explains 26 percent of the variance, and pluralism adds another 4 percent for a total of 30 percent explained variance. The degree of pluralism is again the weaker variable, but it can be regarded as the strongest overall explanation because it can explain a significant portion of the variation in the locations of the thirty-six democracies on both dimensions.[4] Although the joint-power and divided-power aspects of consensus democracy are conceptually and empirically distinct dimensions, they represent complementary institutional mechanisms for the accommodation of deep societal divisions. This finding strengthens Sir Arthur Lewis's recommendation, stated in Chapter 3, that

4. British political heritage is not related to the second dimension. Neither is population size related to the first dimension—contradicting Dahl and Tufte's (1973, 91) argument that "the small system, being more homogeneous, is . . . likely to be more consensual [and that] the larger system, being more heterogeneous, is . . . likely to be more conflictual."

both dimensions of consensus democracy—in particular, Lewis advocates power-sharing cabinets and federalism—are needed in plural societies.

SHIFTS ON THE CONCEPTUAL MAP

The locations of the thirty-six democracies on the conceptual map are *average* locations over a long period: more than sixty years for the twenty older democracies and a minimum of twenty-two years for the three newest democracies (see Table 4.1). These averages conceal any large or small changes that may have taken place. Obviously, political systems can and do change; for instance, in previous chapters I called attention to changes in the party, electoral, and interest group systems of the thirty-six democracies as well as in their degrees of decentralization, the cameral structure of their legislatures, and the activism of their judicial review. To what extent have these changes added up to shifts in the direction of greater majoritarianism or greater consensus on either of both of the dimensions?

To explore this question, I divided the period 1945–2010 in two roughly equal parts: the period until the end of 1980 and the period from 1981 to the middle of 2010. For countries with a sufficiently long time span in the first period, scores on both of the dimensions were calculated for each period. This could be done for the twenty countries covered since the middle or late 1940s and for seven additional countries: Barbados, Botswana, Costa Rica, France, Jamaica, Malta, and Trinidad.[5] The other nine democracies were not included in this part of the analysis. Figure 14.2 shows the shifts that took place in the twenty-seven longer-term democracies from the pre-1980 to the post-1981 period. The

5. These countries are covered starting with the years indicated in Table 4.1. The six countries that became independent and democratic or redemocratized in the 1970s were not included in this analysis because the time span from the beginning of their coverage until 1980 was much too short; the remaining three countries redemocratized after 1981 (see Table 4.1).

arrows point to the positions in the later period. It should be emphasized that these shifts are all relative changes—that is, each country's change is relative to the changes in all of the other countries. The reason is that the scores on each of the dimensions in each period are standardized and add up to zero; therefore, the shifts from left to right as well as up or down have to sum to zero, too. A good example is the slightly upward shift of the United States in Figure 14.2, which appears to indicate a somewhat less extreme position on the federal-unitary dimension. In fact, however, the absolute position of the United States did not change at all: its scores on all five of the variables in this dimension are exactly the same before 1980 and after 1981. The apparent shift is therefore caused by the sum total of movements in the other twenty-six countries toward a lower position on the federal-unitary dimension. Hence Table 14.2 cannot provide an answer to the question of whether there was any overall tendency toward more majoritarianism or more consensus in the 1945–2010 period. There is, however, a different way to answer this question, which I shall discuss below.

The general picture in Figure 14.2 is one of great stability. It shows many relatively small shifts but no radical transformations: not a single country changed from a clearly majoritarian democracy to a clearly consensual democracy or vice versa. There are more shifts from left to right or vice versa than from higher to lower locations or vice versa—a pattern that reflects the greater stability of the institutional characteristics of the federal-unitary dimension because these are more often anchored in constitutional provisions. Nevertheless, four downward movements stand out. The largest of these reflects Belgium's introduction of judicial review in 1984 and full federalism in 1993. The main explanation in the French and Italian cases is the combination of decentralization and stronger judicial review in the second period. The somewhat smaller but still pronounced downward shift in Costa Rica's position is entirely due to the major change from weak to very strong judicial review in 1989. The still smaller downward

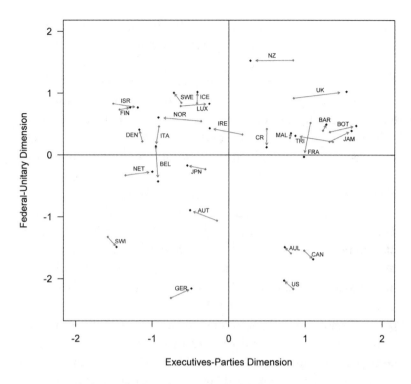

FIG. 14.2 Shifts on the two-dimensional map by twenty-seven democracies from the period before 1981 to the period 1981–2010

movements of Switzerland and Israel are due to the strengthening of their central bank independence. The slight upward movements of many countries do not indicate significant changes because, as in the case of the United States mentioned above, they mainly "compensate" for the significant downward shifts of Belgium, France, Italy, and Costa Rica. However, the adoption of unicameralism in Sweden, Denmark, and Iceland does represent real change and accounts for part of their still relatively small shifts to higher positions in Figure 14.2.

The two big shifts along horizontal lines that stand out in Figure 14.2 are those of our two majoritarian prototypes, New Zealand and the United Kingdom. New Zealand's shift to a less majoritarian position is the result of its adoption in 1996 of PR, which resulted in less electoral disproportionality, more multipartism, a major increase in coalition and minority cabinets, and lower executive dominance, as discussed in Chapter 2. The leftward shift would obviously be even more pronounced had the comparison been between the periods before and after 1996 instead of before and after 1981. The big move to the right by the United Kingdom occurred in spite of a slight increase in the effective number of parties (from 2.10 to 2.27 parties), which was more than counterbalanced, however, by a big increase in disproportionality (from 8.97 to 16.0 percent) and a higher degree of executive dominance. These changes demonstrate that by 2010 the United Kingdom had definitely replaced New Zealand as the closest approximation of the Westminster model. The next two notable shifts are those of Norway and Ireland. Norway moved to more consensual characteristics on four of the five variables in the executives-parties dimension and maintained its high degree of corporatism at the same level. Ireland crossed over from majoritarian into consensual territory in spite of slightly less proportional election results, but increases in multipartism, coalition government, and corporatism, as well as a decrease in executive dominance (Bulsara and Kissane 2009). The other movements from right to left and vice versa are all smaller and reflect a variety of changes in the five variables underlying the executives-parties dimension without any one of these variables standing out as the most influential.

In order to discover whether there was any general trend toward more majoritarianism or consensus on the two dimensions, we need to look at the average *unstandardized* scores on each of the ten basic variables. These averages are presented in Table 14.3. The table also shows the differences between the second-period and first-period scores and whether these differences indicate more majoritarianism or more consensus. On eight of the variables, the trend is toward greater consensus, but only three of these show sizable differences: more multipartism (by about an extra one-third of a party), more than 10 percent fewer minimal

TABLE 14.3

Average values on the ten variables distinguishing majoritarian from consensus democracy in twenty-seven democracies, 1945–80 and 1981–2010, the differences between the second and first periods, and the majoritarian (M) or consensual (C) direction of these differences

	1945–80	1981–2010	Difference
Executives-parties dimension			
Effective number of parliamentary parties	3.06	3.44	+0.38 (C)
Minimal winning one-party cabinets	60.7	54.3	−6.40 (C)
Executive dominance	4.99	4.95	−0.04 (C)
Electoral disproportionality	6.88	7.96	+1.08 (M)
Interest group pluralism	1.92	1.83	−0.09 (C)
Federal-unitary dimension			
Federalism-decentralization	2.28	2.39	+0.11 (C)
Bicameralism	2.29	2.19	−0.10 (M)
Constitutional rigidity	2.59	2.65	+0.06 (C)
Judicial review	1.90	2.13	+0.23 (C)
Central bank independence	0.38	0.39	+0.01 (C)

winning one-party cabinets, and stronger judicial review. Of the two variables that show the opposite trend, only the increase in electoral disproportionality—by more than one percentage point—is an impressive change. The overall trend is toward more consensus democracy, but it is obviously not a very strong trend.

The second-period (1981–2010) scores on the two dimensions are used again in the next two chapters. These scores will differ slightly from those of the twenty-seven democracies used to discover shifts on the conceptual map in the last part of the current chapter, because they will be based on the ten standardized variables and two dimensions for both these twenty-seven countries and the nine countries that could not be included for this purpose. The next two chapters analyze the consequences that type of democracy may have for the effectiveness, democratic character, and general policy orientation of governments. Reliable data on these variables are generally available only for recent decades; moreover, focusing on the more recent period enables us to include as many of the thirty-six democracies as possible in the analysis. It therefore also makes sense to measure the degrees of consensus or majoritarianism of the twenty-seven longer-term democracies in terms of their characteristics in the second period.

CHAPTER 15

EFFECTIVE GOVERNMENT AND
POLICY-MAKING: DOES CONSENSUS
DEMOCRACY MAKE A DIFFERENCE?

In this chapter and the next I deal with the "so what?" question: Does the difference between majoritarian and consensus democracy make a difference for the operation of democracy, especially for how well democracy works? The conventional
wisdom—which is often stated in terms of the relative advantages of PR versus plurality and majority elections but which can
be extended to the broader contrast between consensus and majoritarian democracy along the executives-parties dimension—is
that there is a trade-off between the quality and the effectiveness
of democratic government. On one hand, the conventional wisdom concedes that PR and consensus democracy may provide
more accurate representation and, in particular, better minority
representation and protection of minority interests, as well as
broader participation in decision-making. On the other hand, the
conventional wisdom maintains that the one-party majority governments typically produced by plurality elections are more decisive and hence more effective policy-makers. This view is reflected in the well-known adage that "representative government
must not only represent, it must also govern" (Beer 1998, 25)—

with its clear implication that representativeness comes at the expense of effective government.

Conventional wisdom has long been widely accepted without adequate empirical examination, perhaps because its logic appears to be so strong that no test was thought to be needed. For instance, I have already called attention (in Chapter 5) to Lowell's (1896) assertion that it is a self-evident "axiom" that one-party majority cabinets are needed for effective policy-making. The first part of the conventional wisdom, which concerns democratic quality, is discussed in the next chapter. In this chapter I critically examine the second part, which posits a link between majoritarian democracy and effective decision-making. I use three sets of indicators of government performance. The first and most important of these consists of the Worldwide Governance Indicators, based on expert assessments of six dimensions of good governance in a large number of countries, including all thirty-six of our democracies, from 1996 on. Second, I use the traditional measures of macroeconomic management—especially economic growth, control of inflation, and control of unemployment—as indicators of effective policy-making. My third set consists of indicators of the control of violence. My main focus will be on the effect of the executives-parties dimension of consensus democracy on government performance, and unless indicated otherwise, any statements about consensus democracy in most of the remainder of this chapter will refer to this first dimension. At the end of the chapter, I shall also discuss the effects of the federalist dimension of consensus democracy; this will be a brief discussion because its effects are uniformly minimal and hence not worth reporting in any detail.

HYPOTHESES AND PRELIMINARY EVIDENCE

The theoretical basis for Lowell's axiom is certainly not implausible: concentrating political power in the hands of a narrow majority can promote unified, decisive leadership and hence coherent policies and fast decision-making. But there are several counterarguments. Majoritarian governments may be able to make decisions faster than consensus government, but fast decisions are not necessarily wise decisions. In fact, the opposite may be more valid, as many political theorists—notably the venerable authors of the *Federalist Papers* (Hamilton, Jay, and Madison 1788)—have long argued. The introduction in Britain in the 1980s of the so-called poll tax, a local government tax, is a clear example of a policy, now universally acknowledged to have been disastrous, that was the product of fast decision-making; in all probability, the poll tax would never have been introduced had it been more carefully, and more slowly, debated (Butler, Adonis, and Travers 1994).

Moreover, the supposedly coherent policies produced by majoritarian governments may be negated by the alternation of these governments; this alternation from left to right and vice versa may entail sharp changes in economic policy that are too frequent and too abrupt. In particular, S. E. Finer (1975) has forcefully argued that successful macroeconomic management requires not so much a *strong* hand as a *steady* one and that proportional representation and coalition governments are better able to provide steady, centrist policy-making. Policies supported by a broad consensus are also more likely to be carried out successfully and to remain on course than policies imposed by a "decisive" government against the wishes of important sectors of society. Furthermore, in contrast to PR, single-member district elections can be expected to lead to a greater concern with obtaining government resources for individual districts "at the rest of the country's expense, or protectionist measures for their cornerstone industries" than with policies that encourage nationwide economic growth (Knutsen 2011, 84). Finally, for maintaining civil peace in divided societies, conciliation and compromise—policies that require the greatest possible inclusion of contending groups in the decision-making process—are probably much more important than making snap decisions. These counterarguments appear to be at least slightly stronger than the argument in favor of majori-

tarian government that is based narrowly on the speed and coherence of decision-making.

The empirical evidence is mixed. Peter Katzenstein (1985)
and Ronald Rogowski (1987) have shown that small countries
adopted PR and corporatist practices to compensate for the disadvantages of their small size in international trade; that is, these
consensus elements served as sources of strength instead of weakness. In their classic studies of the macroeconomic effects of electoral systems, Richard Rose (1992) and Francis G. Castles (1994)
find no significant differences in economic growth, inflation, and
unemployment between PR and non-PR systems among the industrialized democracies. Nouriel Roubini and Jeffrey D. Sachs
(1989) do find a clear connection between multiparty coalition
government and governments with a short average tenure—both
characteristic of consensus democracy—on one hand and large
budget deficits on the other; their methods and conclusions, however, have been challenged by Stephen A. Borrelli and Terry A.
Royed (1995) and by Sung Deuk Hahm, Mark S. Kamlet, and
David C. Mowery (1996). In a later study of the effects of electoral
systems in eighty-five democracies in the 1990s, Torsten Persson
and Guido Tabellini (2003, 270–76) find that PR leads to larger
budget deficits than non-PR rules, but they report only ambigu-
ous results for government effectiveness, economic growth, and
corruption.

In a series of articles, Markus M. L. Crepaz and his collabora-
tors (Crepaz 1996, Crepaz and Birchfield 2000, Crepaz and Moser
2004) find that, in the member countries of the Organization for
Economic Development and Cooperation, consensual institutions have significantly favorable effects on inflation, unemployment, and the ability to handle the pressures exerted on national
economies by economic globalization—but neutral effects on economic growth. In the first edition of this book (Lijphart 1999, 264–
69), I also found that consensus democracies have a better record
on inflation and a slightly better record on unemployment but
only mixed results for economic growth. Edeltraud Roller (2005,

233–37) finds positive, but small and statistically insignificant, results for consensus democracy in all three of these indicators of economic performance. Last, in contrast with all of the above findings concerning mixed or neutral effects on economic growth, Carl Henrik Knutsen's (2011, 89) large-scale study covering more than a hundred countries from the nineteenth century on finds that PR systems produce higher growth and hence "generate more prosperity" than non-PR systems; this effect is highly significant, and Knutsen calls it "astonishingly robust."

With regard to the control of violence, G. Bingham Powell (1982) finds that "representational" democracies—similar to what I call consensus democracies—have a better record than majoritarian systems. Two other large-scale statistical analyses confirm the positive effects in this regard of power-sharing institutions: Ted Robert Gurr's (1993) ambitious "global view of ethnopolitical conflicts"—to quote his book's subtitle—and Wolf Linder and André Bächtiger's (2005) comparative study of the relative success of democratization and conflict avoidance in sixty-two African and Asian countries.

The above tests all had to do with macroeconomic management and the control of violence. These are good performance indicators because they involve crucial functions of government and because precise quantitative data are available, but as I shall discuss shortly, they also have several shortcomings and should be treated with caution. Superior measures are provided by the Worldwide Governance Indicators (WGI), produced by three scholars at the Brookings Institution and the World Bank: Daniel Kaufmann, Aart Kraay, and Massimo Mastruzzi (2010). These measures—available for most of the countries in the world, including our thirty-six democracies—are aggregate expert evaluations of the performance of governments, drawn from a variety of survey institutes, think-tanks, nongovernmental organizations, and international organizations. They are much broader than the conventional macroeconomic indicators and cover six dimensions of governance, five of which are relevant for the subject of effective policy-making in this chapter: government effectiveness, regulatory quality, rule of law, control of corruption, and political stability and absence of violence; the sixth dimension, which the authors call "voice and accountability," is an excellent measure of democratic quality that I shall use in the next chapter. The WGI project was started in 1996, and updated datasets were released in 1998, 2000, and annually since 2002.

One problem with regard to the traditional macroeconomic and violence measures is that economic success and the maintenance of civil peace are not solely determined by government policy. As far as British macroeconomic policy is concerned, for instance, Rose (1992, 11) points out that "many influences upon the economy are outside the control of the government . . . Decisions taken independently of government by British investors, industrialists, consumers and workers can frustrate the intention of the government of the day. In an open international economy, Britain is increasingly influenced too by decisions taken in Japan, Washington, New York, Brussels, or Frankfurt." Rose's point should obviously not be exaggerated: the fact that governments are not in full control does not mean that they have no control at all. When the economy performs well—when economic growth is high and inflation, unemployment, and budget deficits are low—governments routinely claim credit for this happy state of affairs. And voters are known to reward government parties in good economic times and to punish them when the economy is in poor shape.

Rose's argument, however, does point up the need to take these other influences into account as much as possible. To the extent that they are identifiable and measurable variables, they should be controlled for in the statistical analyses. For economic performance, the level of economic development is such a potentially important explanatory variable. For the control of violence, the degree of societal division should be controlled for, because deep divisions make the maintenance of public order and peace more difficult. A third variable whose influence must be checked is population size, if only because our democracies differ widely in this respect. It may also be hypothesized that large countries face greater problems of public order than smaller ones. In other respects, it is not clear whether size is a favorable or an unfavorable factor. Large countries obviously have greater power in international relations, which they can use, for instance, to gain economic benefits for their citizens. And yet, greater international influence also means more responsibility and hence higher expenses, especially for military purposes.

Fortuitous events may also affect economic success, such as the good luck experienced by Britain and Norway when they discovered oil in the North Sea. The effects of such fortuitous events as well as external influences that cannot be clearly identified and controlled for can be minimized when economic performance is examined over a long period and for many countries. These two desiderata are frequently in conflict: extending the period of analysis often means that some countries have to be excluded. Therefore, in the analysis below, I usually report the results for different periods, different sets of countries, and different types of data in order to provide as complete and robust a test of the hypotheses as possible. Finally, in testing the influence of the type of democracy on the economic performance variables, I limit the potential disturbing impact of external forces by excluding the five smallest democracies with populations of less than half a million—the Bahamas, Barbados, Iceland, Luxembourg, and Malta—from the analysis because these small countries are obviously extremely vulnerable to international influences.

CONSENSUS DEMOCRACY AND EFFECTIVE DECISION-MAKING

Because the theoretical arguments and the empirical evidence reviewed in the previous section are mixed but give at least a slight edge to consensus democracy, my working hypothesis is that consensus democracy produces better results—but without the expectation that the differences will be very strong and significant. All four of the tables in this chapter and in Chapter 16

present multivariate analyses of the effect of consensus democracy on a series of performance variables with controls for the
effects of the level of economic development (measured by the
human development index, presented in Table 4.3) and population
size (which needs to be logged because of the extreme differences
in the population sizes of our thirty-six democracies). Moreover,
in Table 15.2, which deals with indicators of violence, the degree
of societal division is an additional control variable.

Table 15.1 shows the effect of consensus democracy on four of
the Worldwide Governance Indicators plus an additional measure of corruption and five groups of macroeconomic variables.
The independent variable is the degree of consensus democracy
on the executives-parties dimension; because all of the WGI and
economic variables are for the 1980s or later, the consensus variable used is the degree of consensus democracy in the period
1981–2010. The estimated regression coefficient is the increase
or decrease in the dependent variable for each unit increase in
the independent variable—in our case, each increase by one standard deviation of consensus democracy. Because the range in the
degrees of consensus democracy is close to four standard deviations (see Figure 14.1), the distance between the "average" consensus democracy and the "average" majoritarian democracy is
about two standard deviations. Therefore, in answer to the question, "How much difference does consensus democracy make?" the
reply can be—roughly—twice the value of the estimated regression coefficient. For instance, based on the eighth row of Table
15.1, the effect of consensus democracy on the consumer price
index is approximately twice the regression coefficient of –1.477
percent, or almost 3 percent less inflation than majoritarian democracy. The statistical significance of the correlations depends
on the absolute t-values, shown in the second column, and the
numbers of cases, shown in the third column. Whether the correlations are significant is indicated by asterisks; three levels of
significance are reported, including the least demanding 10 percent level.

TABLE 15.1

Multivariate regression analyses of the effect of consensus democracy (executives-parties dimension) on seventeen government performance variables,
with controls for the effects of the level of economic development and logged
population size, and with extreme outliers removed

Performance variables	Estimated regression coefficient	Absolute t-value	Countries (N)
Government effectiveness (1996–2009)	0.123**	1.749	36
Regulatory quality (1996–2009)	0.066	1.074	36
Rule of law (1996–2009)	0.152**	1.972	36
Control of corruption (1996–2009)	0.182**	1.919	36
Corruption perceptions index (2010)	0.477**	1.813	35
GDP per capita growth (1981–2009)	0.074	0.461	28
GDP per capita growth (1991–2009)	−0.151	0.793	31
Consumer price index (1981–2009)	−1.477**	2.434	26
GDP deflator (1981–2009)	−1.497**	2.208	27
Consumer price index (1991–2009)	−1.483***	2.552	30
GDP deflator (1991–2009)	−1.401***	2.485	30
Unemployment (1981–2009)	−1.792**	1.931	20
Unemployment (1991–2009)	−0.802	1.216	29
Budget balance (2000–2008)	0.351	0.608	22
Budget balance (2003–2007)	0.477	0.954	28
Heritage Foundation freedom index (2009–10)	0.418	0.381	36
Fraser Institute freedom index (2008)	0.004	0.049	36

* Statistically significant at the 10 percent level (one-tailed test)

** Statistically significant at the 5 percent level (one-tailed test)

*** Statistically significant at the 1 percent level (one-tailed test)

Source: Based on data in Kaufmann, Kraay, and Mastruzzi 2010; Transparency International 2010;
World Bank 2011; Miller and Holmes 2011, 6–10; Gwartney, Hall, and Lawson 2010, 7

The four WGI measures at the top of the table are on a scale ranging from −2.5 to +2.5. The country scores are averages of the scores assigned to each country in the eleven datasets produced between 1996 and 2009. Not surprisingly, our long-term democracies receive mainly positive scores, but there are still significant differences among them. The first performance variable, government effectiveness, is a composite measure of the quality of public services, the quality of the civil service and its independence from political pressures, the quality of policy formulation and implementation, and the credibility of the government's commitment to such policies. Regulatory quality measures the government's ability to formulate and implement sound policies and regulations that promote private sector development. Rule of law is a self-explanatory term; it specifically includes the quality of property rights, the police, and the courts, as well as the risk of crime. Control of corruption comprises not only the degree to which public power is used for private gain, including both petty and grand forms of corruption, but also the "capture" of the state by elites and private interests (Kaufmann, Kraay, and Mastruzzi 2010). Consensus democracy has a favorable effect on government performance in all four areas, and the correlations are strong and statistically significant at the 5 percent level in three of them. The link with regulatory quality is weak and not statistically significant even at the 10 percent level, but still positive. To give a few examples of country scores on government effectiveness, the most important of the four WGI indicators, only Argentina (−0.08) and India (−0.05) have negative, but barely negative, scores; the highest scores are Denmark's (2.10), Finland's (2.07), and Switzerland's (1.97); the median value is 1.50, and the two countries closest to the median are France (1.59) and Spain (1.40). Based on the estimated regression coefficient of 0.123, the average consensus democracy scores approximately 0.25 points higher than the average majoritarian democracy after the level of development and population size have been taken into account.

The fifth item in this group of performance variables is an additional measure of the control of corruption: Transparency International's (2010) corruption perceptions index, measured on a ten-point scale on which 10 indicates perfect control of corruption and zero the most corrupt system—available for all of our countries except the Bahamas. Of the other thirty-five democracies, the best performers are Denmark and New Zealand with scores of 9.3; the poorest performers are Argentina (2.9), India and Jamaica (3.3), and Greece (3.5). The correlation with consensus democracy is approximately as strong and at the same level of statistical significance as that of the WGI measure of the control of corruption. The 0.477 regression coefficient indicates that the average consensus democracy is rated almost a whole point higher than the average majoritarian system on the ten-point scale. Corruption could plausibly be hypothesized to be more prevalent in consensus than in majoritarian democracies on the assumption that the consensus systems' tendency to compromise and "deal-making" might foster corrupt practices. Both the WGI's and Transparency International's data demonstrate that the opposite is true.

At this point, it is worth emphasizing again that the effects of consensus democracy on the performance variables shown in Table 15.1 are the effects after the influence of the level of economic development and population size have been taken into account. The very strong impact of the level of development on four of the sets of performance variables in the table deserves additional emphasis. When consensus democracy and the two control variables are simultaneously entered into the equations, the effect of the level of development on the WGI indicators (as well as the Transparency International index), economic growth, inflation, and economic freedom is uniformly significant at the 1 percent level: the more developed countries score significantly higher on the WGI indicators and have much better records on inflation and unemployment, but the less developed countries have considerably higher rates of economic growth. The influence of population size is much smaller and statistically significant (at the 5 percent level) only with regard to inflation, with the smaller countries experiencing higher inflation rates. The effect of the two control variables on unemployment and budget deficits is small and not statistically significant. Taken together, however, these findings clearly demonstrate how necessary it is to use the two control variables, particularly the level of economic development.

The remainder of Table 15.1 reports the effect of consensus democracy on five sets of macroeconomic performance variables. For per capita economic growth, inflation, and unemployment, the results are given for two periods: the longer period 1981–2009 without Argentina, Uruguay, and Korea, which joined our set of democracies only in the 1980s, and the shorter 1991–2009 time span, which does include these three countries. Except for the freedom indexes (at the bottom of the table), all of the data are drawn from the World Bank's (2011) dataset. I dealt with the problem of missing data for particular countries and years by including all countries with no more than two years of missing data but excluding those with three or more missing data points. For the analysis of the effect of consensus democracy on economic growth, all countries could be included: twenty-eight in the 1981–2009 period (that is, thirty-six minus Argentina, Uruguay, Korea, and the five ministates that I deliberately excluded, as explained earlier) and thirty-one in the 1991–2009 period. The table shows that the effect of consensus democracy on economic growth is weak and statistically insignificant in both periods. The negative effect in the second period is stronger than the positive effect in the first, but the regression coefficient of –0.151 indicates that it involves only about 0.3 percent higher annual growth for the majoritarian democracies.

Average annual inflation levels are again reported for the two different periods and slightly different sets of countries, and also in terms of two measures: the GDP deflator and the consumer price index. The consumer price index is the more widely used measure, but the GDP deflator is the more comprehensive index because it measures inflation in the entire economy instead of merely consumer items; the two measures, however, are usually not far apart. In the period from 1981 to 2009, Israel is an extreme outlier as a result of its hyperinflation between 1981 and 1985—almost 400 percent in 1984!—and Uruguay is a similar, although not as extreme, outlier because of its higher than 100 percent inflation levels in 1990–91. When these two outliers are removed from the analysis, the results show strong and significant favorable effects (at the 5 and 1 percent levels) of consensus democracy in both periods and measured by both measures of inflation.[1] The four estimated regression coefficients are remarkably close to each other. They indicate that the average consensus democracy had between 2.8 and 3.0 percentage points lower inflation than the average majoritarian democracy.

The results for unemployment are based on fewer countries because of missing data for several of them, especially in the 1981–2009 period. For the shorter period, the only missing cases are Botswana and India (and, of course, the deliberately excluded five ministates). The consensus democracies have the better record on controlling unemployment in both periods, but only significantly so (at the 5 percent level) in the longer period. The problem of missing data is even more serious with regard to budget balances. Because budget control is not appreciably affected by international influences, I included the five small countries in this part of the analysis. Even so, I had to limit the analysis to two periods after 2000: a longer period (2000–2008) for only twenty-two countries and a shorter period (2003–7) for twenty-eight countries. In both periods, Norway is an extreme outlier and had to be removed: while most countries tend to have budget deficits or modest budget surpluses, Norway had hefty average surpluses of more than 14 percent in both periods. The consensus democracies have a better record of managing their budgets, but not to a statistically significant degree.

1. Germany is not included in the analysis of the consumer price index for 1981–2009 because of missing data in the 1980s.

Finally, Table 15.1 reports the effect of consensus democracy on two measures of economic freedom—not because economic freedom itself is an appropriate indicator of macroeconomic performance but because many economists believe that long-term economic growth depends on it. The two indexes were independently developed by scholars at the Heritage Foundation in Washington, DC, and the Fraser Institute in Vancouver, Canada, and they are available for 2009–10 and 2008, respectively, for all of our thirty-six democracies (Miller and Holmes 2011, Gwartney, Hall, and Lawson 2010). A plausible hypothesis would be that, because majoritarian democracies are more competitive and adversarial in their orientation than consensus democracies, they would also score higher on economic freedom. That hypothesis is disconfirmed by the results shown in Table 15.1, although in both cases the link between consensus democracy and economic freedom is minimal. The estimated regression coefficient for the Fraser Institute's index is very small partly because it uses a ten-point scale (instead of the Heritage Foundation's hundred-point scale), but even so, the effect of consensus democracy, though positive, is miniscule.

The results of these tests of the effect of consensus democracy on sound government and decision-making can be summarized as follows: on sixteen of the seventeen measures, consensus democracy has the better record, and these favorable effects are statistically significant for nine of the sixteen measures; majoritarian democracies have a better record on only one measure (per capita growth in 1991–2009) but not to a statistically significant degree. The overall evidence is therefore in favor of the consensus democracies—and disconfirms the conventional wisdom that majoritarian governments are the superior decision-makers.

CONSENSUS DEMOCRACY AND THE CONTROL OF VIOLENCE

The five performance variables shown in Table 15.2 are measures of violence and the control of violence. The first two are expert assessments of the incidence and likelihood of various forms of violence by the Worldwide Governance Indicators project and the International Country Risk Guide (ICRG). The WGI measure of political stability and absence of violence captures perceptions of the likelihood that the government will be destabilized by unconstitutional or violent means, including terrorism (Kaufmann, Kraay, and Mastruzzi 2010). It uses the same scale of −2.5 to +2.5 as the WGI indicators discussed in the previous section. The ICRG index, available for the years 1990 to 2004, has three components: civil war or coup threat, terrorism and political violence, and civil disorder. Each component is worth four points, and the combined index ranges from 12, indicating very low risk, to zero, indicating very high risk. India and Israel are extreme outliers on both measures. They are given strongly negative scores on the WGI index (−0.89 and −1.07, respectively), much lower than the only other negative scores for Argentina (−0.09) and Jamaica (−0.23). The empirical range on this variable is rather narrow with the top performers, Luxembourg (1.42) and Iceland (1.41), rated well below the maximum of 2.5 points. On the ICRG scale, India and Israel are given 7.44 and 6.58 points, respectively, while most of the other countries have scores higher than nine (PRS Group 2004).

The top two rows of Table 15.2 show the effect of consensus democracy on these two indicators of control of violence with the standard controls for the effects of level of development and population size and the degree of societal division as a third control. Societal division is measured on a three-point scale based on the threefold classification of our thirty-six democracies as plural, semiplural, or nonplural societies (see Table 4.3). The level of development is again a strong and positive explanatory variable at the 1 percent level of statistical significance. Population size exerts an almost equally strong influence: smaller countries are less likely to experience violence than larger ones. Rather surprisingly, the degree of societal division is not an influential variable. Because India and Israel are extreme outliers, they were removed from the analysis. An additional reason for excluding

TABLE 15.2

Multivariate regression analyses of the effect of consensus democracy (executives-parties dimension) on five indicators of violence, with controls for the effects of the level of economic development, logged population size, and degree of societal division, and with extreme outliers removed

Performance variables	Estimated regression coefficient	Absolute t-value	Countries (N)
Political stability and absence of violence (1996–2009)	0.189***	3.360	34
Internal conflict risk (1990–2004)	0.346**	2.097	32
Weighted domestic conflict index (1981–2009)	−105.0*	1.611	30
Weighted domestic conflict index (1990–2009)	−119.7**	2.177	33
Deaths from domestic terrorism (1985–2010)	−2.357**	1.728	33

* Statistically significant at the 10 percent level (one-tailed test)

** Statistically significant at the 5 percent level (one-tailed test)

*** Statistically significant at the 1 percent level (one-tailed test)

Source: Based on data in Kaufmann, Kraay, and Mastruzzi 2010; PRS Group 2004; Banks, 2010: and GTD Team 2010

Israel is the difficulty of separating domestic from international violence in this country.

With the three controls in place and with the two outliers removed, Table 15.2 shows that in the other thirty-four countries—thirty-two in the second row because the ICRG data do not cover the Bahamas and Mauritius—consensus democracy is very strongly correlated with a lower degree of violence: at the 1 percent level of significance for the WGI indicator of political stability and absence of violence and at the 5 percent level for the ICRG measure of internal conflict risk. Based on the estimated regression coefficients, the position of the average consensus democracy on the WGI scale is almost 0.4 points higher than that of the average majoritarian democracy, and almost 0.7 points higher on the ICRG scale.

The next two performance variables shown in Table 15.2 are indices from the Arthur S. Banks (2010) Cross-National Time-Series Data Archive. The domestic conflict index is a weighted measure of conflict events like revolutions, guerrilla warfare, assassinations, and riots, with the more serious events receiving greater weight. These data are available for every year since 1981, and Table 15.1 shows the averages for two periods: 1981–2009 without Argentina, Uruguay, and Korea, and 1990–2009 with these three countries included. Because the number of conflicts is likely to be higher in larger than in smaller countries, it would appear to make sense to use conflicts per, for instance, one million people instead of the raw numbers of conflicts. I use this approach in the next chapter with regard to imprisonment rates: the number of prisoners per 100,000 inhabitants instead of the total number of persons in prisons. This is obviously the correct way of counting individual events, but for group or collective events like riots and violent demonstrations it does not work well. For example, India has experienced a high degree of violent conflict, but its average annual conflict score per million population during 1980–2009 is only 4.26, the sixth lowest score among the thirty-three countries; the similar score per million population for the United States (0.88) is the second lowest; peaceful Iceland (28.21) has the ninth highest score! These numbers are clearly deceptive, and I therefore decided to use the original conflict numbers, to remove the extreme outliers from the analysis, and, of course, to control for the logged population sizes. In addition to India and Israel, the United Kingdom is an outlier on these data. An even better reason for excluding the United Kingdom is that its high numbers are largely the result of the special problem of Northern Ireland. For the analysis of deaths from terrorist attacks, based on data in the Global Terrorism Database (GTD Team 2010), I excluded the same three countries.

The results are shown in the bottom three rows of Table 15.2. To a statistically significant degree, consensus democracy is associated with fewer violent events. In all three cases, the only strongly influential control variable (at the 1 percent level of significance) is population size: larger countries are more conflict-prone than small countries. Because of the inherent problems of dealing with group conflict data, these results should be treated with caution. The evidence based on the WGI and ICRG data in the top two rows of the table, which actually also show a stronger effect of consensus democracy, should be accorded greater weight.

THE EFFECTS OF THE FEDERALIST DIMENSION
OF CONSENSUS DEMOCRACY

In this chapter I have concentrated so far on the consequences of the executives-parties dimension of consensus democracy. These are the effects that the conventional wisdom addresses and posits to be unfavorable. The conventional wisdom does not concern itself explicitly with the federal-unitary dimension, but its logic applies to this second dimension as well. Federalism, second chambers, rigid constitutions, strong judicial review, and independent central banks can all be assumed to inhibit the decisiveness, speed, and coherence of the central government's policy making compared with unitary systems, unicameralism, flexible constitutions, weak judicial review, and weak central banks. For this reason, I repeated the twenty-two regression analyses reported in Tables 15.1 and 15.2 but now with consensus democracy on the federal-unitary dimension as the independent variable—with the same controls and with the same outliers removed from the analysis. With one minor exception, all of the relationships are extremely weak and statistically insignificant. Consensus-federalist democracy does have a slight edge over majoritarianism. In particular, it has a positive effect on five of the six most important variables, the WGI and ICRG indices; its only negative is on the WGI indicator of regulatory quality. Moreover, the positive effect on internal conflict risk is statistically significant but only at the 10 percent level. With regard to the remaining variables, the results are mixed: the ratio of favorable to unfavorable effects is nine to seven. To repeat, however, the effects are so weak that they do not allow any substantive conclusions in favor of one or the other type of democracy.

The findings of this chapter warrant three conclusions. First, on balance, consensus democracies—on the executives-parties dimension—have a better performance record than majoritarian democracies, especially when performance is measured by the five Worldwide Governance Indicators and the ICRG domestic conflict risk assessment and also with regard to inflation; majoritarian democracies do not even have a slightly better record on any of the performance variables except economic growth. Second, however, the favorable effects on unemployment, budget balance, and economic freedom are relatively weak. Hence it is debatable whether the empirical evidence permits the definitive conclusion that consensus democracies are generally the better decision-makers and better policy-makers than majoritarian systems. Therefore, third, the most important conclusion of this chapter is negative: majoritarian democracies are clearly *not* superior to consensus democracies in providing good governance, managing the economy, and maintaining civil peace. This means that the second part of the conventional wisdom does not—or not yet—need to be completely *reversed:* it is not conclusively proven that consensus democracies are actually better at all aspects of governing. What is proven beyond any doubt, however, is that the second part of the conventional wisdom is clearly wrong in claiming that majoritarian democracies are the better governors. The first part of the conventional wisdom, which concedes that consensus democracies are better at representing, is the subject of the next chapter.

CHAPTER 16

THE QUALITY OF DEMOCRACY AND A "KINDER, GENTLER" DEMOCRACY: CONSENSUS DEMOCRACY MAKES A DIFFERENCE

T he conventional wisdom, cited in the previous chapter, argues—erroneously, as I have shown—that majoritarian democracy is better at governing, but admits that consensus democracy is better at representing—in particular, representing minority groups and minority interests, representing everyone more accurately, and representing people and their interests more inclusively. In the first part of this chapter I examine several measures of the quality of democracy and democratic representation and the extent to which consensus democracies perform better than majoritarian democracies according to these measures. In the second part of the chapter I discuss differences between the two types of democracy in broad policy orientations. Here I show that consensus democracy tends to be the "kinder, gentler" form of democracy. I borrow these terms from President George H. W. Bush's acceptance speech at the Republican presidential nominating convention in August 1988, in which he asserted: "I want a kinder, and gentler nation" (*New York Times,* August 19, 1988, A14). Consensus democracies demonstrate these kinder and gentler qualities in the following ways: they are more likely to be welfare states; they have a better record with regard to the protection of the environment; they put fewer people in prison and are less likely to use the death penalty; and the consensus democracies in the developed world are more generous with their economic assistance to the developing nations.

CONSENSUS DEMOCRACY AND DEMOCRATIC QUALITY

Table 16.1 presents the results of multivariate regression analyses of the effect of consensus democracy on six sets of indicators of the quality of democracy. The organization of the table is similar to that of Tables 15.1 and 15.2 in the previous chapter. The independent variable is the degree of consensus democracy on the executives-parties dimension in the period 1981–2010, and the control variables are the level of economic development and logged population size. The first indicator is the overall measure of democratic quality produced by Worldwide Governance Indicators project: "voice and accountability," defined as the extent to which citizens are able to participate in selecting their government, as well as freedom of expression, freedom of association, and a free press (Kaufmann, Kraay, and Mastruzzi 2010). Like the five WGI indicators used in the previous chapter, the scale ranges from −2.5 to +2.5, and the scores are the averages of the eleven scores assigned to each of our thirty-six countries between 1996 and 2009. All of our democracies receive positive scores, and their empirical range is much narrower than the theoretically possible five-point difference: from a low of 0.28 to a high of 1.58. Relatively low performers are Argentina (0.28) and India (0.37) and the best performers are Denmark (1.59) and New Zealand (1.58). The estimated regression coefficient is therefore a modest 0.086, but it is statistically significant at the 5 percent level. The score of the average consensus democracy is approximately one-sixth of a point (twice the regression coefficient) higher than that of the average majoritarian democracy. The level of development and population size have strong impacts as well (at the 1 and 5 percent levels, respectively): the more developed and smaller countries tend to receive the higher ratings.

TABLE 16.1

Multivariate regression analyses of the effect of consensus democracy (executives-parties dimension) on nineteen indicators of the quality of democracy, with controls for the effects of the level of economic development and logged population size, and with extreme outliers removed

Performance variables	Estimated regression coefficient	Absolute t-value	Countries (N)
Voice and accountability (1996–2009)	0.086**	1.955	36
EIU Democracy Index (2006–10)	0.262***	2.493	34
I. Electoral process and pluralism (2006–10)	0.100*	1.647	34
II. Functioning of government (2006–10)	0.413***	2.450	34
III. Political participation (2006–10)	0.466***	2.627	34
IV. Political culture (2006–10)	0.286**	2.134	34
V. Civil liberties (2006–10)	0.222***	2.477	33
Women's parliamentary representation (1990)	4.764***	3.422	36
Women's parliamentary representation (2010)	4.459***	2.507	36
Women's cabinet representation (1995)	3.398**	1.698	36
Women's cabinet representation (2008)	4.062**	1.762	36
Gender inequality index (2008)	−0.038***	4.057	35
Richest 10%/poorest 10% ratio (ca. 2000)	−2.598***	2.491	29

TABLE 16.1 *continued*

Performance variables	Estimated regression coefficient	Absolute t-value	Countries (N)
Richest 20%/poorest 20% ratio (ca. 2000)	−1.230***	2.548	29
Gini index of inequality (ca. 2000)	−3.445***	3.320	30
Voter turnout (1981–2010)	3.185*	1.480	36
Non-mandatory voter turnout (1981–2010)	3.155*	1.404	31
Satisfaction with democracy (1995–96)	6.537*	1.524	17
Satisfaction with democracy (2005–7)	3.888*	1.363	19

* Statistically significant at the 10 percent level (one-tailed test)

** Statistically significant at the 5 percent level (one-tailed test)

*** Statistically significant at the 1 percent level (one-tailed test)

Source: Based on data in Kaufmann, Kraay, and Mastruzzi 2010; Economist Intelligence Unit 2006, 3–5; Economist Intelligence Unit 2008, 4–8; Economist Intelligence Unit 2010, 3–8; United Nations Development Programme 2007, 281–84, 343–46; United Nations Development Programme 2009, 186–89; United Nations Development Programme 2010, 156–60; Banks, Day, and Muller 1996; Inter-Parliamentary Union 2010; International IDEA 2010; Klingemann 1999, 50; World Values Survey Association 2010

In order not to clutter the discussion with repeated references to the two control variables, which, however important, are not our main focus, let me briefly summarize the general pattern for all of the performance variables discussed in this chapter—which is very similar to the situation for "voice and accountability" reported in the previous paragraph. The level of development almost always has the greater impact, usually at the 1 or 5 percent level, and it almost always has a favorable influence (for instance, more voice and accountability, better women's representation, and less inequality). Population size does not have as strong an impact; if significant, the effect is usually at the 5 or 10 percent level; and it usually has an unfavorable influence. Both variables are clearly influential to such an important extent that they must be used as controls in all of the regression analyses. When I report the effects of consensus democracy on the performance variables in this chapter, as in the previous chapter, these are always the effects with level of development and population size controlled for. Without these controls, the bivariate correlations between consensus democracy and the various performance variables would invariably be stronger—but deceptively strong and not at all meaningful.

More detailed measures of democratic quality than the above WGI index have been constructed by the Economist Intelligence Unit (EIU) in 2006, 2008, and 2010. The EIU's overall index of democracy is an average of the scores in the five categories shown in Table 16.1. Each category is composed of an average of twelve subcategories. Most of the countries in the world are covered by the EIU surveys, including thirty-four of our thirty-six countries; only the Bahamas and Barbados are missing. Let me give a few examples of the questions that the EIU asks about each country. In the first category, electoral process and pluralism: "Are elections for the national legislature and head of government free [and fair]?"; "Are municipal elections both free and fair?"; "Do laws provide for broadly equal campaigning opportunities?"; and "Do opposition parties have a realistic prospect of achieving government?" Questions for the second category, the functioning of government, include: "Do freely elected representatives determine government policy?"; "[Do] special economic, religious or other powerful domestic groups . . . exercise significant political power, parallel to democratic institutions?"; "Are sufficient mechanisms and institutions in place for assuring government accountability to the electorate in between elections?"; and "Is the functioning of government open and transparent, with sufficient public access to information?" The third category, political participation, has questions about interest and participation in elections, political parties, other organizations, and lawful demonstrations, and women's legislative representation. The fourth category, political culture, focuses on the degree to which citizens express faith in and support for democracy. The fifth category, civil liberties, looks at the traditional freedoms of expression, association, and religion, a free and robust press and other media of communication, equal treatment under the law, and an independent judiciary (Economist Intelligence Unit 2010, 33–42).

Table 16.1 shows the effect of consensus democracy on the five categories of democratic quality and on the overall EIU democracy index (averaged over the years 2006, 2008, and 2010), which are measured on a ten-point scale, after the effects of level of development and population size have been taken into account. Consensus democracy has very strong effects on four of the performance variables (at the 1 percent level) and somewhat weaker but still significant effects on the first and fourth categories. Israel is an extreme outlier on the civil liberties variable and was therefore removed from the analysis; its score of 5.29 is far below those of all of the other countries that are in a narrow range between 8.04 and 10.00. The highest scores on the overall EIU democracy index are Sweden's (9.75) and Norway's (9.68), and the lowest are Argentina's (6.70) and Trinidad's (7.18). The average consensus democracy scores more than half a point higher than the average majoritarian democracy.

Both the Worldwide Governance Indicators project and the Economist Intelligence Unit use accountability as one of their criteria for high-quality democracy. This is indeed a crucial democratic desideratum, and a frequent claim in favor of majoritarian democracy is that its typically one-party majority governments offer clearer responsibility for policy-making and hence better accountability of the government to the citizens—who can use elections either to "renew the term of the incumbent government" or to "throw the rascals out" (Powell 1989, 119). The claim is undoubtedly valid for majoritarian systems with pure or almost pure two-party competition like the Barbadian prototype discussed in Chapter 2. However, in two-party systems with significant third parties, "rascals" may be repeatedly returned to office in spite of clear majorities of the voters voting for other parties and hence against the incumbent government. All reelected British cabinets since 1945 fit this description; in 2005 the negative vote of almost two-thirds (64.8 percent) of the voters against the incumbent Labour party was insufficient to dislodge it from power. Moreover, it is actually easier to change governments in consensus democracies than in majoritarian democracies, as shown by the shorter duration of cabinets in consensus systems (see the first column of Table 7.1). Admittedly, of course, changes in consensus democracies tend to be partial changes in the composition of cabinets, in contrast with the more frequent complete turnovers in majoritarian democracies.

WOMEN'S REPRESENTATION

The next five performance variables in Table 16.1 measure women's political representation and the inequality between women and men. The representation of women in parliaments and cabinets is an important measure of the quality of democratic representation in their own right, and it can also serve as an indirect proxy of how well minorities are represented generally. That there are so many kinds of ethnic and religious minorities in different countries makes comparisons extremely difficult, and it therefore makes sense to focus on the "minority" of women—a political rather than a numerical minority—that is found everywhere and that can be compared systematically across countries. As Rein Taagepera (1994, 244) states, "What we know about women's representation should [also] be applicable to ethnoracial minorities."

I chose years in the 1990s and in the first decade of the twenty-first century for the measurement of the percentages of women elected to the lower or only houses of parliament and the percentages of women's participation in cabinets. Women's parliamentary representation has increased at a rapid rate according to several studies (Sawer, Tremblay, and Trimble 2006, Tremblay 2008); I deliberately selected 1990 and 2010 in order to discover the exact extent to which women succeeded in improving their share of representation in our long-term democracies over these twenty years.[1] They more than doubled their representation: the respective percentages are 12.0 and 24.9. For cabinet representation, the same long time span was not available, but from 1995 to 2008 women also improved their participation in cabinets from 15.5 to 26.5 percent. In spite of these overall improvements, major differences have persisted between consensus and majoritarian democracies. The effect of consensus democracy on women's legislative representation in both years is strong and highly significant (at the 1 percent level). In 2010, the highest percentages were those of Sweden (45.0 percent), Iceland (42.9 percent), and the Netherlands (40.7 percent). The lowest were Botswana's (7.9 percent) and Malta's (8.7 percent). In both years, there were more than 9 percentage points more women in the first or only chambers in the average consensus than in the average majoritarian democracy. The results for women's cabinet representation are similar although less strong (at the 5 instead of the 1 percent level of significance). Women were better represented in the average consensus democracy than in the average majoritarian democracy by about 8 percentage points.

The tables also shows the gender inequality index devised by the United Nations Development Programme (2010, 219). It "reflects women's disadvantage in three dimensions—reproductive health, empowerment and the labour market—for as many countries as data of reasonable quality allow." It is a good overall measure of the status of women and is available for all of our democ-

---

1. The increase in women's legislative representation is partly due to the introduction of gender quotas by political parties and legislatures. Mona Lena Krook's (2009) comparative study of this subject presents both a global perspective and detailed case studies of legislative and party quotas in four of our democracies: Argentina, France, Sweden, and the United Kingdom.

racies except the Bahamas. For the other thirty-five countries the scale ranges from 0.174 (indicating low inequality) to 0.748 (indicating high inequality). At the high end are India (0.748), Botswana (0.663), and Jamaica (0.638); at the low end are the Netherlands (0.174), Denmark (0.209), and Sweden (0.212). The effect of consensus democracy on the gender inequality index is strongly negative and highly significant (at the 1 percent level). The average consensus democracy has an index score that is about 0.075 lower than the average majoritarian system.

POLITICAL EQUALITY

Political equality is a basic goal of democracy, and the degree of political equality is therefore an important indicator of democratic quality. Political equality is difficult to measure directly, but economic equality can serve as a valid proxy, since political equality is more likely to prevail in the absence of great economic inequalities: "Many resources that flow directly or indirectly from one's position in the economic order can be converted into political resources" (Dahl 1996, 645). Table 16.1 shows three measures of income inequality for varying years around 2000 provided by the United Nations Development Programme (2007, 281–84). The first compares the income share of the richest 10 percent to the poorest 10 percent of the population. The second is a similar measure comparing the richest to the poorest 20 percent. These data are available for all of our democracies except the five smallest countries and Mauritius. Botswana is an outlier with extremely high inequality and was removed from the analysis. The 10/10 ratio ranges from a high of 31.8 for Argentina to a low of 4.5 for Japan; the 20/20 ratio ranges from 16.3 to a low of 3.4, with Argentina and Japan again at opposite ends of the scale. The effect of consensus democracy on both variables is very strong and significant (at the 1 percent level). An even better and more comprehensive measure is the Gini index of inequality which has a theoretical range of 100, indicating extreme inequality (with one person receiving all of the country's income) to zero, indicating complete equality. Botswana has the highest inequality (60.5) but cannot be considered an extreme outlier and is therefore included in this part of the analysis. After Botswana the highest inequalities, above 40.0, occur in the Western hemisphere: Argentina (51.3), Costa Rica (49.8), Jamaica (45.5), Uruguay (44.9), and the United States (40.8). The lowest inequalities are found in Denmark (24.7), Japan (24.9), and Sweden (25.0). The effect of consensus democracy on this measure of inequality is even stronger and more highly significant than on the two ratio measures. The average consensus democracy has a Gini index that is more than 9 points lower than the average majoritarian democracy.

ELECTORAL PARTICIPATION

Voter turnout is an excellent indicator of democratic quality for two reasons. First, it shows the extent to which citizens are actually interested in being represented. Second, turnout is strongly correlated with socioeconomic status and can therefore also serve as an indirect indicator of political equality: high turnout means more equal participation and hence greater political equality; low turnout spells unequal participation and hence more inequality (Lijphart 1997). Table 16.1 uses the turnout percentages in legislative elections in parliamentary democracies and the average turnout percentages in presidential and legislative elections in presidential systems. The percentage for each country is the mean turnout in all elections between 1981 and 2010. The basic measure is the number of voters as a percentage of voting-age population.[2]

2. This is a more accurate measure of turnout than actual voters as a percent of registered voters, because voter registration procedures and reliability differ greatly from country to country. The only problem with the voting-age measure is that it includes noncitizens and hence tends to depress the turnout percentages of countries with large noncitizen populations. Because this problem assumes extreme proportions in Luxembourg with its small citizen and relatively very large noncitizen population, I made an exception in this case and used the turnout percentage based on registered voters.

Average voter turnout varies a great deal from country to country in our thirty-six democracies—from a low of 38.3 to a high of 95.0 percent. The countries with the highest voter turnout are Malta (95.0 percent), Uruguay (94.5 percent), and Luxembourg (88.5 percent). At the low end of the range are Switzerland (38.3 percent), Botswana (46.5 percent), Jamaica (50.6 percent), and the United States (51.3 percent). Consensus democracy has a significant positive effect on voter turnout, but the effect is relatively weak and significant only at the 10 percent level. One possible explanation for the weak relationship is that turnout is also affected by the presence or absence of compulsory voting, which tends to increase turnout. Of the three highest-turnout countries above, Uruguay and Luxembourg have mandatory voting laws with sanctions—usually modest fines—that are actually enforced. Three other countries have such laws: Argentina, Australia, and Belgium (International IDEA 2010, Birch 2009). In order to check whether compulsory voting changes the effect of consensus democracy on voter turnout, it can be entered as a dummy control variable (in addition to the two standard controls of level of development and population size) in the multivariate regression analysis. The result is an estimated regression coefficient of 3.178—almost identical to the 3.185 without mandatory voting as a control—and the level of significance is barely changed. A second check is to run the regression analysis without the five countries with compulsory voting. Table 16.1 shows that for the thirty-one countries with voluntary voting, the results are again almost the same: all three regression coefficients are remarkably close to each other, and they are all statistically significant only at the 10 percent level.

Another potential disturbing influence is suggested by the fact that in two countries with the lowest turnouts—Switzerland and the United States—turnout is severely depressed by the high frequency of elections and the multitude of electoral choices to be made. When the frequency of elections as well as compulsory voting and the two standard control variables are controlled for, the effect of consensus democracy on total turnout becomes much stronger and is now significant at the 5 percent level. The effect on nonmandatory turnout when the frequency of elections is controlled for is about the same. The estimated regression coefficients are 3.719 and 3.634, respectively, both significant at the 5 percent level. The two coefficients show that the average consensus democracy has a voter turnout that is more than 7 percentage points higher than the turnout in the average majoritarian democracy.

SATISFACTION WITH DEMOCRACY

Does type of democracy affect citizens' satisfaction with democracy? Hans-Dieter Klingemann (1999) reports the responses to the following survey question asked in many countries, including eighteen of our democracies, in 1995 and 1996: "On the whole, are you very satisfied, fairly satisfied, not very satisfied, or not at all satisfied with the way democracy works in (your country)?" The Danes and Norwegians expressed the highest percentage of satisfaction with their democracies: 83 and 82 percent, respectively, said that they were very or fairly satisfied. The Italians and Greeks were the least satisfied: only 19 and 28 percent, respectively, expressed satisfaction. The low percentage in the Italian survey conducted in 1995 is due at least in part to the political turbulence in Italy following the first election after Italy's drastic electoral reform. Table 16.1 reports the effect of consensus democracy on satisfaction with democracy after Italy is removed as an outlier. The correlation is positive, but only at the 10 percent level. When Italy is included in the analysis, the statistical significance falls below 10 percent, but the effect of consensus democracy is still clearly positive.

A similar question was asked in the World Values Survey in a large number of countries, including nineteen of our democracies, in 2005–7: "How democratically is [your] country being governed today? . . . [U]sing a scale from 1 to 10, where 1 means that it is 'not at all democratic' and 10 means that it is 'completely democratic,' what position would you choose?" Respondents who chose the high numbers 8 to 10 can be counted as being satisfied with their democratic system. The highest percentage is Norway's 74.1 percent, and the lowest—again—is Italy's 24.5 percent. Italy is no longer an outlier in this respect, however, because several other countries have only slightly higher percentages of satisfaction: Korea (29.5 percent), the Netherlands (30.1 percent), Trinidad (32.1 percent), the United Kingdom (33.3 percent), and the United States (35.5 percent). With all nineteen countries included in the multivariate analysis, democracy has a positive effect on satisfaction with democracy, but only at the 10 percent level of significance. Pippa Norris (2011, 214) reports a similar positive but small impact of proportional representation.

These results should be treated with caution because they are based on only seventeen to nineteen countries. Moreover, the results of the 1995–96 and 2005–7 surveys are not strictly comparable, because the questions about democratic satisfaction were phrased differently and also because the surveys were conducted in different countries: only eleven of our democracies were included in both surveys. The average percentage of respondents expressing approval in 2005–7 is also considerably lower than in 1995–96: 44.3 percent versus 54.6 percent (including Italy's low percentage). However, these differences can also be interpreted as strengthening the conclusion in favor of consensus democracy: in two surveys held ten years apart, in different sets of countries, with different questions, and with different overall levels of approval, consensus democracy still has roughly the same positive and statistically significant effect on citizens' satisfaction with the operation of their democratic systems.

The general conclusion is that consensus democracies have a better record than majoritarian democracy on all of the measures of democratic quality in Table 16.1, that all of the favorable effects of consensus democracy are statistically significant, and that more than half are significant at the most demanding 1 percent level. This conclusion applies to the effect of consensus democracy on the executives-parties dimension. In order to test the effect of consensus democracy on the federal-unitary dimension, I re-peated the nineteen regression analyses reported in Table 16.1 with consensus-federalist democracy as the independent variable—with the same controls and with the same outliers removed from the analysis. Without only a few slight exceptions, the relation-ships are extremely weak and statistically insignificant even at the 10 percent level. Consensus-federalist democracy has more unfavorable than favorable effects, but this finding is counter-balanced by the positive—but far from statistically significant—effects it has on the WGI indicator of voice and accountability and the overall EIU democracy index, which are the broadest and most comprehensive indicators of the quality of democracy. As in the previous chapter, I should emphasize that the effects are so weak that they do not allow any substantive conclusions in favor of one or the other type of democracy—and that they are not worth reporting in detail.

CONSENSUS DEMOCRACY AND ITS KINDER, GENTLER QUALITIES

The democratic qualities discussed so far in this chapter should appeal to all democrats: it is hard to find fault with better performance on the fundamental criteria of democracy used by the Worldwide Governance Indicators and the Economist Intel-ligence Unit, and with better results for women's representation, political equality, and participation in elections. In addition, consensus democracy (on the executives-parties dimension) is associated with some other attributes that I believe most, though not necessarily all, democrats will also find attractive: a strong com-munity orientation and social consciousness—the kinder, gentler qualities mentioned at the beginning of this chapter. These char-acteristics are also consonant with feminist conceptions of de-mocracy that emphasize, in Jane Mansbridge's (1996, 123) words, "connectedness" and "mutual persuasion" instead of self-interest and power politics: "The processes of persuasion may be related to a more consultative, participatory style that seems to characterize women more than men." Mansbridge further relates these differences to her distinction between "adversary" and "unitary" democracy, which is similar to the majoritarian-consensus contrast. Accordingly, consensus democracy may also be thought of as the more feminine model and majoritarian democracy as the more masculine model of democracy.

There are four areas of government activity in which the kinder and gentler qualities of consensus democracy are likely to manifest themselves: social welfare, the protection of the environment, criminal justice, and foreign aid. My hypothesis is that consensus democracy will be associated with kinder, gentler, and more generous policies. Table 16.2 presents the results of the multivariate regression analyses of the effect of consensus democracy on eight indicators of the policy orientations in these four areas. The independent variable in all cases is the degree of consensus democracy on the executives-parties dimension in the period 1981–2010. The control variables are again the level of economic development and logged population size.

Determining the degree to which democracies are welfare states is an extremely difficult task (Castles, Leibfried, Lewis, Obinger, and Pierson 2010). In particular, it is not sufficient simply to count the total amount of direct public social expenditure as a percentage of gross domestic product, because this amount is invariably reduced by direct and/or indirect taxes paid by the recipients of social benefits. The most careful analysis of the funds that should be included and that should be subtracted to arrive at the net expenditure on social welfare is the study "How Expensive Is the Welfare State?" by Willem Adema and Maxime Ladaique (2009), which covers the member countries of the Organization for Economic Development and Cooperation (OECD), including twenty-two of our democracies, in the year 2005. The first two rows of Table 16.2 are based on their calculations. Net public social expenditure consists of all direct public social expenses plus "tax breaks for social purposes that mirror cash benefits," minus all direct and indirect taxes and social contributions paid

by beneficiaries. The second row in the table, net publicly mandated social expenditure, adds private social expenditure that is
mandated by the state, again minus direct and indirect taxes and
social contributions.[3] Although the second total is only slightly
higher than the first in most countries, it is worth testing the effect of consensus democracy on both percentages. France has the
highest social expenditures as percentages of GDP (30.4 and 30.7
percent), followed by Germany (28.1 and 28.8 percent), and Sweden (27.3 and 27.5 percent). Korea has by far the lowest percentages (8.0 and 8.6 percent); the next lowest are Ireland (twice 17.2
percent), New Zealand (twice 18.4 percent), the United States
(18.4 and 18.8 percent) and Iceland (18.1 and 19.3 percent). The
effect of consensus democracy on both of the social expenditure
totals is strongly positive and statistically significant at the 5 percent level. The social expenditures of the average consensus democracy are about 4.75 percentage points higher than those of
the typical majoritarian democracy.

The best indicator of how well countries do with regard to
protecting the environment is the Environmental Performance
Index, produced by a team of environmental experts at Yale University and Columbia University. It is a broad and comprehensive
index that rates the performance of most of the countries in the
world on twenty-five indicators in ten policy areas, including
environmental health, air quality, water resource management,
biodiversity and habitat, forestry, fisheries, agriculture, and climate
change (Yale Center for Environmental Law and Policy 2010).
The first report was based on a pilot project and was published in
2006. Updates were released in 2008 and 2010. I used the ratings
in the 2010 report in Table 16.2 because it includes the largest
number of the world's countries and thirty-four of our democracies; only the Bahamas and Barbados are missing.

3. Adema and Ladaique present a third total that also includes *voluntary* private social expenditure which, in my opinion, is at odds with the
basic concept of the welfare state in which it is the *state* that directly or
indirectly serves as the provider of social protection.

TABLE 16.2

Multivariate regression analyses of the effect of consensus democracy (executives-parties dimension) on eight indicators of social welfare expenditures, environmental performance, criminal justice, and foreign aid, with controls for the effects of the level of economic development and logged population size, and with extreme outliers removed

Performance variables	Estimated regression coefficient	Absolute t-value	Countries (N)
Net public social expenditure (2005)	2.372**	2.092	22
Net publicly mandated social expenditure (2005)	2.382**	2.110	22
Environmental performance index (2010)	3.147**	1.724	34
Incarceration (2010)	−29.566***	2.463	35
Death penalty (2010)	−0.231**	1.779	36
Foreign aid (1990)	0.137**	1.874	21
Foreign aid (2005)	0.085*	1.608	22
Aid versus defense (2005)	8.328**	2.100	21

* Statistically significant at the 10 percent level (one-tailed test)

** Statistically significant at the 5 percent level (one-tailed test)

*** Statistically significant at the 1 percent level (one-tailed test)

Source: Based on data in Adema and Ladaique 2009, 48; Yale Center for Environmental Law and Policy 2010; International Centre for Prison Studies 2011; Amnesty International 2011; United National Development Programme 2007, 289, 294

Countries are rated on a scale from 100, indicating the best performance, to zero, indicating the poorest performance, although in practice no country is rated even close to zero; the worst performer, Sierra Leone, ranked number 163, still has a score of 32.1. Among our thirty-four democracies, Iceland receives the highest score (93.5), followed by Switzerland (89.1), Costa Rica (86.4), Sweden (86.0), Norway (81.1), and Mauritius (80.6). The poorest performers are Botswana (41.3), India (48.3), Trinidad (54.2), Korea (57.0), Jamaica (58.0), and Belgium (58.1). Table 16.2 shows that consensus democracy has a positive and statistically significant effect (at the 5 percent level) on environmental performance. Consensus democracies score more than six points higher than majoritarian democracies. As in all of the tables in Chapters 15 and 16, levels of development and population size are controlled for, and the former has a significant positive effect on environmental performance, too. The above examples show, however, that it is not always the most developed countries that receive the highest scores: Costa Rica and Mauritius are among the better and Korea and Belgium are among the poorer protectors of the environment.

One would also expect the qualities of kindness and gentleness in consensus democracies to show up in criminal justice systems that are less punitive than those of majoritarian democracies, with fewer people in prison and with less or no use of capital punishment. To test the hypothesis with regard to incarceration rates, I used the numbers collected by the International Centre for Prison Studies (2011), available for all of our democracies. These rates represent the number of inmates per hundred thousand population. The highest and lowest rates are those of the United States and India: 743 and 32 inmates per hundred thousand population, respectively. In fact, the United States is an extreme outlier: its 743 prisoners per hundred thousand people is about twice as many as the 376 inmates in the next most punitive country, the Bahamas. After the United States and the Bahamas, the next most punitive countries are Barbados (326), Israel (325), and Trinidad (276). The least punitive countries after India are Japan (59), and Finland and Iceland (both with 60 inmates per hundred thousand population). When the United States is removed from the analysis, the effect of consensus democracy on incarceration rates is strongly negative and significant at the 1 percent level. The consensus democracies put almost 60 fewer people per hundred thousand population in prison than the majoritarian democracies.

As of the end of 2010, according to the data collected by Amnesty International, eight of our thirty-six democracies retained and used the death penalty: the Bahamas, Barbados, Botswana, India, Jamaica, Japan, Trinidad, and the United States. The laws of twenty-six countries did not provide for the death penalty for any crime. The remaining two countries—Israel and Korea— were in the intermediate category of countries with the death penalty only for exceptional crimes, such as crimes under military law, or having a policy of not carrying out executions. On the basis of these differences, I constructed a three-point scale with a score of two for the active use of the death penalty, zero for the absence of the death penalty, and one for the intermediate cases. The effect of consensus democracy on the use of capital punishment is strongly negative and significant at the 5 percent level.

In the field of foreign policy, one might plausibly expect the kind and gentle characteristics of consensus democracy to be manifested by generosity with foreign aid and a reluctance to rely on military power.[4] Table 16.2 uses three indicators for more than twenty OECD countries: foreign aid—that is, economic development assistance, not military aid—as a percentage of gross na-

---

4. This hypothesis can also be derived from the "democratic peace" literature (Lijphart and Bowman 1999). The fact that democracies are more peaceful, especially in their relationships with each other, than nondemocracies is often attributed to their stronger compromise-oriented political cultures and their institutional checks and balances. If this explanation is correct, one should expect consensus democracies to be even more peace-loving than majoritarian democracies.

tional product at the end of the Cold War in 1990; foreign aid in 2005, fifteen years later; and foreign aid in 2005 as a percent of defense expenditures. In 1990, foreign aid ranged from a high of 1.17 percent of gross national product (Norway) to a low of 0.11 percent (Austria); in 2005, the highest percentage was 0.98 percent (Sweden) and the lowest 0.19 (Japan and the United States). The highest foreign aid as a percent of defense expenditure was Ireland's 70 percent, and the lowest was that of the United States, 5 percent.

In the analysis of the effect of consensus democracy on these three performance variables it is especially important to use the standard controls for level of development and population size: wealthier countries can better afford to give foreign aid than less wealthy countries, and large countries tend to assume greater military responsibilities and hence tend to have larger defense expenditures—which can be expected to limit their ability and willingness to provide foreign aid. In the multivariate analyses, consensus democracy has a positive effect on giving foreign aid and on foreign aid as a percentage of military expenditures, which is statistically significant at the 5 percent level for two of the performance variables and at the 10 percent level for the third. The average consensus democracy gave about 0.27 percent more of its gross national product in foreign aid than the average majoritarian democracy in 1990 and about 0.17 percent more in 2005. Its aid as a percent of defense spending was more than 16 percentage points higher.

Similar regression analyses can be performed to test the effects of the other (federal-unitary) dimension of consensus democracy on the above eight indicators, with the same controls in place and with the United States removed from the analysis of imprisonment rates. These analyses yield no interesting results. Consensus-federalist democracy has a favorable effect on five of the performance variables and an unfavorable effect on three—but the effects are all small and not statistically significant.

As the subtitle of this chapter states: consensus democracy

makes a difference. Indeed, the results could hardly be clearer: consensus democracy—on the executives-parties dimension—makes a big and highly favorable difference with regard to almost all of the indicators of democratic quality and with regard to all of the kinder and gentler qualities.

CHAPTER 17

CONCLUSIONS AND RECOMMENDATIONS

Two conclusions of this book stand out as most important. The first is that the enormous variety of formal and informal rules and institutions that we find in democracies can be reduced to a clear two-dimensional pattern on the basis of the contrasts between majoritarian and consensus government. The second important conclusion has to do with the policy performance of democratic governments: as far as the executives-parties dimension is concerned, majoritarian democracies do not outperform the consensus democracies on effective government and effective policy-making—in fact, the consensus democracies have the better record—but the consensus democracies do clearly outperform the majoritarian democracies with regard to the quality of democracy and democratic representation as well as with regard to what I have called the kindness and gentleness of their public policy orientations. On the second dimension, the federalist institutions of consensus democracy have little effect on the performance variables examined in the previous two chapters, but they do have obvious advantages for large countries and for countries with deep religious and ethnic divisions.

These conclusions have an extremely important practical implication: because the overall performance record of the consensus democracies is clearly superior to that of the majoritarian democracies, the consensus option is the more attractive choice for countries designing their first democratic constitutions or contemplating democratic reform. This recommendation is particularly pertinent, and even urgent, for societies that have deep cultural and ethnic cleavages, but it is also relevant for more homogeneous countries.

THE GOOD NEWS

Two pieces of good news and two pieces of bad news are attached to this practical constitutional recommendation. The first bit of good news is that, contrary to the conventional wisdom, there is no trade-off at all between governing effectiveness and high-quality democracy—and hence no difficult decisions to be made on giving priority to one or the other objective. Consensus democracy on the executives-parties dimension has advantages that are not offset by countervailing disadvantages—almost too good to be true, but the empirical results presented in Chapters 15 and 16 demonstrated that it *is* true. The mixed and neutral findings with regard to the effects of consensus-federalist democracy on the performance variables similarly mean that, if federal-type institutions are desirable for countries because of their size or internal divisions, there are no significant disadvantages attached to this choice.

Additional good news is that it is not difficult to write constitutions and other basic laws in such a way as to introduce consensus democracy. Divided-power institutions—strong federalism, strong bicameralism, rigid amendment rules, judicial review, and independent central banks—can be prescribed by means of constitutional stipulations and provisions in central bank charters. How these constitutional provisions work also depends on how they are interpreted and shaped in practice, of course, but the independent influence of explicit written rules should not be underestimated. It may also be possible to strengthen these institutions by choosing a particular form of them; for instance, if one wants to stimulate active and assertive judicial review, the best way to do so is to set up a special constitutional court (see Chapter 12). A central bank can be made particularly strong if its independence is enshrined not just in a central bank charter but in the constitution—or to outsource the central bank function to a strong supranational central bank like the European Central Bank (see Chapter 13).

The institutions of consensus democracy on the executives-parties dimension do not depend as directly on constitutional provisions as the divided-power institutions. But two formal elements are of crucial indirect importance: proportional representation and a parliamentary system of government. Especially when they are used in combination, and if the PR system is proportional not just in name but reasonably proportional in practice, they provide a potent impetus toward consensus democracy. On the conceptual map of democracy (see Figure 14.1), almost all of the democracies that have both PR and parliamentary systems are on the left, consensual side of the map, and almost all of the democracies that have plurality or majority elections or presidential systems of government or both are on the right, majoritarian side.

Because the hybrid Swiss system can be regarded as more parliamentary than presidential (see Chapter 7) and because the Japanese SNTV electoral system, which was used until 1996, can be regarded as closer to PR than to plurality (see Chapter 8), there are, among our thirty-six democracies, only four major and two minor exceptions to the proposition that PR and parliamentarism produce consensus democracy. Three parliamentary-PR systems are on the majoritarian side of the map: Greece, Malta, and Spain. Greece and Spain are the two PR countries with notoriously impure PR systems (see Chapter 8) and are therefore not major exceptions. The only major exception is Malta, where the proportional STV system has not prevented the development and persistence of an almost pure two-party system. The three exceptions on the other side—clear and significant exceptions—are India, Mauritius, and Uruguay. The ethnic and religious pluralism and the multiplicity of ethnic and religious groups in India and Mauritius have produced multiparty systems and coalition or minority cabinets in spite of plurality elections. Uruguay is the only presidential system on the consensus side of the map for several special reasons: its almost purely proportional system for legislative elections, its multipartism and factionalism, its corporatist tendencies, and its strong but not dominant presidency. It should also be noted that all of the exceptional democracies are only moderately exceptional in one respect: they are not located at either of the extreme ends of the majoritarian-consensus continuum; in fact, they are all within one standard deviation from the center. A final case that needs to be highlighted is New Zealand, which has become a parliamentary-PR democracy, but is still on the majoritarian side. However, as Figure 14.2 shows, it has moved a considerable distance toward the center on the strength of its electoral reform in the 1990s. If PR is retained, it is bound to cross into consensual territory where most of the other parliamentary-PR democracies are also located.

Both parliamentarism and PR can be fine-tuned to fit the conditions of particular countries and also to allay any fears that the combination of PR and parliamentary government will lead to weak and unstable cabinets and ineffective policy-making—however exaggerated such fears may be, given the analysis in Chapter 15 of this book. An important reinforcement of parliamentary government that has been introduced in several countries is the German-style constructive vote of no confidence, which requires that parliament can dismiss a cabinet only by simultaneously electing a new cabinet. One problem with this rule is that a parliament that has lost confidence in the cabinet but is too divided internally to elect a replacement may render the cabinet impotent by rejecting all or most of its legislative proposals; this scenario is similar to the divided-government situation that often afflicts presidential democracies. The problem can be solved, however, by adding the French rule that gives the cabinet the right to make its legislative proposals matters of confidence—which means that parliament can reject such proposals only by voting its lack of confidence in the cabinet by an absolute majority (see Chapter 6). The combination of these German and French rules can prevent both cabinet instability and executive-legislative deadlock without taking away parliament's ultimate power to install a cabinet in which it does have confidence.

Similarly, PR systems can be designed so as to control the degree of multipartism. The evidence does not support fears that PR, if it is too proportional, will inevitably lead to extreme party proliferation. Nevertheless, if, for instance, one wants to exclude small parties with less than 5 percent of the vote from legislative representation, it is easy to do so by writing a threshold clause into the election law and (unlike the German election law) not allowing any exceptions to this rule. The only cautionary advice that needs to be given about electoral thresholds, especially if they are as high as 5 percent or even higher, is that in unconsolidated party systems there may be many small parties that will be denied representation—leading to a major overrepresentation of the larger parties and an extremely high degree of disproportionality.

AND THE (SEEMINGLY) BAD NEWS

Unfortunately, there are also two pieces of bad news: both institutional and cultural traditions may present strong resistance to consensus democracy. As far as the four institutional patterns defined by the PR-plurality and parliamentary-presidential contrasts are concerned, there is a rough but remarkable congruence with four geographical regions of the world, defined in terms of the Eastern, Western, Northern, and Southern hemispheres (Powell 1982, 66–68). In the Eastern hemisphere, the "North" (western and central Europe) is mainly PR-parliamentary, whereas the "South" (especially the former British dependencies in Africa, Asia, and Australasia) is characterized by the plurality-parliamentary form of government. In the Western hemisphere, the "South" (Latin America) is largely PR-presidential in character, whereas the "North" (the United States) is the world's principal example of plurality-presidential government.

Most of the older democracies, but only a few of the newer (like the Czech Republic, Hungary, Slovenia, and Estonia), are in the PR-parliamentary "North-East." Most of the newer democracies—both those analyzed in this book and the somewhat younger ones—as well as most of the democratizing countries are in the "South-East" and "South-West." These two regions are characterized by either plurality elections or presidentialism. The majoritarian propensities of these institutions and the strength of institutional conservatism are obstacles to consensus democracy that may not be easy to overcome.

The second piece of bad news appears to be that consensus democracy may not be able to take root and thrive unless it is supported by a consensual political culture. Although the focus of this book has been on institutions rather than culture, it is clear that a consensus-oriented culture often provides the basis for and connections between the institutions of consensus democracy. For instance, four of the five elements of the executives-parties dimension are structurally connected—PR leading to multipartism, multipartism to coalitions cabinets, and so on—but there is no such structural connection between these four and the fifth element of interest group corporatism. The most plausible explanation is cultural. Consensus democracy and majoritarian democracy are alternative sets of political institutions, but more than that: they also represent what G. Bingham Powell (2000) calls the two "visions" of democracy.

Similarly, four of the five elements of the second dimension of consensus democracy are structurally and functionally linked to the requirement of operating a federal system, as theorists of federalism have long insisted (see Chapter 1). But there is no such link with central bank independence. Instead, the most likely connection is a political-cultural predisposition to think in terms of dividing power among separate institutions. My final example concerns the connection found in Chapter 16 between consensus democracy and several kinder and gentler public policies. It appears more plausible to assume that both consensus democracy and these kinder, gentler policies stem from an underlying consensual and communitarian culture than that these policies are the direct result of consensus institutions.

GROUNDS FOR OPTIMISM

These two items of bad news do not necessarily mean that consensus democracy has no chance in newly democratic and democratizing countries, because there are three important counterarguments. One is that South Africa, a former British colony and located in the "South-East," adopted a parliamentary-PR system when it became democratic in 1994. The provisional constitution that went into effect in 1994 prescribed both a standard parliamentary system with a prime minister and cabinet subject to parliamentary confidence—although the prime minister is formally called "president" and also serves as head of state, as in Botswana—and with one of the most proportional PR systems for parliamentary elections used anywhere in the world. This system remained unchanged in the permanent constitution that went into effect in 1999. South Africa has become one of the most successful and stable democracies on the African continent and hence a prominent model—considerably more prominent than Botswana, Namibia, and Mauritius because of its much larger size—for other aspiring democracies in Africa.

Second, we tend to think of culture and structure in terms of cause and effect, respectively, but there is actually a great deal of interaction between them; this is especially true of political culture and political structure. As Gabriel A. Almond and Sidney Verba (1963, 35) argue in *The Civic Culture,* structural and cultural phenomena are variables in "a complex, multidirectional system of causality." This means that, although a consensual culture may lead to the adoption of consensus institutions, these institutions also have the potential of making an initially adversarial culture less adversarial and more consensual. Consensus democracies like Switzerland and Austria may have consensual cultures today, but they have not always been so consensual: the Swiss fought five civil wars from the sixteenth to the middle of the nineteenth century, and the Austrians fought a brief but bloody civil war as recently as 1934. In the early twenty-first century, Belgium, India, and Israel have—and clearly need—consensus institutions, but they do not have consensual cultures. Observers of the Belgian political scene often wonder whether the country can stay together or will fall apart. Israel and India, too, can only be described as having highly contentious and conflictual political cultures.

Third, although the institutional traditions in the "South-East" and "South-West," where most of the newly democratic and democratizing countries are located, are not favorable to consensus democracy—but note the countervailing example of South Africa— the prevalent political cultures in these areas of the world are much more consensual than majoritarian. In his classic work *From Empire to Nation,* Rupert Emerson (1960, 284) argued that the assumption that the majority has the "right to overrule a dissident minority after a period of debate does violence to conceptions basic to non-Western peoples." While he conceded that there were important differences among the traditions of Asian and African peoples, "their native inclination is generally toward extensive and unhurried deliberation aimed at ultimate consensus. The gradual discovery of areas of agreement is the significant feature and not the ability to come to a speedy resolution of issues by counting heads." Sir Arthur Lewis (1965, 86), a native of St. Lucia in the Caribbean and of African descent, not only strongly advocated consensus democracy for the West African countries (see Chapter 3) but also emphasized their strong consensually oriented traditions: "The tribe has made its decisions by discussion, in much the way that coalitions function; this kind of democratic procedure is at the heart of the original institutions of the people."

The same point has been made forcefully and repeatedly in the book *Will of the People: Original Democracy in Non-Western*

Societies by Philippine statesman and scholar Raul S. Manglapus (1987, 69, 78, 82, 103, 107, 123, 129). He argues not only that the non-West has strong democratic traditions but that these traditions are much more consensual than majoritarian: "the common characteristic [is] the element of consensus as opposed to adversarial decisions." And time and again he describes the non-Western democratic process as a "consensual process" based on a strong "concern for harmony." My final example is a statement by Nigerian scholar and former United Nations official Adebayo Adedeji (1994, 126): "Africans are past masters in consultation, consensus, and consent. Our traditions abhor exclusion. Consequently, there is no sanctioned and institutionalized opposition in our traditional system of governance. Traditionally, politics for us has never been a zero-sum game."

Such statements are often regarded as suspect because they have been abused by some non-Western political leaders to justify deviations from democracy (Bienen and Herbst 1991, 214). But the fact that they have sometimes been used for illegitimate purposes does not make them less valid. All of the authors I have cited are both sincere democrats and sensitive observers without ulterior nondemocratic motives. Hence the consensus-oriented political cultures of the non-Western world can be regarded as a strong counterforce to its majoritarian institutional conservatism, and they may be able to provide fertile soil for consensus democracy.

APPENDIX

TWO DIMENSIONS AND TEN BASIC VARIABLES, 1945–2010 AND 1981–2010

The following list contains the values of the executives-parties and federal-unitary dimensions and of the ten basic variables during the periods 1945–2010 and 1981–2010. On the two dimensions, high values indicate consensus/federal and low values majoritarian/unitary characteristics. Please note that the exact years that mark the beginning of the 1945–2010 period differ from country to country and, in fact, range from 1945 to 1988 (see Table 4.1). For the 1981–2010 period, the years are the same for all countries, with the exception of the first year for Argentina (1984), Uruguay (1985), and Korea (1988). The two periods for central bank independence are 1945–94 and 1981–94, as explained in Chapter 13. The thirty-six democracies are identified by the first three characters of their English names, except that AUL means Australia, AUT Austria, CR Costa Rica, JPN Japan, NZ New Zealand, UK United Kingdom, and US United States.

The values of the "so what?" variables analyzed in Chapter 15 and 16 are not included in this appendix for reasons of space but may be accessed on the website of the Department of Political Science, University of California, San Diego, under the author's name: http://polisci.ucsd .edu/faculty/lijphart.html/data. Disaggregated data on the basic ten variables (for instance, the effective number of parliamentary parties and electoral disproportionality for each election instead of averaged over several elections) can be found in a second dataset on the same website.

	First (executives-parties dimension)		Second (federal-unitary dimension)		Effective number of parliamentary parties		Minimal winning one-part cabinets (%)	
	1945–2010	1981–2010	1945–2010	1981–2010	1945–2010	1981–2010	1945–2010	1981–2010
ARG	−0.93	−1.01	1.38	1.34	3.15	3.15	82.4	82.4
AUL	−0.73	−0.65	1.63	1.58	2.22	2.19	80.7	86.5
AUT	0.43	0.64	1.07	0.97	2.68	3.23	43.3	47.4
BAH	−1.50	−1.33	−0.15	−0.18	1.69	1.74	100.0	100.0
BAR	−1.28	−1.20	−0.49	−0.53	1.68	1.62	100.0	100.0
BEL	1.14	1.10	0.10	0.44	4.72	6.13	37.3	36.3
BOT	−1.43	−1.62	−0.48	−0.52	1.38	1.43	100.0	100.0
CAN	−1.00	−1.03	1.73	1.81	2.52	2.66	88.4	89.9
CR	−0.37	−0.38	−0.28	−0.12	2.67	2.81	85.8	85.2
DEN	1.31	1.35	−0.34	−0.42	4.57	4.95	23.6	5.7
FIN	1.58	1.48	−0.83	−0.83	5.04	5.05	10.0	1.4
FRA	−0.86	−0.89	−0.22	0.02	3.26	2.94	54.8	50.8
GER	0.78	0.63	2.41	2.33	3.09	3.30	37.8	43.4
GRE	−0.64	−0.55	−0.74	−0.77	2.27	2.32	98.1	97.7
ICE	0.53	0.55	−1.00	−1.09	3.72	4.01	46.3	47.8
IND	0.65	0.63	1.14	1.08	4.80	5.25	30.5	32.0
IRE	0.17	0.38	−0.42	−0.46	2.89	2.95	49.5	31.0
ISR	1.53	1.38	−0.90	−0.81	5.18	5.65	14.0	18.6
ITA	1.12	1.13	−0.39	−0.16	4.84	5.36	11.7	8.3
JAM	−1.49	−1.56	−0.40	−0.43	1.67	1.65	100.0	100.0
JPN	0.60	0.71	0.17	0.15	3.62	3.66	40.1	14.1
KOR	−1.22	−1.29	−0.07	−0.10	2.85	2.85	86.0	86.0
LUX	0.61	0.38	−0.88	−0.89	3.48	3.78	45.4	50.0
MAL	−0.83	−0.75	−0.33	−0.36	1.99	2.00	100.0	100.0
MAU	0.42	0.42	−0.13	−0.17	2.85	2.90	15.3	10.6
NET	1.34	1.17	0.30	0.28	4.87	4.86	26.8	39.7

continued

	First (executives-parties dimension)		Second (federal-unitary dimension)		Effective number of parliamentary parties		Minimal winning one-part cabinets (%)	
	1945–2010	1981–2010	1945–2010	1981–2010	1945–2010	1981–2010	1945–2010	1981–2010
NOR	0.80	1.09	−0.66	−0.67	3.64	4.11	55.3	36.6
NZ	−0.47	−0.17	−1.67	−1.65	2.28	2.66	81.4	60.0
POR	0.22	0.04	−0.61	−0.63	3.13	2.85	53.4	55.4
SPA	−0.62	−0.63	0.47	0.42	2.66	2.61	69.3	71.6
SWE	0.79	0.87	−1.03	−1.09	3.47	3.82	48.1	42.6
SWI	1.72	1.67	1.46	1.59	5.20	5.50	4.0	1.7
TRI	−1.01	−0.79	−0.24	−0.34	1.87	1.88	94.3	90.7
UK	−1.09	−1.48	−1.06	−1.12	2.16	2.27	97.3	99.8
URU	0.39	0.31	−0.79	−0.84	4.40	4.40	80.3	80.3
US	−0.67	−0.63	2.25	2.18	2.39	2.37	80.4	78.9

	Index of executive dominance		Index of disproportion-ality (%)		Index of interest group pluralism		Index of federalism	
	1945–2010	1981–2010	1945–2010	1981–2010	1945–2010	1981–2010	1945–2010	1981–2010
ARG	8.00	8.00	17.98	17.98	2.70	2.70	4.5	4.5
AUL	9.10	7.37	9.44	10.07	2.12	1.88	5.0	5.0
AUT	8.07	5.90	2.51	2.02	0.38	0.38	4.5	4.5
BAH	9.44	7.37	16.48	15.90	3.00	3.00	1.0	1.0
BAR	8.87	7.37	17.27	18.72	2.20	2.00	1.0	1.0
BEL	2.57	4.21	3.35	3.75	1.15	1.33	3.5	4.2
BOT	9.90	9.90	14.61	18.48	2.60	2.60	1.0	1.0
CAN	8.10	7.37	11.56	13.14	3.25	3.17	5.0	5.0

	Index of executive dominance		Index of disproportionality (%)		Index of interest group pluralism		Index of federalism	
	1945–2010	1981–2010	1945–2010	1981–2010	1945–2010	1981–2010	1945–2010	1981–2010
CR	3.00	3.00	14.38	14.77	2.20	2.20	1.0	1.0
DEN	3.23	3.69	1.71	1.60	0.78	0.88	2.0	2.0
FIN	1.55	2.68	2.96	3.34	0.85	0.67	2.0	2.0
FRA	8.00	8.00	20.88	19.56	2.90	2.75	1.3	1.5
GER	3.80	4.92	2.67	2.55	0.88	0.88	5.0	5.0
GRE	4.45	3.69	7.88	6.64	3.12	3.12	1.0	1.0
ICE	3.20	3.28	3.85	2.48	2.20	2.17	1.0	1.0
IND	3.33	3.69	9.60	8.51	2.15	2.15	4.5	4.5
IRE	4.16	2.95	3.93	4.17	2.55	2.42	1.0	1.0
ISR	1.46	1.13	2.60	3.76	1.15	1.50	3.0	3.0
ITA	1.49	2.01	3.61	4.82	2.42	2.08	1.3	1.5
JAM	9.64	9.83	15.66	15.41	3.00	3.00	1.0	1.0
JPN	3.37	2.46	7.00	10.50	1.48	1.38	2.0	2.0
KOR	8.00	8.00	21.97	21.97	2.90	2.90	1.5	1.5
LUX	5.87	7.37	3.43	4.14	0.88	0.88	1.0	1.0
MAL	8.85	7.37	2.07	1.65	3.00	3.00	1.0	1.0
MAU	2.39	2.11	15.61	16.57	1.30	1.30	1.0	1.0
NET	2.91	2.68	1.21	1.08	0.98	1.00	3.0	3.0
NOR	4.04	2.95	4.53	3.79	0.38	0.38	2.0	2.0
NZ	4.54	3.28	9.25	9.11	2.68	2.71	1.0	1.0
POR	3.26	3.69	4.43	4.85	2.62	2.62	1.0	1.0
SPA	8.26	7.37	7.28	6.53	3.04	3.04	3.0	3.0
SWE	5.61	4.92	2.04	1.95	0.35	0.42	2.0	2.0
SWI	1.00	1.00	2.55	3.08	0.88	0.88	5.0	5.0
TRI	6.95	4.21	11.33	11.67	3.00	3.00	1.3	1.5
UK	8.12	9.83	11.70	16.00	3.02	3.08	1.2	1.4
URU	4.00	4.00	6.05	6.05	1.70	1.70	1.0	1.0
US	4.00	4.00	14.28	13.35	3.02	2.88	5.0	5.0

	Index of bicameralism		Index of constitutional rigidity		Index of judicial review		Index of central bank independence	
	1945–2010	1981–2010	1945–2010	1981–2010	1945–2010	1981–2010	1945–94	1981–94
ARG	4.0	4.0	4.0	4.0	2.7	2.7	0.39	0.39
AUL	4.0	4.0	4.0	4.0	3.0	3.0	0.42	0.42
AUT	2.0	2.0	3.0	3.0	3.0	3.0	0.55	0.53
BAH	2.0	2.0	3.0	3.0	2.0	2.0	0.41	0.41
BAR	2.0	2.0	2.0	2.0	2.0	2.0	0.38	0.38
BEL	2.8	2.5	3.0	3.0	1.8	2.7	0.27	0.30
BOT	2.5	2.5	2.0	2.0	2.0	2.0	0.33	0.33
CAN	3.0	3.0	4.0	4.0	3.4	3.9	0.52	0.52
CR	1.0	1.0	3.0	3.0	2.7	3.4	0.37	0.37
DEN	1.2	1.0	2.0	2.0	2.0	2.0	0.46	0.46
FIN	1.0	1.0	3.0	3.0	1.0	1.0	0.28	0.28
FRA	3.0	3.0	1.7	2.0	2.4	3.0	0.35	0.35
GER	4.0	4.0	3.5	3.5	4.0	4.0	0.69	0.69
GRE	1.0	1.0	2.0	2.0	2.0	2.0	0.38	0.38
ICE	1.4	1.2	1.0	1.0	2.0	2.0	0.34	0.34
IND	3.0	3.0	3.0	3.0	4.0	4.0	0.34	0.34
IRE	2.0	2.0	2.0	2.0	2.0	2.0	0.41	0.41
ISR	1.0	1.0	1.0	1.0	1.0	1.0	0.41	0.46
ITA	3.0	3.0	2.0	2.0	2.1	2.5	0.28	0.33
JAM	2.0	2.0	3.0	3.0	2.0	2.0	0.30	0.30
JPN	3.0	3.0	4.0	4.0	2.0	2.0	0.25	0.25
KOR	1.0	1.0	4.0	4.0	3.0	3.0	0.27	0.27
LUX	1.0	1.0	3.0	3.0	1.0	1.0	0.33	0.33
MAL	1.0	1.0	3.0	3.0	2.0	2.0	0.44	0.44
MAU	1.0	1.0	3.0	3.0	3.0	3.0	0.40	0.40
NET	3.0	3.0	3.0	3.0	1.0	1.0	0.48	0.48
NOR	1.5	1.5	3.0	3.0	2.0	2.0	0.17	0.17

	Index of bicameralism		Index of constitutional rigidity		Index of judicial review		Index of central bank independence	
	1945–2010	1981–2010	1945–2010	1981–2010	1945–2010	1981–2010	1945–94	1981–94
NZ	1.1	1.0	1.0	1.0	1.0	1.0	0.21	0.24
POR	1.0	1.0	3.0	3.0	2.0	2.0	0.32	0.32
SPA	3.0	3.0	3.0	3.0	3.0	3.0	0.29	0.29
SWE	1.7	1.0	1.5	2.0	1.0	1.0	0.29	0.29
SWI	4.0	4.0	4.0	4.0	1.0	1.0	0.61	0.68
TRI	2.0	2.0	3.0	3.0	2.0	2.0	0.35	0.30
UK	2.5	2.5	1.0	1.0	1.0	1.0	0.31	0.28
URU	3.0	3.0	1.0	1.0	2.5	2.5	0.19	0.19
US	4.0	4.0	4.0	4.0	4.0	4.0	0.56	0.56

References

Adedeji, Adebayo. 1994. "An Alternative for Africa." *Journal of Democracy* 5, no. 4 (October): 119–32.

Adema, Willem, and Maxime Ladaique. 2009. "How Expensive Is the Welfare State? Gross and Net Indicators in the OECD Social Expenditure Database (SOCX)." *OECD Social, Employment and Migration Working Papers,* no. 92. Paris: OECD.

Agius, Carmel A., and Nancy A. Grosselfinger. 1995. "The Judiciary and Politics in Malta." In C. Neal Tate and Torbjörn Vallinder, eds., *The Global Expansion of Judicial Power,* 381–402. New York: New York University Press.

Alen, André, and Rusen Ergec. 1994. *Federal Belgium After the Fourth State Reform of 1993.* Brussels: Ministry of Foreign Affairs.

Almond, Gabriel A. 1983. "Corporatism, Pluralism, and Professional Memory." *World Politics* 35, no. 2 (January): 245–60.

Almond, Gabriel A., and Sidney Verba. *The Civic Culture: Political Attitudes and Democracy in Five Nations.* Princeton, NJ: Princeton University Press.

Altman, David. 2008. "Collegiate Executives and Direct Democracy in Switzerland and Uruguay: Similar Institutions, Opposite Political Goals, Distinct Results." *Swiss Political Science Review* 14, no. 3 (Autumn): 483–520.

———. 2011. *Direct Democracy Worldwide.* Cambridge: Cambridge University Press.

Ambler, John S. 1971. *The Government and Politics of France.* Boston: Houghton Mifflin.

Amnesty International. 2011. *Abolitionist and Retentionist Countries.* London: http://www.amnesty.org/en/death-penalty.

Amorim Neto, Octavio. 2006. "The Presidential Calculus: Executive Policy Making and Cabinet Formation in the Americas." *Comparative Political Studies* 39, no. 4 (May): 415–40.

Amorim Neto, Octavio, and Marina Costa Lobo. 2009. "Portugal's Semi-Presidentialism (Re)Considered: An Assessment of the President's Role in the Policy Process, 1976–2006." *European Journal of Political Research* 48, no. 2 (March): 234–55.

Anckar, Dag. 2008. "Microstate Democracy: Majority or Consensus; Diffusion or Problem-Solving?" *Democratization* 15, no. 1 (February): 67–85.

Anderson, Liam. 2001. "The Implications of Institutional Design for Macroeconomic Performance: Reassessing the Claims of Consensus Democracy." *Comparative Political Studies* 34, no. 4 (May): 429–52.

Andeweg, Rudy B. 1997. "Institutional Reform in Dutch Politics: Elected Prime Minister, Personalized PR, and Popular Veto in Comparative Perspective." *Acta Politica* 32, no. 2 (Autumn): 227–57.

Armingeon, Klaus. 1997. "Swiss Corporatism in Comparative Perspective." *West European Politics* 20, no. 4 (October): 164–79.

———. 2002. "Interest Intermediation: The Cases of Consociational Democracy and Corporatism." In Hans Keman, ed., *Comparative Democratic Politics: A Guide to Contemporary Theory and Research,* 143–65. London: Sage.

Aron, Raymond. 1982. "Alternation in Government in the Industrialized Countries." *Government and Opposition* 17, no. 1 (Winter): 3–21.

Axelrod, Robert. 1970. *Conflict of Interest: A Theory of Divergent Goals with Applications to Politics.* Chicago: Markham.

Baar, Carl. 1991. "Judicial Activism in Canada." In Kenneth M. Holland, ed., *Judicial Activism in Comparative Perspective,* 53–69. New York: St. Martin's.

———. 1992. "Social Action Litigation in India: The Operation and Limits of the World's Most Active Judiciary." In Donald W. Jackson and C. Neal Tate, eds., *Comparative Judicial Review and Public Policy*, 77–87. Westport, CT: Greenwood.

Bale, Tim, and Daniele Caramani, eds. 2010. "Political Data Yearbook 2009." *European Journal of Political Research* 49, nos. 7–8 (December): 855–1212.

Banaian, King, Leroy O. Laney, and Thomas D. Willett. 1986. "Central Bank Independence: An International Comparison." In Eugenia Froedge Toma and Mark Toma, eds., *Central Bankers, Bureaucratic Incentives, and Monetary Policy*, 199–217. Dordrecht: Kluwer Academic.

Banks, Arthur S. 2010. *Cross-National Time-Series Data Archive.* Binghamton, NY: http://databanksinternational.com.

Banks, Arthur S., Alan J. Day, and Thomas C. Muller. 1996. *Political Handbook of the World, 1995–1996*. Binghamton, NY: CSA.

Beer, Samuel. 1998. "The Roots of New Labour: Liberalism Rediscovered." *Economist* (February 7): 23–25.

Bienen, Henry, and Jeffrey Herbst. 1991. "Authoritarianism and Democracy in Africa." In Dankwart Rustow and Kenneth Paul Erickson, eds., *Comparative Political Dynamics: Global Research perspectives*, 211–32. New York: HarperCollins.

Bienen, Henry, and Nicolas van de Walle. 1991. *Of Time and Power: Leadership Duration in the Modern World.* Stanford, CA: Stanford University Press.

Birch, Sarah. 2009. *Full Participation: A Comparative Study of Compulsory Voting.* Tokyo: United Nations University Press.

Blondel, Jean. 1968. "Party Systems and Patterns of Government in Western Democracies." *Canadian Journal of Political Science* 1, no. 2 (June): 180–203.

Borrelli, Stephen A., and Terry A. Royed. 1995. "Government 'Strength' and Budget Deficits in Advanced Democracies." *European Journal of Political Research* 28, no. 2 (September): 225–60.

Boston, Jonathan, Stephen Levine, Elizabeth McLeay, and Nigel S. Roberts, eds. 1996. *New Zealand Under MMP: A New Politics?* Auckland: Auckland University Press.

Bowman, Larry W. 1991. *Mauritius: Democracy and Development in the Indian Ocean.* Boulder, CO: Westview.

Brass, Paul R. 1990. *The Politics of India Since Independence.* Cambridge: Cambridge University Press.

Bräutigam, Deborah. 1997. "Institutions, Economic Reform, and Democratic Consolidation in Mauritius." *Comparative Politics* 30, no. 1 (October): 45–62.

Brewer-Carías, Allan R. 1989. *Judicial Review in Comparative Law.* Cambridge: Cambridge University Press.

Brinks, Daniel M. 2008. *The Judicial Response to Police Killings in Latin America: Inequality and the Rule of Law.* Cambridge: Cambridge University Press.

Buchanan, Paul G. 2008. "Preauthoritarian Institutions and Postauthoritarian Outcomes: Labor Politics in Chile and Uruguay." *Latin American Politics and Society* 50, no. 1 (Spring): 59–89.

Budge, Ian, and Valentine Herman. 1978. "Coalitions and Government Formation: An Empirically Relevant Theory." *British Journal of Political Science* 8, no. 4 (October): 459–77.

Bulsara, Hament, and Bill Kissane. 2009. "Arend Lijphart and the Transformation of Irish Democracy." *West European Politics* 32, no. 1 (January): 172–95.

Busch, Andreas. 1994. "Central Bank Independence and the Westminster Model." *West European Politics* 17, no. 1 (January): 53–72.

Butler, David. 1978. "Conclusion." In David Butler, ed., *Coalitions in British Politics,* 112–18. New York: St. Martin's.

Butler, David, and Austin Ranney. 1978. "Theory." In David Butler and Austin Ranney, eds., *Referendums: A Comparative Study of Practice and Theory,* 23–37. Washington, DC: American Enterprise Institute.

Butler, David, Andrew Adonis, and Tony Travers. 1994. *Failure in British Government: The Politics of the Poll Tax.* Oxford: Oxford University Press.

Cappelletti, Mauro. 1989. *The Judicial Process in Comparative Perspective.* Oxford: Clarendon.

Carnota, Walter F. 2010. "Judicial Globalization: How the International Law of Human Rights Changed the Argentine Supreme Court." In Donald W. Jackson, Michael C. Tolley, and Mary L. Volcansek, eds., *Globalizing Justice: Critical Perspectives on Transnational Law and the Cross-Border Migration of Legal Norms,* 255–66. Albany: State University of New York Press.

Cason, Jeffrey. 2002. "Electoral Reform, Institutional Change, and Party Adaptation in Uruguay." *Latin American Politics and Society* 44, no. 3 (Autumn): 89–109.

Castles, Francis G. 1994. "The Policy Consequences of Proportional Representation: A Sceptical Commentary." *Political Science* 46, no. 2 (December): 161–71.

Castles, Francis G., Stephan Leibfried, Jane Lewis, Herbert Obinger, and Christopher Pierson, eds. 2010. *The Oxford Handbook of the Welfare State.* Oxford: Oxford University Press.

Chubb, Basil. 1982. *The Government and Politics of Ireland,* 2nd ed. Stanford, CA: Stanford University Press.

Church, Clive H., and Adrian Vatter. 2009. "Opposition in Consensual Switzerland: A Short but Significant Experiment." *Government and Opposition* 44, no. 4 (October): 412–37.

Codding, George Arthur, Jr. 1961. *The Federal Government of Switzerland.* Boston: Houghton Mifflin.

Colomer, Josep M., ed. 2004. *Handbook of Electoral System Choice.* Houndmills: Palgrave Macmillan.

———. 2010. *Europe, Like America: The Challenges of Building a Continental Federation.* Barcelona: La Caixa.

———. 2011. *The Science of Politics: An Introduction.* New York: Oxford University Press.

Committee on the Constitutional System. 1987. *A Bicentennial Analysis of the American Political Structure: Report and Recommendations.* Washington, DC: Committee on the Constitutional System.

Coombs, David. 1977. "British Government and the European Community." In Dennis Kavanagh and Richard Rose, eds., *New Trends in British Politics: Issues for Research,* 83–103. London: Sage.

Coppedge, Michael, and John Gerring. 2011. "Conceptualizing and Measuring Democracy: A New Approach." *Perspectives on Politics* 9, no. 2 (June): 247–67.

Crepaz, Markus M. L. 1996. "Consensus Versus Majoritarian Democracy: Political Institutions and Their Impact on Macroeconomic Performance and Industrial Disputes." *Comparative Political Studies* 29, no. 1 (February): 4–26.

Crepaz, Markus M. L., and Vicki Birchfield. 2000. "Global Economics, Local Politics: Lijphart's Theory of Consensus Democracy and the Politics of Inclusion." In Markus M. L. Crepaz, Thomas A. Koelble, and David Wilsford, eds., *Democracy and Institutions: The Life Work of Arend Lijphart,* 197–224. Ann Arbor: University of Michigan Press.

Crepaz, Markus M. L., and Ann W. Moser. 2004. "The Impact of Collective and Competitive Veto Points on Public Expenditures in the Global Age." *Comparative Political Studies* 37, no. 3 (April): 259–85.

Crepaz, Markus M. L., and Jürg Steiner. 2011. *European Democracies,* 7th ed. Boston: Longman.

Croissant, Aurel, and Teresa Schächter. 2010. "Institutional Patterns in the New Democracies of Asia: Forms, Origins and Consequences." *Japanese Journal of Political Science* 11, no. 2 (August): 173–97.

Crowe, Christopher, and Ellen E. Meade. 2007. "The Evolution of Central Bank Governance around the World." *Journal of Economic Perspectives* 21, no. 4 (Fall): 69–90.

Crowe, Edward W. 1980. "Cross-Voting in the British House of Commons: 1945–74." *Journal of Politics* 42, no. 2 (May): 487–510.

Cukierman, Alex, Steven B. Webb, and Bilin Neyapti. 1994. *Measuring Central Bank Independence and Its Effect on Policy Outcomes.* San Francisco: ICS.

Dahl, Robert A. 1956. *A Preface to Democratic Theory.* Chicago: University of Chicago Press.

———. 1971. *Polyarchy: Participation and Opposition.* New Haven: Yale University Press.

———. 1996. "Equality versus Inequality." *PS: Political Science and Politics* 29, no. 4 (December): 639–48.

Dahl, Robert A., and Edward R. Tufte. 1973. *Size and Democracy.* Stanford, CA: Stanford University Press.

Damgaard, Erik. 2008. "Cabinet Termination." In Kaare Strøm, Wolfgang C. Müller, and Torbjörn Bergman, eds., *Cabinets and Coalition Bargaining: The Democratic Life Cycle in Western Europe,* 301–26. Oxford: Oxford University Press.

Deschouwer, Kris. 2009. *The Politics of Belgium: Governing a Divided Society.* New York: Palgrave Macmillan.

de Swaan, Abram. 1973. *Coalition Theories and Cabinet Formations: A Study of Formal Theories of Coalition Formation Applied to Nine European Parliaments After 1918.* Amsterdam: Elsevier.

De Winter, Lieven, and Patrick Dumont. 2009. "Do Belgian Parties Undermine the Democratic Chain of Delegation?" In Marleen Brans, Lieven De Winter, and Wilfried Swenden, eds., *The Politics of Belgium: Institutions and Policy Under Bipolar and Centrifugal Federalism,* 95–114. London: Routledge.

De Winter, Marc Swyngedouw, and Patrick Dumont. 2009. "Party System(s) and Electoral Behaviour in Belgium: From Stability to Balkanisation." In Marleen Brans, Lieven De Winter, and Wilfried Swenden, eds., *The Politics of Belgium: Institutions and Policy Under Bipolar and Centrifugal Federalism,* 71–94. London: Routledge.

Diamond, Larry. 1989. "Introduction: Persistence, Erosion, Breakdown, and Reversal." In Larry Diamond, Juan J. Linz, and Seymour Martin Lipset, eds., *Democracy in Developing Countries: Asia,* 1–52. Boulder, CO: Lynne Rienner.

———. 1992. "Economic Development and Democracy Reconsidered." In Gary Marks and Larry Diamond, eds., *Reexamining Democracy: Essays in Honor of Seymour Martin Lipset,* 93–139. Newbury Park, CA: Sage.

Diamond, Larry, and Marc F. Plattner, eds. 2006. *Electoral Systems and Democracy.* Baltimore: Johns Hopkins University Press.

Dicey, A. V. 1915. *Introduction to the Study of the Law of the Constitution,* 8th ed. London: Macmillan.

Dixon, Robert G., Jr. 1968. *Democratic Representation: Reapportionment in Law and Politics.* New York: Oxford University Press.

Dodd, Lawrence C. 1976. *Coalitions in Parliamentary Government.* Princeton, NJ: Princeton University Press.

Dogan, Mattei. 1989. "Irremovable Leaders and Ministerial Instability in European Democracies." In Mattei Dogan, ed., *Pathways to Power: Selecting Rulers in Pluralist Democracies,* 239–75. Boulder, CO: Westview.

———. 1994. "Use and Misuse of Statistics in Comparative Research: Limits to Quantification in Comparative Politics." In Mattei Dogan and Ali Kazancigil, eds., *Comparing Nations: Concepts, Strategies, Substance,* 35–71. Oxford: Blackwell.

Downes, Andrew S., and Lawrence Nurse. 2004. "Macroeconomic Management and Building Social Consensus: An Evaluation of the Barbados Protocols." *Journal of Eastern Caribbean Studies* 29, no. 4 (December): 1–41.

Druckman, James N. 1996. "Party Factionalism and Cabinet Durability." *Party Politics* 2, no. 3 (July): 397–407.

Duchacek, Ivo. 1970. *Comparative Federalism: The Territorial Dimension of Politics.* New York: Holt, Rinehart and Winston.

Duncan, Neville. 1994. "Barbados: Democracy at the Crossroads." In

Carlene J. Edie, ed., *Democracy in the Caribbean: Myths and Realities,* 75–91. Westport, CT: Praeger.

Dunleavy, Patrick, and Françoise Boucek. 2003. "Constructing the Number of Parties." *Party Politics* 9, no. 3 (May): 291–315.

Duverger, Maurice. 1964. *Political Parties: Their Organization and Activity in the Modern State,* 3rd ed. London: Methuen.

———. 1980. "A New Political System Model: Semi-Presidential Government." *European Journal of Political Research* 8, no. 2 (June): 165–87.

———. 1986. "Duverger's Law: Forty Years Later." In Bernard Grofman and Arend Lijphart, eds., *Electoral Laws and Their Political Consequences,* 69–84. New York: Agathon.

Economist Intelligence Unit. 2006. *Index of Democracy.* London: The Economist.

———. 2008. *Index of Democracy, 2008.* London: The Economist.

———. 2010. *Democracy Index, 2010.* London: The Economist.

Edinger, Lewis J. 1986. *West German Politics.* New York: Columbia University Press.

Elazar, Daniel J. 1968. "Federalism." In David L. Sills, ed., *International Encyclopedia of the Social Sciences,* vol. 5, 353–67. New York: Macmillan and Free Press.

———. 1987. *Exploring Federalism.* Tuscaloosa: University of Alabama Press.

———. 1997. "Contrasting Unitary and Federal Systems." *International Political Science Review* 18, no. 3 (July): 237–51.

Elder, Neil, Alastair H. Thomas, and David Arter. 1988. *The Consensual Democracies? The Government and Politics of the Scandinavian States,* rev. ed. Oxford: Basil Blackwell.

Elster, Jon. 1994. "Constitutional Courts and Central Banks: Suicide Prevention or Suicide Pact?" *East European Constitutional Review* 3, nos. 3–4 (Summer–Fall): 66–71.

Emerson, Rupert. 1960. *From Empire to Nation: The Rise to Self-Assertion of Asian and African Peoples.* Cambridge, MA: Harvard University Press.

Emmanuel, Patrick A. M. 1992. *Elections and Party Systems in the Commonwealth Caribbean, 1944–1991.* St. Michael, Barbados: Caribbean Development Research Services.

Erk, Jan, and Edward Koning. 2010. "New Structuralism and Institutional Change: Federalism Between Centralization and Decentralization." *Comparative Political Studies* 43, no. 3 (March): 353–78.

Etchemendy, Sebastián, and Ruth Berins Collier. 2007. "Down but Not Out: Union Resurgence and Segmented Neocorporatism in Argentina (2003–2007)." *Politics and Society* 35, no. 3 (September): 363–401.

Falkner, Gerda. 2006. "Collective Participation in the European Union: The 'Euro Corporatism' Debate." In Colin Crouch and Wolfgang Streeck, eds., *The Diversity of Democracy: Corporatism, Social Order and Political Conflict,* 223–42. Cheltenham: Edward Elgar.

Farrell, David M. 2011. *Electoral Systems: A Comparative Introduction,* 2nd ed. Houndmills: Palgrave Macmillan.

Feldstein, Martin. 1997. "EMU and International Conflict." *Foreign Affairs* 76, no. 6 (November–December): 60–73.

Fenno, Richard F., Jr. 1959. *The President's Cabinet: An Analysis in the Period from Wilson to Eisenhower.* Cambridge, MA: Harvard University Press.

Finer, S. E., ed. 1975. *Adversary Politics and Electoral Reform.* London: Anthony Wigram.

Fish, M. Steven, and Matthew Kroenig. 2009. *The Handbook of National Legislatures: A Global Survey.* Cambridge: Cambridge University Press.

Fitzmaurice, John. 1996. *The Politics of Belgium: A Unique Federalism.* Boulder, CO: Westview.

Flinders, Matthew. 2010. *Democratic Drift: Majoritarian Modification and Democratic Anomie in the United Kingdom.* Oxford: Oxford University Press.

Franck, Matthew J. 1996. *Against the Imperial Judiciary: The Supreme Court vs. the Sovereignty of the People.* Lawrence: University Press of Kansas.

Freedom House. 2011. *Freedom in the World 2011.* Lanham, MD: Rowman and Littlefield.

Friedrich, Carl J. 1950. *Constitutional Government and Democracy,* rev. ed. Boston: Ginn.

Gallagher, Michael. 1991. "Proportionality, Disproportionality and Electoral Systems." *Electoral Studies* 10, no. 1 (March): 33–51.

———. 1995. "Conclusion." In Michael Gallagher and Pier Vincenzo Uleri, eds., *The Referendum Experience in Europe,* 226–52. London: Macmillan.

Gallagher, Michael, and Paul Mitchell, eds. 2005. *The Politics of Electoral Systems.* Oxford: Oxford University Press.

Gallagher, Michael, Michael Laver, and Peter Mair. 2011. *Representative Government in Modern Europe,* 5th ed. Maidenhead: McGraw-Hill.

Ganesh, Janan. 2010. "Over to You." *The Economist: The World in 2011* (December): 108.

García Montero, Mercedes. 2009. *Presidentes y parlamentos: Quién controla la actividad legislativa en América Latina?* Madrid: Centro de Investigaciones Sociológicas.

Gastil, Raymond D. 1989. *Freedom in the World: Political Rights and Civil Liberties, 1988–1989.* New York: Freedom House.

———. 1991. "The Comparative Survey of Freedom: Experiences and Suggestions." In Alex Inkeles, ed., *On Measuring Democracy: Its Consequences and Concomitants,* 21–46. New Brunswick, NJ: Transaction.

Gerlich, Peter. 1992. "A Farewell to Corporatism." *West European Politics* 15, no. 1 (January): 132–46.

Gerring, John, and Strom C. Thacker. 2008. *A Centripetal Theory of Democratic Governance.* Cambridge: Cambridge University Press.

Gobeyn, Mark James. 1993. "Explaining the Decline of Macro-Corporatist Political Bargaining Structures in Advanced Capitalist Societies." *Governance* 6, no. 1 (January): 3–22.

Goldey, David, and Philip Williams. 1983. "France." In Vernon Bogdanor and David Butler, eds., *Democracy and Elections: Electoral Systems and Their Political Consequences,* 62–83. Cambridge: Cambridge University Press.

Goodin, Robert E. 1996. "Institutionalizing the Public Interest: The Defense of Deadlock and Beyond." *American Political Science Review* 90, no. 2 (June): 331–43.

Goodman, John B. 1991. "The Politics of Central Bank Independence." *Comparative Politics* 23, no. 3 (April): 329–49.

Gorges, Michael J. 1996. *Euro-Corporatism? Interest Intermediation in the European Community.* Lanham, MD: University Press of America.

Grau i Creus, Mireia. 2000. "Spain: Incomplete Federalism." In Ute Wachendorfer-Schmidt, ed., *Federalism and Political Performance,* 58–77. London: Routledge.

Grilli, Vittorio, Donato Masciandaro, and Guido Tabellini. 1991. "Political and Monetary Institutions and Public Financial Policies in the Industrial Countries." *Economic Policy: A European Forum* 6, no. 2 (October): 342–92.

Grosser, Alfred. 1964. "The Evolution of European Parliaments." In Stephen R. Graubard, ed., *A New Europe?* 219–44. Boston: Houghton Mifflin.

GTD Team. 2010. *Global Terrorism Database.* College Park, MD: http://www.start.umd.edu/gtd.

Gurr, Ted Robert. 1993. *Minorities at Risk: A Global View of Ethnopolitical Conflicts.* Washington, DC: United States Institute of Peace Press.

Gutmann, Emanuel. 1988. "Israel: Democracy Without a Constitution." In Vernon Bogdanor, ed., *Constitutions in Democratic Politics, 290-308.* Aldershot: Gower.

Gwartney, James, Joshua Hall, and Robert Lawson. 2010. *Economic Freedom of the World: 2010 Annual Report.* Vancouver: Fraser Institute.

Haggard, Stephan, and Robert R. Kaufman. 1995. *The Political Economy of Democratic Transitions.* Princeton, NJ: Princeton University Press.

Hahm, Sung Deuk, Mark S. Kamlet, and David C. Mowery. 1996. "The Political Economy of Deficit Spending in Nine Industrialized Parliamentary Democracies: The Role of Fiscal Institutions." *Comparative Political Studies* 29, no. 1 (February): 52–77.

Hailsham, Lord. 1978. *The Dilemma of Democracy: Diagnosis and Prescription.* London: Collins.

Hall, Peter A. 1994. "Central Bank Independence and Coordinated Wage Bargaining: Their Interaction in Germany and Europe." *German Politics and Society* 31 (Spring): 1–23.

Hamilton, Alexander, John Jay, and James Madison. 1788. *The Federalist.* New York: McLean.

Hattenhauer, Hans, and Werner Kaltefleiter, eds. 1986. *Mehrheitsprinzip, Konsens und Verfassung.* Heidelberg: C. F. Müller Juristischer Verlag.

Hazan, Reuven Y. 1997. "Executive-Legislative Relations in an Era of Accelerated Reform: Reshaping Government in Israel." *Legislative Studies Quarterly* 22, no. 3 (August): 329–50.

Helmke, Gretchen. 2005. "Enduring Uncertainty: Court-Executive Relations in Argentina During the 1990s and Beyond." In Steven Levitsky and María Victoria Murillo, eds., *Argentine Democracy: The Politics of Institutional Weakness,* 139–62. University Park: Pennsylvania State University Press.

Hendriks, Frank. 2010. *Vital Democracy: A Theory of Democracy in Action.* Oxford: Oxford University Press.

Hix, Simon. 1994. "The Study of the European Community." *West European Politics* 17, no. 1 (January): 1–30.

———. 2005. *The Political System of the European Union,* 2nd ed. New York: Palgrave Macmillan.

Holm, John D. 1989. "Elections and Democracy in Botswana." In John D. Holm and Patrick Molutsi, eds., *Democracy in Botswana: The Proceedings of a Symposium Held in Gabarone, 1–5 August 1988,* 189–202. Gabarone: Macmillan Botswana.

Holm, John D., Patrick P. Molutsi, and Gloria Somolekae. 1996. "The Development of Civil Society in a Democratic State: The Botswana Model." *African Studies Review* 39, no. 2 (September): 43–69.

Horwill, George. 1925. *Proportional Representation: Its Dangers and Defects.* London: Allen and Unwin.

Huber, John D. 1996. *Rationalizing Parliament: Legislative Institutions and Party Politics in France.* Cambridge: Cambridge University Press.

Hueglin, Thomas O., and Alan Fenna. 2006. *Comparative Federalism: A Systematic Inquiry.* Peterborough, ON: Broadview.

Huntington, Samuel P. 1991. *The Third Wave: Democratization in the Late Twentieth Century.* Norman: University of Oklahoma Press.

Inglehart, Ronald. 1977. *The Silent Revolution: Changing Values and Political Styles Among Western Publics.* Princeton, NJ: Princeton University Press.

Inglehart, Ronald, and Christian Welzel. 2005. *Modernization, Cultural Change, and Democracy: The Human Development Sequence.* Cambridge: Cambridge University Press.

International Centre for Prison Studies. 2011. *World Prison Brief.* London: http://www.prisonstudies.org.

International IDEA. 2010. *Voter Turnout.* Stockholm: http://www.idea.int/vt.

Inter-Parliamentary Union. 2010. *Women in National Parliaments.* Geneva: http://www.ipu.org.

Jackson, Keith, and Alan McRobie. 1998. *New Zealand Adopts Pro-*

portional Representation: Accident? Design? Evolution? Aldershot: Ashgate.

Jain, M. P. 2000. "The Supreme Court and Fundamental Rights." In S. K. Verma and Kusum, eds., *Fifty Years of the Supreme Court of India: Its Grasp and Reach,* 1–100. New Delhi: Oxford University Press.

Johnson, Nevil. 1998. "The Judicial Dimension in British Politics." *West European Politics* 21, no. 1 (January): 148–66.

Jones, Charles O. 1994. *The Presidency in a Separated System.* Washington, DC: Brookings Institution.

Jones, Mark P. 1995. *Electoral Laws and the Survival of Presidential Democracies.* Notre Dame, Ind.: University of Notre Dame Press.

Kaiser, André. 1997. "Types of Democracy: From Classical to New Institutionalism." *Journal of Theoretical Politics* 9, no. 4 (October): 419–44.

Kasenally, Roukaya. 2011. "Mauritius: Paradise Reconsidered." *Journal of Democracy* 22, no. 2 (April): 160–69.

Katzenstein, Peter J. 1985. *Small States in World Markets: Industrial Policy in Europe.* Ithaca, NY: Cornell University Press.

Kaufmann, Daniel, Aart Kraay, and Massimo Mastruzzi. 2010. *Worldwide Governance Indicators.* Washington, DC: http://govindicators.org.

Kavanagh, Dennis. 1974. "An American Science of British Politics." *Political Studies* 22, no. 3 (September): 251–70.

Keeler, John T. S., and Martin Schain. 1997. "Institutions, Political Poker, and Regime Evolution in France." In Kurt von Mettenheim, ed., *Presidential Institutions and Democratic Politics: Comparing Regional and National Contexts,* 84–105. Baltimore: John Hopkins University Press.

Kenworthy, Lane. 2003. "Quantitative Indicators of Corporatism." *International Journal of Sociology* 33, no. 3 (Fall): 10–44.

Kim, Taekyoon. 2008. "Variants of Corporatist Governance: Differences in the Korean and Japanese Approaches in Dealing with Labor." *Yale Journal of International Affairs* 3, no. 1 (Winter): 78–94.

King, Anthony. 1976. "Modes of Executive-Legislative Relations: Great Britain, France, and West Germany." *Legislative Studies Quarterly* 1, no. 1 (February): 11–36.

Kirchner, Emil J. 1994. "The European Community: A Transnational

Democracy?" In Ian Budge and David McKay, eds., *Developing Democracy: Comparative Research in Honour of J. F. P. Blondel,* 253–66. London: Sage.

Klingemann, Hans-Dieter. 1999. "Mapping Political Support in the 1990s: A Global Analysis." In Pippa Norris, ed., *Critical Citizens: Global Support for Democratic Government,* 31–56. Oxford: Oxford University Press.

Klingemann, Hans-Dieter, ed. 2009. *The Comparative Study of Electoral Systems.* Oxford: Oxford University Press.

Knutsen, Carl Henrik. 2011. "Which Democracies Prosper? Electoral Rules, Form of Government and Economic Growth." *Electoral Studies* 30, no. 1 (March): 83–90.

Kothari, Rajni. 1970. *Politics in India.* Boston: Little, Brown.

Krauss, Ellis S. 1984. "Conflict in the Diet: Toward Conflict Management in Parliamentary Politics." In Ellis S. Krauss, Thomas P. Rohlen, and Patricia G. Steinhoff, eds., *Conflict in Japan,* 243–93. Honolulu: University of Hawaii Press.

Krauss, Ellis S., and Robert Pekkanen. 2004. "Explaining Party Adaptation to Electoral Reform: The Discreet Charm of the LDP?" *Journal of Japanese Studies* 30, no. 1 (Winter): 1–34.

Krook, Mona Lena. 2009. *Quotas for Women in Politics: Gender and Candidate Selection Reform Worldwide.* Oxford: Oxford University Press.

Laakso, Markku, and Rein Taagepera. 1979. "'Effective' Number of Parties: A Measure with Application to West Europe." *Comparative Political Studies* 12, no. 1 (April): 3–27.

Lane, Jan-Erik, and Svante Ersson. 1994. *Comparative Politics: An Introduction and New Approach.* Cambridge: Polity.

LaPalombara, Joseph. 1987. *Democracy, Italian Style.* New Haven: Yale University Press.

Laver, Michael, and Norman Schofield. 1990. *Multiparty Government: The Politics of Coalition in Europe.* Oxford: Oxford University Press.

Laver, Michael, and Kenneth A. Shepsle. 1996. *Making and Breaking Governments: Cabinets and Legislatures in Parliamentary Democracies.* Cambridge: Cambridge University Press.

Lawson, Stephanie. 1993. "Conceptual Issues in the Comparative Study of Regime Change and Democratization." *Comparative Politics* 25, no. 2 (January): 183–205.

Lehmbruch, Gerhard. 1993. "Consociational Democracy and Corporatism in Switzerland." *Publius* 23, no. 2 (Spring): 43–60.

Lehner, Franz. 1984. "Consociational Democracy in Switzerland: A Political-Economic Explanation and Some Empirical Evidence." *European Journal of Political Research* 12, no. 1 (March): 25–42.

Leiserson, Michael. 1970. "Coalition Government in Japan." In Sven Groennings, E. W. Kelley, and Michael Leiserson, eds., *The Study of Coalition Behavior: Theoretical Perspectives and Cases from Four Continents,* 80–102. New York: Holt, Rinehart, and Winston.

Levine, Stephen. 1979. *The New Zealand Political System: Politics in a Small Society.* Sydney: George Allen and Unwin.

Lewin, Leif. 1994. "The Rise and Decline of Corporatism: The Case of Sweden." *European Journal of Political Research* 26, no. 1 (July): 59–79.

Lewis, W. Arthur. 1965. *Politics in West Africa.* London: George Allen and Unwin.

Lijphart, Arend. 1977. *Democracy in Plural Societies: A Comparative Exploration.* New Haven: Yale University Press.

———. 1984. *Democracies: Patterns of Majoritarian and Consensus Government in Twenty-One Countries.* New Haven: Yale University Press.

———. 1994. *Electoral Systems and Party Systems: A Study of Twenty-Seven Democracies, 1945–1990.* Oxford: Oxford University Press.

———. 1997. "Unequal Participation: Democracy's Unresolved Dilemma." *American Political Science Review* 91, no. 1 (March): 1–14.

———. 1999. *Patterns of Democracy: Government Forms and Performance in Thirty-Six Countries.* New Haven: Yale University Press.

Lijphart, Arend, and Peter J. Bowman. 1999. "Types of Democracy and Generosity with Foreign Aid: An Indirect Test of the Democratic Peace Proposition." In Erik Beukel, Kurt Klaudi Klausen, and Poul Erik Mouritzen, eds., *Elites, Parties, and Democracy: Festschrift for Professor Mogens N. Pedersen,* 193–206. Odense: Odense University Press.

Lijphart, Arend, and Markus M. L. Crepaz. 1991. "Corporatism and Consensus Democracy in Eighteen Countries: Conceptual and Empirical Linkages." *British Journal of Political Science* 21, no. 2 (April): 235–46.

Lim, Jibong. 2004. "The Korean Constitutional Court, Judicial Activism, and Social Change." In Tom Ginsburg, ed., *Legal Reform in Korea,* 19–35. London: RoutledgeCurzon.

Linder, Wolf. 2010. *Swiss Democracy: Possible Solutions to Conflict in Multicultural Societies,* 3rd ed. New York: Palgrave Macmillan.

Linder, Wolf, and André Bächtiger. 2005. "What Drives Democratisation in Asia and Africa?" *European Journal of Political Research* 44, no. 6 (October): 861–80.

Linz, Juan J., and Arturo Valenzuela, eds. 1994. *The Failure of Presidential Democracy.* Baltimore: Johns Hopkins University Press.

Longley, Lawrence D., and David M. Olson, eds. 1991. *Two into One: The Politics and Processes of National Legislative Cameral Change.* Boulder, CO: Westview.

Loosemore, John, and Victor J. Hanby. 1971. "The Theoretical Limits of Maximum Distortion: Some Analytical Expressions for Electoral Systems." *British Journal of Political Science* 1, no. 4 (October): 467–77.

Lorenz, Astrid. 2005. "How to Measure Constitutional Rigidity: Four Concepts and Two Alternatives." *Journal of Theoretical Politics* 17, no. 3 (July): 339–61.

Loughlin, John, and Sonia Mazey, eds. 1995. *The End of the French Unitary State? Ten Years of Regionalization in France (1982–1992).* London: Frank Cass.

Lowell, A. Lawrence. 1896. *Governments and Parties in Continental Europe.* Boston: Houghton Mifflin.

Lundell, Krister. 2010. *The Origin of Electoral Systems in the Post-War Era: A Worldwide Approach.* London: Routledge.

———. 2011. "Accountability and Patterns of Alternation in Pluralitarian, Majoritarian and Consensus Democracies." *Government and Opposition,* 46, no. 2 (April): 145–67.

Lutz, Donald S. 2006. *Principles of Constitutional Design.* Cambridge: Cambridge University Press.

MacDonald, Scott B. 1986. *Trinidad and Tobago: Democracy and Development in the Caribbean.* New York: Praeger.

Mackie, Thomas T., and Richard Rose. 1991. *The International Almanac of Electoral History,* 3rd ed. London: Macmillan.

Maddex, Robert L. 2008. *Constitutions of the World,* 3rd ed. Washington, DC: CQ Press.

Mahler, Gregory S. 1997. "The 'Westminster Model' Away from Westminster: Is It Always the Most Appropriate Model?" In Abdo I. Baaklini and Helen Desfosses, eds., *Designs for Democratic Stability: Studies in Viable Constitutionalism,* 35–51. Armonk, NY: M. E. Sharpe.

Manglapus, Raul S. 1987. *Will of the People: Original Democracy in Non-Western Societies.* New York: Greenwood.

Mansbridge, Jane. 1980. *Beyond Adversary Democracy.* New York: Basic Books.

———. 1996. "Reconstructing Democracy." In Nancy J. Hirschmann and Christine Di Stefano, eds., *Revisioning the Political: Feminist Reconstructions of Traditional Concepts in Western Political Theory,* 117–38. Boulder, CO: Westview.

Mathur, Hansraj. 1991. *Parliament in Mauritius.* Stanley, Rose-Hill, Mauritius: Éditions de l'Océan Indien.

———. 1997. "Party Cooperation and the Electoral System in Mauritius." In Brij V. Lal and Peter Larmour, eds., *Electoral Systems in Divided Societies: The Fiji Constitution Review,* 135–46. Canberra: National Centre for Development Studies, Australian National University.

Maxfield, Sylvia. 1997. *Gatekeepers of Growth: The International Political Economy of Central Banking in Developing Countries.* Princeton, NJ: Princeton University Press.

May, Clifford D. 1987. "Political Speechmaking: Biden and the Annals of Raised Eyebrows." *New York Times* (September 21): B8.

Maundeni, Zibani. 2004. *Civil Society, Politics and the State in Botswana.* Gabarone: Medi.

McRae, Kenneth D. 1983. *Conflict and Compromise in Multilingual Societies: Switzerland.* Waterloo, ON: Wilfrid Laurier University Press.

———. 1997. "Contrasting Styles of Democratic Decision-Making: Adversarial versus Consensual Politics." *International Political Science Review* 18, no. 3 (July): 279–95.

Meyer, Peter J. 2010. *Uruguay: Political and Economic Conditions and U.S. Relations.* Washington, DC: Congressional Research Service.

Miller, Terry, and Kim R. Holmes. 2011. *2011 Index of Economic Freedom: Promoting Economic Opportunity and Prosperity.* Washington, DC: Heritage Foundation.

Mitchell, Paul, and Benjamin Nyblade. 2008. "Government Formation and Cabinet Type." In Kaare Strøm, Wolfgang C. Müller, and Torbjörn Bergman, eds., *Cabinets and Coalition Bargaining: The Democratic Life Cycle in Western Europe,* 201–35. Oxford: Oxford University Press.

Moreno, Luís. 1994. "Ethnoterritorial Concurrence and Imperfect Federalism in Spain." In Bertus de Villiers, ed., *Evaluating Federal Systems,* 162–93. Dordrecht: Martinus Nijhoff.

Muller, Thomas C., William R. Overstreet, Judith F. Isacoff, and Tom Lansford. 2011. *Political Handbook of the World, 2011.* Washington, DC: CQ Press.

Müller, Wolfgang C., Torbjörn Bergman, and Kaare Strøm. 2008. "Coalition Theory and Cabinet Governance: An Introduction." In Kaare Strøm, Wolfgang C. Müller, and Torbjörn Bergman, eds., *Cabinets and Coalition Bargaining: The Democratic Life Cycle in Western Europe,* 1–50. Oxford: Oxford University Press.

Munroe, Trevor. 1996. "Caribbean Democracy: Decay or Renewal?" In Jorge I. Domínguez and Abraham F. Lowenthal, eds., *Constructing Democratic Governance: Mexico, Central America, and the Caribbean in the 1990s,* 104–17. Baltimore: Johns Hopkins University Press.

Muravchik, Joshua. 1991. *Exporting Democracy: Fulfilling America's Destiny.* Washington, DC: AEI.

Murillo, M. Victoria, and Andrew Schrank. 2010. "Labor Organizations and Their Role in the Era of Political and Economic Reform." In Carlos Scartascini, Ernesto Stein, and Mariano Tommasi, eds., *How Democracy Works: Political Institutions, Actors, and Arenas in Latin American Policymaking,* 247–68. Washington, DC: Inter-American Development Bank.

Nohlen, Dieter. 1984. "Changes and Choices in Electoral Systems." In Arend Lijphart and Bernard Grofman, eds., *Choosing an Electoral System: Issues and Alternatives,* 217–24. New York: Praeger.

Nohlen, Dieter, ed. 2005. *Elections in the Americas: A Data Handbook,* 2 vols. Oxford: Oxford University Press.

Nohlen, Dieter, and Philip Stöver, eds. 2010. *Elections in Europe: A Data Handbook.* Baden-Baden: Nomos.

Nohlen, Dieter, Florian Grotz, and Christof Hartmann, eds. 2001. *Elections in Asia and the Pacific: A Data Handbook,* 2 vols. Oxford: Oxford University Press.

Nohlen, Dieter, Michael Krennerich, and Bernhard Thibaut, eds. 1999.

Elections in Africa: A Data Handbook. Oxford: Oxford University Press.

Norris, Pippa. 2004. *Electoral Engineering: Voting Rules and Political Behavior.* Cambridge: Cambridge University Press.

———. 2011. *Democratic Deficit: Critical Citizens Revisited.* Cambridge: Cambridge University Press.

O'Donnell, Guillermo. 1994. "Delegative Democracy." *Journal of Democracy* 5, no. 1 (January): 55–69.

Pauwels, Teun. 2011. "Explaining the Strange Decline of the Populist Radical Right Vlaams Belang in Belgium: The Impact of Permanent Opposition." *Acta Politica* 46, no. 1 (January): 60–82.

Payne, Anthony. 1993. "Westminster Adapted: The Political Order of the Commonwealth Caribbean." In Jorge I. Domínguez, Robert A. Pastor, and R. DeLisle Worrell, eds., *Democracy in the Caribbean: Political, Economic, and Social Perspectives,* 57–73. Baltimore: Johns Hopkins University Press.

Pekkarinen, Jukka, Matty Pohjola, and Bob Rowthorn, eds. 1992. *Social Corporatism: A Superior Economic System?* Oxford: Clarendon.

Pempel, T. J. 1992. "Japanese Democracy and Political Culture: A Comparative Perspective." *PS: Political Science and Politics* 25, no. 1 (March): 5–12.

Persson, Torsten, and Guido Tabellini. 2003. *The Economic Effects of Constitutions.* Cambridge, MA: MIT Press.

Peters, B. Guy. 1997. "The Separation of Powers in Parliamentary Systems." In Kurt von Mettenheim, ed., *Presidential Institutions and Democratic Politics: Comparing Regional and National Contexts,* 67–83. Baltimore: Johns Hopkins University Press.

Polillo, Simone, and Mauro F. Guillén. 2005. "Globalization Pressures and the State: The Global Spread of Central Bank Independence." *American Journal of Sociology* 110, no. 6 (May): 1764–1802.

Powell, G. Bingham, Jr. 1982. *Contemporary Democracies: Participation, Stability, and Violence.* Cambridge, MA: Harvard University Press.

———. 1989. "Constitutional Design and Citizen Electoral Control." *Journal of Theoretical Politics* 1, no. 2 (April): 107–30.

———. 2000. *Elections as Instruments of Democracy: Majoritarian and Proportional Visions.* New Haven: Yale University Press.

Premdas, Ralph. 2007. *Trinidad and Tobago: Ethnic Conflict, Inequality, and Public Sector Governance.* Houndmills: Palgrave Macmillan.

PRS Group. 2004. *International Country Risk Guide*. East Syracuse, NY: http://www.prsgroup.com.

Qvortrup, Matt. 2012. "Voting on Electoral Reform: A Comparative Perspective on the AV Referendum in the United Kingdom." *Political Quarterly* 83, no. 1 (January–March): 62–74.

Rae, Douglas W. 1967. *The Political Consequences of Electoral Laws*. New Haven: Yale University Press.

Rae, Douglas W., and Michael Taylor. 1970. *The Analysis of Political Cleavages*. New Haven: Yale University Press.

Reed, Steven R., and John M. Bolland. 1999. "The Fragmentation Effect of SNTV in Japan." In Bernard Grofman, Sung-Chull Lee, Edwin Winckler, and Brian Woodall, eds., *Elections in Japan, Korea, and Taiwan Under the Single Non-Transferable Vote: The Comparative Study of an Embedded Institution*, 211–26. Ann Arbor: University of Michigan Press.

Reich, Robert B. 1997. *Locked in the Cabinet*. New York: Alfred A. Knopf.

Reynolds, Andrew, Ben Reilly, and Andrew Ellis. 2005. *Electoral System Design: The New International IDEA Handbook*. Stockholm: International Institute for Democracy and Electoral Assistance.

Riker, William H. 1962. *The Theory of Political Coalitions*. New Haven: Yale University Press.

———. 1975. "Federalism." In Fred I. Greenstein and Nelson W. Polsby, eds., *Handbook of Political Science 5: Governmental Institutions and Processes*, 93–172. Reading, MA: Addison-Wesley.

———. 1982. *Liberalism Against Populism: A Confrontation Between the Theory of Democracy and the Theory of Social Choice*. San Francisco: Freeman.

Rodden, Jonathan. 2004. "Comparative Federalism and Decentralization: On Meaning and Measurement." *Comparative Politics* 36, no. 4 (July): 481–500.

Rogowski, Ronald. 1987. "Trade and the Variety of Democratic Institutions." *International Organization* 41, no. 2 (Spring): 203–23.

Roller, Edeltraud. 2005. *The Performance of Democracies: Political Institutions and Public Policies*. Oxford: Oxford University Press.

Rose, Richard. 1974. "A Model Democracy?" In Richard Rose, ed., *Lessons from America: An Exploration*, 131–61. New York: Wiley.

———. 1992. *What Are the Economic Consequences of PR?* London: Electoral Reform Society.

Rose, Richard, and Dennis Kavanagh. 1976. "The Monarchy in Contemporary Political Culture." *Comparative Politics* 8, no. 4 (July): 548–76.

Roubini, Nouriel, and Jeffrey D. Sachs. 1989. "Political and Economic Determinants of Budget Deficits in the Industrial Democracies." *European Economic Review* 33, no. 5 (May): 903–38.

Sadeh, Tal. 2006. *Sustaining European Monetary Union: Confronting the Cost of Diversity.* Boulder, CO: Lynne Rienner.

Saiegh, Sebastián M. 2011. *Ruling by Statute: How Uncertainty and Vote Buying Shape Lawmaking.* Cambridge: Cambridge University Press.

Samuels, David, and Richard Snyder. 2001. "The Value of a Vote: Malapportionment in Comparative Perspective." *British Journal of Political Science* 31, no. 4 (October): 651–71.

Sandiford, Sir Lloyd Erskine. 2004. "Reflections on the Barbados Protocols." *Journal of Eastern Caribbean Studies* 29, no. 4 (December): 86–94.

Sartori, Giovanni. 1976. *Parties and Party Systems: A Framework for Analysis.* Cambridge: Cambridge University Press.

———. 1994. "Neither Presidentialism nor Parliamentarism." In Juan J. Linz and Arturo Valenzuela, eds., *The Failure of Presidential Democracy,* 106–18. Baltimore: Johns Hopkins University Press.

Sawer, Marian, Manon Tremblay, and Linda Trimble, eds. 2006. *Representing Women in Parliament: A Comparative Study.* London: Routledge.

Schmidt, Manfred G. 1996. "Germany: The Grand Coalition State." In Josep M. Colomer, ed., *Political Institutions in Europe,* 62–98. London: Routledge.

Schmidt, Vivien A. 2006. *Democracy in Europe: The EU and National Polities.* Oxford: Oxford University Press.

Schmitter, Philippe C. 1982. "Reflections on Where the Theory of Neo-Corporatism Has Gone and Where the Praxis of Neo-Corporatism May Be Going." In Gerhard Lehmbruch and Philippe C. Schmitter, eds., *Patterns of Corporatist Policy-Making,* 259–79. London: Sage.

———. 1989. "Corporatism Is Dead! Long Live Corporatism!" *Government and Opposition* 24, no. 1 (Winter): 54–73.

———. 2008. "The Changing Politics of Organised Interests." *West European Politics* 31, nos. 1–2 (January–March): 195–210.

Scott, K. J. 1962. *The New Zealand Constitution.* Oxford: Clarendon.

Seligson, Mitchell A., and Juliana Martínez Franzoni. 2010. "Limits to Costa Rican Heterodoxy: What Has Changed in 'Paradise'?" In Scott Mainwaring and Timothy R. Scully, eds., *Democratic Governance in Latin America*, 307–37. Stanford, CA: Stanford University Press.

Sen, Amartya. 2010. "Introduction." In United Nations Development Programme, *Human Development Report 2010*, vi–vii. New York: Palgrave Macmillan.

Shugart, Matthew Soberg, and John M. Carey. 1992. *Presidents and Assemblies: Constitutional Design and Electoral Dynamics.* Cambridge: Cambridge University Press.

Shugart, Matthew Soberg, and Stephan Haggard. 2001. "Institutions and Public Policy in Presidential Systems." In Stephan Haggard and Mathew D. McCubbins, eds., *Presidents, Parliaments, and Policy*, 64–102. Cambridge: Cambridge University Press.

Shugart, Matthew Soberg, and Scott Mainwaring. 1997. "Presidentialism and Democracy in Latin America: Rethinking the Terms of the Debate." In Scott Mainwaring and Matthew Soberg Shugart, eds., *Presidentialism and Democracy in Latin America*, 12–54. Cambridge: Cambridge University Press.

Siaroff, Alan. 1999. "Corporatism in 24 Industrial Democracies: Meaning and Measurement." *European Journal of Political Research* 36, no. 2 (October): 175–205.

———. 2003a. "Two-and-a-Half-Party Systems and the Comparative Role of the 'Half.'" *Party Politics* 9, no. 3 (May): 267–90.

———. 2003b. "Comparative Presidencies: The Inadequacy of the Presidential, Semi-Presidential and Parliamentary Distinction." *European Journal of Political Research* 42, no. 3 (May): 287–312.

———. 2009. *Comparing Political Regimes: A Thematic Introduction to Comparative Politics*, 2nd ed. Toronto: University of Toronto Press.

Siegfried, André. 1956. "Stable Instability in France." *Foreign Affairs* 34, no. 3 (April): 394–404.

Spiller, Pablo T., and Mariano Tommasi. 2008. "Political Institutions, Policymaking Processes, and Policy Outcomes in Argentina." In Ernesto Stein and Mariano Tommasi, eds., *Policymaking in Latin America: How Politics Shapes Policy*, 69–110. Washington, DC: Inter-American Development Bank.

Steiner, Jürg. 1971. "The Principles of Majority and Proportionality." *British Journal of Political Science* 1, no. 1 (January): 63–70.

———. 1974. *Amicable Agreement Versus Majority Rule: Conflict Resolution in Switzerland.* Chapel Hill: University of North Carolina Press.

Stepan, Alfred. 2001. *Arguing Comparative Politics.* Oxford: Oxford University Press.

Stone, Alec. 1992. *The Birth of Judicial Politics in France: The Constitutional Council in Comparative Perspective.* New York: Oxford University Press.

Stone Sweet, Alec. 2004. *The Judicial Construction of Europe.* Oxford: Oxford University Press.

Strøm, Kaare. 1990. *Minority Government and Majority Rule.* Cambridge: Cambridge University Press.

———. 1997. "Democracy, Accountability, and Coalition Bargaining." *European Journal of Political Research* 31, nos. 1–2 (February): 47–62.

Strøm, Kaare, Ian Budge, and Michael J. Laver. 1994. "Constraints on Cabinet Formation in Parliamentary Democracies." *American Journal of Political Science* 38, no. 2 (May): 303–35.

Strøm, Kaare, Wolfgang C. Müller, and Torbjörn Bergman, eds. 2008. *Cabinets and Coalition Bargaining: The Democratic Life Cycle in Western Europe.* Oxford: Oxford University Press.

Studlar, Donley S., and Kyle Christensen. 2006. "Is Canada a Westminster or Consensus Democracy? A Brief Analysis." *PS: Political Science and Politics* 39, no. 4 (October): 837–41.

Swenden, Wilfried, Marleen Brans, and Lieven De Winter. 2009. "The Politics of Belgium: Institutions and Policy Under Bipolar and Centrifugal Federalism." In Marleen Brans, Lieven De Winter, and Wilfried Swenden, eds., *The Politics of Belgium: Institutions and Policy Under Bipolar and Centrifugal Federalism,* 1–11. London: Routledge.

Taagepera, Rein. 1994. "Beating the Law of Minority Attrition." In Wilma Rule and Joseph F. Zimmerman, eds., *Electoral Systems in Comparative Perspective: Their Impact on Women and Minorities,* 236–45. Westport, CT: Greenwood.

———. 2003. "Arend Lijphart's Dimensions of Democracy: Logical Connections and Institutional Design." *Political Studies* 51, no. 1 (March): 1–19.

———. 2007. *Predicting Party Sizes: The Logic of Simple Electoral Systems.* Oxford: Oxford University Press.

Taagepera, Rein, and Bernard Grofman. 1985. "Rethinking Duverger's Law: Predicting the Effective Number of Parties in Plurality and PR Systems—Parties Minus Issues Equals One." *European Journal of Political Research* 13, no. 4 (December): 341–52.

Taagepera, Rein, and Matthew Soberg Shugart. 1989. *Seas and Votes: The Effects and Determinants of Electoral Systems.* New Haven: Yale University Press.

Tarlton, Charles D. 1965. "Symmetry and Asymmetry as Elements of Federalism: A Theoretical Speculation." *Journal of Politics* 27, no. 4 (November): 861–74.

Tate, C. Neal, and Torbjörn Vallinder, eds. 1995. *The Global Expansion of Judicial Power.* New York: New York University Press.

Taylor, Michael, and Valentine M. Herman. 1971. "Party Systems and Government Stability." *American Political Science Review* 65, no. 1 (March): 28–37.

Therborn, Göran. 1977. "The Rule of Capital and the Rise of Democracy." *New Left Review* 103 (May–June): 3–41.

Thorndike, Tony. 1993. "Revolution, Democracy, and Regional Integration in the Eastern Caribbean." In Anthony Payne and Paul Sutton, eds., *Modern Caribbean Politics,* 147–75. Baltimore: Johns Hopkins University Press.

Transparency International. 2010. *Corruption Perceptions Index, 2010.* Berlin: http://www.transparency.org.

Tremblay, Manon, ed. 2008. *Women and Legislative Representation: Electoral Systems, Political Parties, and Sex Quotas.* New York: Palgrave Macmillan.

Trench, Alan, ed. 2007. *Devolution and Power in the United Kingdom.* Cambridge: Cambridge University Press.

Tschaeni, Hanspeter. 1982. "Constitutional Change in Swiss Cantons: An Assessment of a Recent Phenomenon." *Publius* 12, no. 1 (Winter): 113–30.

Tsebelis, George. 2002. *Veto Players: How Political Institutions Work.* New York: Russell Sage Foundation.

Tsebelis, George, and Jeannette Money. 1997. *Bicameralism.* Cambridge: Cambridge University Press.

Tummala, Krishna K. 1996. "The Indian Union and Emergency Powers." *International Political Science Review* 17, no. 4 (October): 373–84.

Tuozzo, Maria F. 2009. "World Bank Influence and Institutional Reform in Argentina." *Development and Change* 40, no. 3 (May): 467–85.

Uleri, Pier Vincenzo. 2002. "On Referendum Voting in Italy: YES, NO or Non-Vote: How Italian Parties Learned to Control Referendums." *European Journal of Political Research* 41, no. 6 (October): 863–83.

United Nations Development Programme. 2007. *Human Development Report, 2007/2008.* New York: Palgrave Macmillan.

———. 2009. *Human Development Report, 2009.* New York: Palgrave Macmillan.

———. 2010. *Human Development Report, 2010.* New York: Palgrave Macmillan.

Vanberg, Georg. 2005. *The Politics of Constitutional Review in Germany.* Cambridge: Cambridge University Press.

Vanhanen, Tatu. 1997. *Prospects of Democracy: A Study of 172 Countries.* London: Routledge.

Varshney, Ashutosh. 1995. *Democracy, Development, and the Countryside: Urban-Rural Struggles in India.* Cambridge: Cambridge University Press.

Vatter, Adrian. 2000. "Consensus and Direct Democracy: Conceptual and Empirical Linkages." *European Journal of Political Research* 38, no. 2 (October): 171–92.

———. 2008. "Swiss Consensus Democracy in Transition: A Re-Analysis of Lijphart's Concept of Democracy for Switzerland from 1997 to 2007." *World Political Science Review* 4, no. 2 (July): 1–38.

———. 2009. "Lijphart Expanded: Three Dimensions of Democracy in Advanced OECD Countries?" *European Political Science Review* 1, no. 1 (March): 125–54.

Vatter, Adrian, and Julian Bernauer. 2009. "The Missing Dimension of Democracy: Institutional Patterns in 25 EU Member States Between 1997 and 2006." *European Union Politics* 10, no. 3 (September): 335–59.

———. 2010. *Consensus Democracy Indicators in 35 Advanced Democracies: Political Data Set, 1997–2006.* Bern: Institute of Political Science, University of Bern; Konstanz: Department of Politics and Management, University of Konstanz.

Verba, Sidney. 1967. "Some Dilemmas in Comparative Research." *World Politics* 20, no. 1 (October): 111–27.

Verney, Douglas V. 1959. *The Analysis of Political Systems.* London: Routledge and Kegan Paul.

Verzichelli, Luca. 2008. "Portfolio Allocation." In Kaare Strøm, Wolfgang C. Müller, and Torbjörn Bergman, eds., *Cabinets and Coalition Bargaining: The Democratic Life Cycle in Western Europe,* 237–67. Oxford: Oxford University Press.

Volcansek, Mary L. 1994. "Political Power and Judicial Review in Italy." *Comparative Political Studies* 26, no. 4 (January): 492–509.

———. 2000. *Constitutional Politics in Italy: The Constitutional Court.* New York: St. Martin's Press.

von Beyme, Klaus. 1985. *Political Parties in Western Democracies.* New York: St. Martin's.

von Mettenheim, Kurt. 1997. "Introduction: Presidential Institutions and Democratic Politics." In Kurt von Mettenheim, ed., *Presidential Institutions and Democratic Politics: Comparing Regional and National Contexts,* 1–15. Baltimore: Johns Hopkins University Press.

Vowles, Jack, Peter Aimer, Susan Banducci, and Jeffrey Karp, eds. 1998. *Voters' Victory? New Zealand's First Election Under Proportional Representation.* Auckland: Auckland University Press.

Wada, Junichiro. 1996. *The Japanese Election System: Three Analytical Perspectives.* London: Routledge.

Warwick, Paul V. 1994. *Government Survival in Parliamentary Democracies.* Cambridge: Cambridge University Press.

Watts, Ronald L. 2008. *Comparing Federal Systems,* 3rd ed. Montreal: McGill-Queen's University Press.

Wheare, K. C. 1946. *Federal Government.* London: Oxford University Press.

———. 1964. *Federal Government,* 4th ed. Oxford: Oxford University Press.

Whitehead, Lawrence. 2009. "Europe's Democratization: Three 'Clusters' Compared." *Taiwan Journal of Democracy* 5, no. 2 (December): 1–19.

Wiarda, Howard J. 1997. *Corporatism and Comparative Politics: The Other Great "Ism."* Armonk, NY: M. E. Sharpe.

———. 2004. "Conclusion: New Directions in Research, Theory, and Policy." In Howard J. Wiarda, ed., *Authoritarianism and Corporatism in Latin America—Revisited,* 282–304. Gainesville: University Press of Florida.

Wilson, Bruce M. 2009. "Institutional Reform and Rights Revolutions in Latin America: The Cases of Costa Rica and Colombia." *Journal of Politics in Latin America* 1, no. 2: 59–85.

Wilson, Graham. 1990. *Interest Groups.* Oxford: Basil Blackwell.

———. 1994. "The Westminster Model in Comparative Perspective." In Ian Budge and David McKay, eds., *Developing Democracy: Comparative Research in Honour of J. F. P. Blondel,* 189–201. London: Sage.

———. 1997. "British Democracy and Its Discontents." In Metin Heper, Ali Kazancigil, and Bert A. Rockman, eds., *Institutions and Democratic Statecraft,* 59–76. Boulder, CO: Westview.

Wilson, Woodrow. 1884. "Committee or Cabinet Government?" *Overland Monthly,* 2nd ser., 3 (January): 17–33.

———. 1885. *Congressional Government: A Study in American Politics.* Boston: Houghton Mifflin.

Woldendorp, Jaap. 2011. "Corporatism in Small North-West European Countries: Business as Usual, Decline, or a New Phenomenon?" Working Paper Series, no. 30. Amsterdam: Department of Political Science, Free University: http://www.fsw.vu.nl/en/departments/political-science/working-papers/index.asp.

Woldendorp, Jaap, Hans Keman, and Ian Budge. 2000. *Party Government in 48 Democracies (1945–1998): Composition-Duration-Personnel.* Dordrecht: Kluwer.

———. 2010. *Party Government in 40 Democracies (1945–2008): Composition-Duration-Personnel* (dataset available from the authors on request).

World Bank. 2011. *Indicators.* Washington, DC: http://data.worldbank.org/indicator.

World Values Survey Association. 2010. *World Values Survey, 2005–2007.* Stockholm: http://worldvalues.org.

Yale Center for Environmental Law and Policy. 2010. *Environmental Performance Index, 2010.* New Haven: http://epi.yale.edu.

Yoon, Dae-Kyu. 2010. *Law and Democracy in South Korea: Democratic Development Since 1987.* Seoul: Kyungnam University Press.

INDEX